CO-CREATIVE TRANSACTIONAL ANALYSIS

CO-CREATIVE TRANSACTIONAL ANALYSIS
Papers, Responses, Dialogues, and Developments

*Keith Tudor and
Graeme Summers*

Routledge
Taylor & Francis Group

LONDON AND NEW YORK

First published 2014 by Karnac Books Ltd.

Published 2018 by Routledge
2 Park Square, Milton Park, Abingdon, Oxon OX14 4RN
711 Third Avenue, New York, NY 10017, USA

Routledge is an imprint of the Taylor & Francis Group, an informa business

British Library Cataloguing in Publication Data

A C.I.P. for this book is available from the British Library

ISBN-13: 9781782201571 (pbk)

Typeset by V Publishing Solutions Pvt Ltd., Chennai, India

MIX
Paper from
responsible sources
FSC
www.fsc.org FSC® C013985

Printed in the United Kingdom
by Henry Ling Limited

CONTENTS

FIGURES AND TABLES   ix

ABBREVIATIONS   xiii

ABOUT THE AUTHORS AND CONTRIBUTORS   xv

INTRODUCTION   xix
Keith Tudor

INTRODUCTION   xxxi
Graeme Summers

CHAPTER ONE
Co-creative transactional analysis   1
Graeme Summers and Keith Tudor

CHAPTER TWO
The neopsyche: the integrating Adult ego state   29
Keith Tudor

CHAPTER THREE
Response to "The neopsyche: the integrating Adult
    ego state", and rejoinder   69
Graeme Summers and Keith Tudor

CHAPTER FOUR
Dynamic ego states: the significance of non-conscious and
    unconscious patterns, as well as conscious patterns   89
Graeme Summers

CHAPTER FIVE
Response to "Dynamic ego states", and rejoinder   99
Keith Tudor and Graeme Summers

CHAPTER SIX
Empathy: a co-creative perspective   119
Keith Tudor

CHAPTER SEVEN
Response to "Empathy: a co-creative perspective",
    and rejoinder   141
Graeme Summers and Keith Tudor

CHAPTER EIGHT
Co-creative contributions   157
*Helena Hargaden, Laurie Hawkes, Marco Mazzetti, Trudi
    Newton, and Gregor Žvelc*

CHAPTER NINE
Response to "Co-creative contributions"   183
Graeme Summers and Keith Tudor

CHAPTER TEN
Implications, developments, and possibilities   201
Graeme Summers and Keith Tudor

AFTERWORD   223
Graeme Summers

AFTERWORD   227
Keith Tudor

APPENDIX ONE
Introducing co-creative transactional analysis   235
Graeme Summers and Keith Tudor

APPENDIX TWO
A co-creative "TA 101": notes on the syllabus   251
Keith Tudor

GLOSSARY   263
Keith Tudor and Graeme Summers

REFERENCES   269

INDEX   293

FIGURES AND TABLES

FIGURE I.1
The co-creative transactional analysis literature and
Keith Tudor's related publications   xxv

FIGURE 1.1
Co-creative therapeutic relating   7

FIGURE 1.2
Co-creative therapeutic relationships: Mapping a client's
crossed transactions   9

FIGURE 1.3
Co-creative script matrix (developed from Cornell, 1988)   23

FIGURE 1.4
A script helix   24

FIGURE 2.1
Articles on ego states published in the *Transactional Analysis
Journal* 1971–2009   31

FIGURE 2.2
Psychic organs and corresponding ego states (Berne, 1961/1975a)   34

FIGURE 2.3
Second order structure of the Adult (Berne, 1961)   43

FIGURE 2.4
The integrating Adult model   51

FIGURE 2.5
Physis and integration   56

FIGURE 2.6
Ego state development in the integrating Adult model
    (developed from Gobes in Novey, Porter-Steele,
    Gobes, & Massey, 1993)   57

FIGURE 3.1
The neo–archaeopsyche, two ego state model   87

FIGURE 3.2
The neo–archaeopsyche, two ego state model, including
    second and third order analysis   88

FIGURE 4.1
Dynamic ego states (Summers, 2008)   90

FIGURE 6.1
Co-creative empathic transacting   132

FIGURE 7.1
Social and ulterior level transactions between
    integrating Adults   150

FIGURE 7.2
Co-creative empathic transacting (showing the client's work
    with the Parent)   151

FIGURE 7.3
Double contamination (three ego state model)   152

FIGURE 7.4
Contaminations (integrating Adult model)   153

FIGURE 9.1
Healthy contact with self and openness to others via Adult   191

FIGURE 9.2
Defensive Parent–Child intrapsychic loop   191

FIGURE 10.1
Intrapsychic impasses in co-creative transactional analysis   204

FIGURE 10.2
A Past–Past interpersonal impasse within the co-transferential
    psychological field   206

FIGURE 10.3
An intersubjective impasse   208

FIGURE 10.4
A co-creative script matrix (representing a power dynamic
    with regard to one polarity of influence)   211

FIGURE A1.1
Three types of ego states   237

FIGURE A1.2
Parallel transactions: two types   241

FIGURE A1.3
Crossed transactions: two types   242

FIGURE A1.4
Ulterior transactions: two types   243

FIGURE A1.5
The drama triangle (Karpman, 1968)   245

FIGURE A1.6
Co-creative script matrix (Summers & Tudor, 2000)   248

TABLE 2.1
Articles on ego states published in the *Transactional Analysis
    Journal* 1971–2012   30

TABLE 2.2
Locating transactional analysis as an organismic psychology   40

TABLE 2.3
The properties, description, and associated disciplines of psychic
    organs (summarised from Berne, 1961/1975a)   47

TABLE 5.1
Senses of self and domains of relatedness and consciousness
    (based on Stern, 1998)   102

TABLE 6.1
Assumptions about the nature of social science applied to the
    development of co-creative transactional analysis   121

TABLE 6.2
Similarities between the theory of the Integrated Adult
    (Erskine, 1988, 1991) and of the integrating Adult
    (Tudor, 2003) and co-creative transactional analysis
    (Summers & Tudor, 2000)   133

TABLE 6.3
Differences between the theory of the Integrated Adult
    (Erskine, 1988, 1991) and of the integrating Adult (Tudor,
    2003) and co-creative transactional analysis (Summers &
    Tudor, 2000)   134

TABLE 10.1
Game theory analysed   214

TABLE A2.1
Differences between the four fields of application in
    transactional analysis   254

TABLE A2.2
Transactional methodology and method (from Tudor, 1999)   260

ABBREVIATIONS

CTA—Certified Transactional Analyst

EATA—The European Association for Transactional Analysis

IARTA—The International Association of Relational Transactional Analysis

ITA—The (UK) Institute of Transactional Analysis (now the UK Association for Transactional Analysis)

ITAA—The International Transactional Analysis Association

PTSTA—Provisional Teaching and Supervising Transactional Analyst

STA—Supervising Transactional Analyst

T&CC—Training and Certification Council of Transactional Analysis

TA 101—Transactional Analysis "101" Introductory Course

TAJ—The *Transactional Analysis Journal*

TSTA—Teaching and Supervising Transactional Analyst

TTA—Teaching Transactional Analyst

UKCP—The United Kingdom Council for Psychotherapy

Note: There are four fields of application in transactional analysis: counselling (C), education (E), organisational (O), and psychotherapy (P). In terms of a transactional analyst's qualifications, these are represented after the qualification, thus, for example, CTA(C), PTSTA(E), STA(O), TTA(P), and TSTA(C).

ABOUT THE AUTHORS AND CONTRIBUTORS

Authors

Graeme Summers is a freelance Executive Coach and Trainer based in the United Kingdom. He works for several international business schools including London Business School and Ashridge in the UK, and IMD in Switzerland. He coaches senior executives working in many different sectors from all over the globe and has worked in Europe, Asia, the Middle East, and Africa. He is a member of the Steering Group of the International Association of Relational Transactional Analysis. He is a Certified Transactional Analyst (Psychotherapy) and, prior to his coaching career, was a psychotherapist for nineteen years. He was also Director of Training for the Counselling and Psychotherapy Training Institute in Edinburgh where he led a United Kingdom Council for Psychotherapy recognised Transactional Analysis training programme. He is married, has four children and lives in Gloucestershire, UK, where he enjoys countryside walks, especially when it is not raining.

Keith Tudor is an Associate Professor at Auckland University of Technology, Auckland, where he is also the Head of the Department of Psychotherapy & Counselling. He is a Certified Transactional Analyst and a Teaching and Supervising Transactional Analyst, a Provisional Member of the New Zealand Association of Psychotherapists, and has a small private practice in West Auckland. He is the series editor of *Advancing Theory in Therapy* (Routledge), the editor of *Psychotherapy and Politics International*, and the co-editor of *Ata: Journal of Psychotherapy Aotearoa New Zealand*. He is the author/editor of over 250 publications, including twelve books, the previous of which, *The Turning Tide* (LC Publications, 2011), is concerned with pluralism and partnership in psychotherapy in Aotearoa New Zealand.

Contributors

Helena Hargaden, MSc, DPsych, Teaching and Supervising Transactional Analyst, is a psychotherapist, writer, coach and supervisor. In collaboration with others she has developed relational perspectives in and of transactional analysis, and has been widely published and translated into a number of languages. She lives on the South Coast in the UK where she has a clinical practice, and can be contacted at: helenahargaden27@hotmail.com

Laurie Hawkes, CTA, TTA(P), CTA(P) Trainer, is a psychotherapist in private practice in Paris. She is fortunate to teach and train in a private institute, L'Ecole d'Art Paris-Ile de France, which is co-led by seven colleagues, including herself. She has published six books in French and three articles, one of which received the Raymond Hostie award in 2013. She is also an avid tango dancer.

Marco Mazzetti, MD, is a psychiatrist, a Teaching and Supervising Transactional Analyst (Psychotherapy), a university lecturer, and the President of the European Association for Transactional Analysis. He is the author of several books and scientific papers, and received the Eric Berne Memorial Award in 2012, in recognition of his original, innovative, and significant advancement in the theory and practice of transactional analysis supervision. Among his main interests are cross-cultural psychotherapy and psycho-traumatology, and he is the Head of Invisible Wounds, Rome, a rehabilitation service for torture victims. He works in private practice in Milan, Italy, and may be contacted at: marcom.imat@gmail.com

Trudi Newton is an Educational TSTA working internationally to facilitate radical approaches to learning and community development. Co-author of several books for educators, including (with Rosemary Napper) *TACTICS* (TA Resources, 2003), which looks in detail at the process of learning and teaching, she is currently co-editing an international collection of educational TA writing. As well as writing regularly for the *Transactional Analysis Journal*, Trudi has been the guest editor for two issues: on Transactional Analysis and Education (Newton, 2004) and on Transactional Analysis Training (Newton & Napper, 2009). She has provided training in the UK and Russia, and contributes to training programmes in several countries including South Africa.

Gregor Žvelc, PhD, is a clinical psychologist and Assistant Professor in the Department of Psychology in both the University of Ljubljana and of Primorska in Slovenia. He is a Certified Transactional Analyst and a Provisional Teaching and Supervising Transactional Analyst (Psychotherapy). He is also International Integrative Psychotherapy Trainer & Supervisor. He is the Director of the Institute for Integrative Psychotherapy and Counselling in Ljubljana, where he has a private practice and leads trainings in integrative psychotherapy and Transactional Analysis. He is co-editor of *International Journal of Integrative Psychotherapy* and author of the book *Relational Theories in Psychotherapy: Integrative Model of Interpersonal Relationship*. He can be reached at Institute IPSA, Stegne 7, 1000 Ljubljana, Slovenia, e-mail: gregor.zvelc@guest.arnes.si, homepage: www.institut-ipsa.si

INTRODUCTION

Keith Tudor

Co-creative transactional analysis is an approach to this particular branch of psychology that, as the phrase suggests, emphasises the "co" (mutual, joint) aspect of professional relationships, whether therapeutic, educative, and/or consultative—and, by implication, of personal relationships. The "co" of co-creative acknowledges the transactional, interrelational, mutual, joint, and co-operative, as well as partnership. That the term contains the word "creative" is an intentional reference to what is, can, and should be, original, imaginative, intuitive and spontaneous about the encounter between human beings—with all our wisdom, intellect, and emotions, and in all our complexities and contexts. Together, the suffix and the root word describe what emerges—and is emergent—between therapist, practitioner, facilitator, educator, supervisor, consultant, helper, and client.

Co-creative transactional analysis emerged, appropriately enough, in and from a relationship between colleagues and friends: Graeme Summers and me. Graeme and I had originally met in 1984 through mutual friends who were associated with the (then) metanoia Psychotherapy Training Institute in London, UK (now Metanoia Institute). Graeme and I hit it off and met a few times on our own, meetings that were marked by the beginnings of what were to become passionate debates about psychology and psychotherapy. In 1985 I went to live in Italy, and it was not until 1987 that I began my formal training in transactional analysis, also at the Metanoia Institute; I turned up for the first weekend of the Foundation Year—and was delighted to see Graeme again. We reconnected; we engaged thoroughly in the training; we attended local and national conferences; and began working together around bringing transactional analysis to children, running several workshops for children at national conferences of the United Kingdom's Institute of Transactional Analysis (ITA), and international conferences organised by EATA and ITAA. For various reasons, after that initial year, we were in different training year groups; I took some time out during my training; Graeme moved away from London and, in 1992, I moved to Sheffield. Nevertheless, we kept up, and, despite some geographical distance, we used to meet and, again, discuss our responses to training and to therapy (a generic term I use to encompass psychotherapy, counselling, and counselling psychology). Whilst we still identified with transactional analysis, significantly for our future collaboration and co-creation, we had each also become interested and involved in different modalities of therapy: Graeme in gestalt therapy (see his Introduction), I in person-centred psychology. By the early 1990s we had each married; our partners had become friends; we each had had children; and our children had become friends. Another point of contact was our preparation for our qualifying examination as certified transactional analysts, an exam we both took—and passed—in the same venue: in Maastricht, in the Netherlands, in 1994. In our preparation for our exams and in our subsequent meetings, and in the context of deciding whether or not we would continue in the career path that transactional analysis offers—to becoming Provisional and then full Training and Supervising Transactional Analysts—both Graeme and I had shared some reservations about, and critiques of, transactional analysis. Whilst we each had, for the most part, enjoyed and appreciated the personal, developmental and professional impact of our training, we had a number of concerns about transactional analysis. For me, these were:

• That some of its language and ideas were outdated and, in one or two instances, offensive; examples included Berne's views on homosexuality (for a discussion of which see Barnes, 2004), and the designation of RAPO to describe a game whereby a woman falsely cries "Rape".

- That it was full of jargon; this was somewhat ironic given Berne's motivation to make especially psychoanalytic ideas more accessible.
- That in its emphasis on the contract, functionality, and (quick) "cure", it overemphasised the cognitive and the behavioural at the expense of a more psychological and relational dynamic, especially with regard to the therapeutic relationship.
- That it was overly concerned to name or nominalise things, rather than explore multiple, constructed, and more fluid meanings, and, thus, that transactional analysts often came across as being too definite, defining, certain, and, at worst, dogmatic—a theme I later explored in a conference paper (Tudor, 2007b).
- That, for the most part, and with the exception of the radical psychiatry tradition, it tended to discount the impact of the social/political world on clients, one aspect of which was, at worst, the pathologising of clients—and trainees—who were active in the social/political sphere.
- That despite the radical psychiatry tradition and that fact that transactional analysis had developed in the 1960s it appeared somewhat "straight" and conservative; as Andrew Samuels has expressed this with regard to psychotherapists: "we deal with the kinky—and yet we are a very conventional group of people" (Samuels & Williams, 2001, p. 3; also see below, p. 53).
- That a number of trainers and supervisors tended to encourage trainees to conform to "received wisdom", rather than to think for themselves and to critique theory and practice; this was also ironic given that, in the field of psychotherapy, such training was—and is—viewed as postgraduate, one of the features of which—and, indeed, the requirements of postgraduate education—is the development of the student's critical abilities.
- That the predominant theory and model of training—and it was training as distinct from education—was one based on child development whereby trainees were encouraged to view trainers and supervisors as parent (even Parent) figures and encouraged to regress, as distinct from a model of training based on adult development and adult education in which adult students are encouraged to learn and to progress.
- That in some respects it appeared irrelevant to the people with whom we were working (young people, working-class people, and people from different cultures).

In response to these critiques I/we wanted to find a way of integrating what we were bringing from our different perspectives about the importance and impact of the social sphere, as well as what we had learned from gestalt and person-centred psychologies, and to be able to identify with a more contemporary transactional analysis. Our discussions began to focus on this theme in 1998, and over the next two years we worked on a paper that was published as an article, "Co-creative transactional analysis" in the *Transactional Analysis Journal*, Vol. *30*, No. 1, January 2000, pp. 23–40, © International Transactional Analysis Association (ITAA), which forms the first chapter in this volume, and is reprinted with permission. In the original article, and drawing on field theory, social constructivism, and positive health psychology, we (re) presented a dynamic, co-creative approach to transactional analysis that offered a revision of the foundations of transactional analysis— that is, transactions, which we renamed as "co-creative reality" to emphasise the co-construction of "reality" or realities; ego states or "co-creative personality"; scripts or "co-creative identity"; and games or "co-creative confirmations".

In the article, we had drawn on the model of the Integrated Adult ego state as first suggested by Berne (1961/1975a) and developed by James and Jongeward (1971) and Erskine (1988). We considered that this model served as a useful basis for the co-creative approach because of its clear distinction between Adult integration and unintegrated introjections and fixated archaic responses. However, we also recognised that there was more work to do in elaborating this, and, as then Graeme was less interested in undertaking further writing, I took this forward by researching the concept of the Adult ego state; research that led to the publication of a chapter on "The neopsyche: The integrating Adult ego state" (Tudor, 2003), which was first published in the book *Ego States: Key Concepts in Transactional Analysis*, edited by my good friends and colleagues, Charlotte Sills and Helena Hargaden, and published by Worth Publishing, London, in 2003 (Sills & Hargaden, 2003a). This forms Chapter Two in this book and is reproduced here by kind permission of Worth Publishing.

Early on in my psychotherapy career I had been referred a couple of children, mainly, I suspect, as I had been a social worker and was, therefore, seen as "a safe pair of hands" and, as a man, perhaps something of a rarity. I undertook some additional training in working with children and had specialist supervision on this work with Sue Fish, one of the founders of Metanoia. For a number of years (from 1988 to around 2004) I always had a small number of children and young people as part of my clinical caseload, and at my qualifying CTA exam in 1994 presented my work with a child as my first tape extract and verbatim (the first UK CTA candidate to do so). When I became a supervisor I set up and ran a specialised supervision group for practitioners who were working with children, young people and families in both public and private practice. The experience of that group and the (then) widespread ambivalence in the UK transactional analysis community about transactional analysts working with children led me to propose and edit a book on the subject, which was published in 2007 (Tudor, 2007b). Historically, a number of books on transactional analysis have included a chapter introducing transactional analysis theory and concepts, and, as I wanted to retain this tradition but to update such an introduction, I asked Graeme to collaborate on an introductory chapter that would present key concepts from transactional analysis (ego states, transactions, games, and scripts) that were consistent with our co-creative approach, and would stand as a useful introduction to the subject of the book. Graeme had previously initiated our collaboration on an introduction to co-creative transactional analysis, which had been published online (Summers & Tudor, 2005b), and we used this as the basis of the chapter in the book on children and young people (Summers & Tudor, 2007), an edited version of which forms the basis of Appendix One and is reproduced here with our acknowledgement to Russell House Publishing, Lyme Regis, UK. I particularly appreciate the work Graeme did on the original introductory article, which, in effect, stands or could stand as the handout for a co-creative "TA 101" introductory course (see also Appendix Two).

As part of the preparation for the Teaching and Supervising Transactional Analysis (TSTA) Examinations (which I took and passed in Rome in 2004), I reviewed the required syllabus (Training and Certification Council (T&CC), 2010, Section 11) from a co-creative perspective and made notes on the various topics on "cue cards". Over the years I have taught 101s I have refined these and have shared these with colleagues, especially those who, in turn, are preparing for their TSTA exams. The current iteration of these notes form Appendix Two.

More recently, Graeme was invited to contribute a chapter to a volume on the application of the principles of relational transactional analysis (Fowlie & Sills, 2011) in which he developed his ideas on "dynamic ego states", which forms Chapter Four of this volume, and, again, we are grateful to Karnac Books for its permission to reproduce that chapter here.

Shortly after my chapter on ego states was published, I remember having a conversation with Graeme in which he encouraged me to complete the work we had started in our co-authored article by elaborating the method and practice of co-creative transactional analysis. In the chapter on the neopsyche/integrating Adult, I had made some points about the implications for practice on which I subsequently elaborated in an article that was originally published in the *Transactional Analysis Journal*, Vol. 41, No. 4, October 2011, pp. 322–335, © ITAA. This article, which outlines both the methodology and the method of co-creative transactional analysis, at least, from my perspective, forms Chapter Six in this volume, and is also reprinted with permission.

From the time of our initial work, beginning in 1998, the publication of this book thus represents some fifteen years of the co-creative perspective in and on transactional analysis.

Although these four contributions constitute the co-creative literature or tradition in transactional analysis, this work does not stand in isolation.

My own intellectual journey between 2003 and 2011 has encompassed being involved in a number of writing projects, specifically five publications—Cornell et al. (2006), Tudor and Worrall (2006), and Tudor (2008a, 2008d, 2011d)—which have informed the development of this co-creative theory, and, of course, the co-creative approach has, in turn, informed other work (see Figure I.1). These influences were informed also by my doctoral study *The Fight for Health* (Tudor, 2010a) in which I conducted a piece of heuristic research, drawing the connections between my work on positive mental health and its promotion (Tudor, 1996a), the chapter on the neopsyche (Tudor, 2003), and an article (and later chapter) I had written on psychological health (Tudor, 2007a, 2008a), involving both autonomy and homonomy (Angyal, 1941). Here I am describing my own development; Graeme describes his own development with regard to this material in his Introduction.

In terms of how influential this work has been, the original, co-creative article has been cited in thirty-six subsequent articles published in the *Transactional Analysis Journal* (2003–2012); by authors in eleven chapters (that I know of) in a number of books; and by Grégoire (2007), Tangolo (2010), Lapworth and Sills (2011), and Stewart and Joines (2012) in their books. It has been translated into French

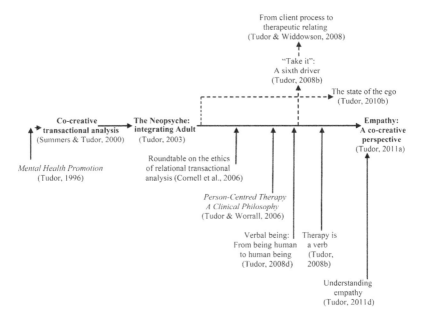

Figure I.1. The co-creative transactional analysis literature and Keith Tudor's related publications.

(Summers & Tudor, 2001) and Spanish (Summers & Tudor, 2012), and another publication on the same subject (Summers & Tudor, 2005b), originally published online then later published as a chapter (Summers & Tudor, 2008) and reproduced here as Appendix One, has been translated into Serbian (Summers & Tudor, 2005c). Co-creative transactional analysis is clearly part of the contemporary interest in and beyond transactional analysis in the "relational turn" in psychoanalysis, psychotherapy, and counselling. This was recognised by Bill Cornell and Helena Hargaden when they included the article in a collection titled *From Transactions to Relations: The Emergence of a Relational Tradition in Transactional Analysis* (Cornell & Hargaden, 2005)—that is, Summers and Tudor (2005a). The chapter on the neopsyche/integrating Adult has been cited in twenty articles in the *Transactional Analysis Journal* (2003–2012); by authors in a couple of book chapters, and by Hall (2008), Widdowson (2009), Fowlie and Sills (2011), Lapworth and Sills (2011), Mohr (2011), and Novellino (2012) in their books, and has been translated into German (Tudor, 2005). Whilst it is too early to assess the specific influence of the two most recent publications of the quartet, co-creative transactional analysis has been discussed as a recent "orientation" within transactional analysis by Grégoire (2007), and in a recent article in the *Transactional Analysis Journal* van Rijn and Wild (2013) acknowledged that: "All the approaches used at Metanoia Institute are based on relational principles (Fowlie & Sills, 2011a)[1] and share an emphasis on the centrality of the therapeutic relationship and cocreation in the therapeutic process (Summers & Tudor, 2000)" (p. 151).

Since 2000, as I have thought about, developed and taught this material, and researched and published related material, I have sometimes been asked about what constitutes "the co-creative literature". My response to this has been to name the four papers that form the basis of this book—and, now, with Graeme, to collect them together in one volume. Although Graeme and I have followed different paths and now live in different countries—he in the United Kingdom (UK) and I in Aotearoa New Zealand—we have each and both held our co-creative orientation and continued to develop and offer this critique and reading of transactional analysis. For some time I have thought about publishing a book on co-creative transactional analysis, and following a meeting with Graeme at the ITAA Congress in Bilbao in August 2011 I began to think more specifically about this. In considering the content and structure of the book, I wanted:

a. To offer some background and context to co-creative transactional analysis, which is the purpose of the two Introductions.
b. To reproduce the four co-creative papers together and to use the opportunity to edit them together; these form Chapters One, Two, Four, and Six.
c. To create some form of dialogue with colleagues within different fields of application in transactional analysis who have been influenced by, or responsive to, co-creative transactional analysis— responses that form Chapter Eight.
d. To elaborate and develop some of the arguments and implications of co-creative transactional analysis begun in all four papers—a project that now forms Chapter Ten.

At this point, I contacted Graeme to share my plans about the book. His response—typical of him, and of our relationship—was engaged, passionate, and creative. He suggested including his chapter on dynamic ego states both in its own right (as part of the literature), and, in part, as a response to my chapter on the integrating Adult. Similarly, he had some critique of my recent work on empathy as the principal method of co-creative transactional analysis. We began talking (by Skype) and, as a result, we both became excited about creating some dialogue between ourselves, which, in both its content and process, reflected our co-creativity. This led to a fifth aim for the book:

e. To co-create a dialogue between us; not only to further our thinking about co-creative transactional analysis, but also to represent and reflect on our differences, the result of which form three new and interleaving contributions (Chapters Three, Five, and Seven) between the original work.

I think the effect of this has been quite transformative, both in terms of our thinking and the development of co-creative transactional analysis, and also of the book itself, as we have opened up space between us—which, of course, now also includes you, the reader—that allows for reflection, contribution, disagreement, and diversity.

Finally, we discussed how we would introduce the book, and decided that we would write two Introductions, thereby acknowledging and honouring our separate and individual, though interrelated, journeys to this point; and, as the project progressed, we also decided to conclude with two separate Afterwords.

In aiming to produce a coherent book, we have edited the original papers for consistency and house style, and have updated references that were then noted as being "in press"; any substantive editions and additions are noted by square brackets [...]. With regard to our original article (Chapter One), we have taken the opportunity to make two significant revisions. In presenting the four pillars of transactional analysis, Berne tended to maintain the sequence: ego states, transactions, games, and scripts, on the basis that "Structural analysis, which must precede Transactional Analysis, is concerned with the segregation and analysis of ego states" (Berne, 1961/1975a, p. 22). In *Transactional Analysis in Psychotherapy* he followed his discussion of ego states (Chapters Two–Seven) by the "Analysis of Transactions" (Chapter Nine), "Games" (Chapter Ten), and "Scripts" (Chapter Eleven); he reproduced this structure in *Principles of Group Treatment* (Berne, 1966) and in his last book, *What Do You Say After You Say Hello?* (Berne, 1972/1975b). Given our constructivist approach, and the opportunity this book affords us to play with the structure of our original article, our first revision is to reorder the material so that the sequence of the parts is now: transactions, followed by ego states, then scripts, and games. (We have, nevertheless, retained Berne's sequence in our introductory article, which forms Appendix One.) Our second revision is to reformulate our original script matrix so that it is more in line with the logic of our ego state theory. In the chapter on the neopsyche (Chapter Two) I have also taken the opportunity to elaborate some aspects of theory. As a part of making this a whole book, and to avoid repetition, we have collected all the references from the original individual papers, together with the new chapters, in one list of References. The exception to this is Chapter Eight in which, as it comprises contributions from other colleagues, we have combined their citations in a reference list at the end of that chapter. Also, for coherence and ease of reference for the reader, when referring to text originally published elsewhere (i.e., in Chapters One, Two, Four, and Six) we use the page numbers in this present book. Since I wrote the original chapter on the neopsyche, I have further refined the term "Integrating Adult" by writing the adjective in lower case, thus "integrating Adult", in order to avoid reification of this nominal "state", and have incorporated this change throughout, again for consistency. Since I moved to Aotearoa New Zealand in 2009, I have had the good fortune to meet a new group of colleagues, one of whom is Charlotte Daellenbach, who, amongst her many other contributions, promotes the use of the term "transactional analysis" over its abbreviated form "TA"; I agree with her, and we have thus adopted this convention in the book. I am also grateful that she, together with several other colleagues from both within and outside transactional analysis, accepted our invitation to offer their endorsements for the book which may be found on the publishers website at http://www.karnacbooks.com/Product.asp?PID=35472&MATCH=1. Finally, with regard to language, in most cases we use the term "therapist" to refer to the practitioner. This reflects the fact that our approach was originally developed in the context of psychotherapy and largely informed by psychotherapeutic literature. We think that the practitioner might also be a counsellor, coach, educator or consultant who may utilise this framework in a manner appropriate to their professional context. In terms of clarifying language, concepts, and terms, we have also provided a Glossary.

In the original article (Summers & Tudor, 2000), Graeme and I noted our gratitude to a number of colleagues for their support in the course of our development and writing of the paper, especially Helena Hargaden and Charlotte Sills, and, specifically, Jim Allen, Robin Hobbes, and Peter Philippson. In the chapter on the neopsyche, I acknowledged that it had been enriched by continuing discussions with Graeme, as well as with Helena and Charlotte, to all of whom I was—and still am—grateful for their continued support, encouragement, feedback, and friendships. As regards this book, I want to acknowledge first Graeme for his creativity and contribution to our "co-"relationship, and, indeed, to the evolving project that has become this book; second, our colleagues who have contributed to Chapter Eight; third, my transactional analysis colleagues in Aoteaora New Zealand, and, specifically in terms of the development of my ideas for this book, Jo Stuthridge, as well as for her welcome, collegiality, and friendship; Al Freed Saboonchi for his interest in, and questions about, the co-creative approach to impasses and impasse theory; and "the Wellington Group", comprising Andrea Broadhurst, Dianne Brooker, Patricia Ford, Karen Horrocks, Kate Jacobsen, Mark Pope, and Rob Surtees, who were kind enough to invite me to facilitate a two-day training course on co-creative transactional analysis, and with whom I enjoyed a delightful and stimulating time "road-testing" some of the new ideas in this book; fourth, Sue Eusden for her questions about power, which stimulated me/us to clarify some of our ideas about this subject; fifth, to colleagues at Auckland University of Technology, Auckland, who are supportive and encouraging of my research, writing, and publishing, and my enthusiasm for the field; and, last but by no means least, my family, who, as ever, support me with what the Irish poet Brendan Behan affectionately referred to as his "writing problem"! In particular I want to acknowledge, and thank, my son Saul, who (I may say) is not only an intuitive philosopher and psychologist, but also someone with whom— along with his friends—I and my wife, Louise, enjoy great conversations about life and the universe—if not love! A couple of years ago, Saul came to a talk I gave in Auckland about co-creative transactional analysis (Tudor, 2011) at which I presented the history, development and influences outlined in this Introduction; a talk that marked my decision to pursue and publish this book, which, therefore, I dedicate to him with much love, paternal—that is, integrating Adult!—pride, and respect.

Note

1. These relational principles were developed in 2009/2010 by the founding members of the International Association for Relational Transactional Analysis (IARTA) (see Chapter Six).

INTRODUCTION

Graeme Summers

I welcome the opportunity to share some of my reflections about co-creative transactional analysis within this book, and to thank you, the reader, for your interest in this approach. I have appreciated how others have responded to our work over the years, and hope that we can provide here some space for a range of perspectives that express a vitalising mix of convergence and divergence in how people under-stand, adapt and use these ideas.

Keith continues to be a significant advocate and provocateur in my own development. From the beginning of our friendship, over twenty-five years ago, we spent many hours indulging our mutual love for psychological ideas and their application in passionate and engaging conversations.

In our original article we consistently utilised the "we" pronoun as "we" articulated "our" thinking. This reflected our overlapping frames of reference and interests, which continue to resonate meaningfully with me. However, I see it as a mark of health that Keith and I have both common and different interests. For this reason we have chosen to each write separate Introductions to give space for our individual voices and to allow for our personal and intertwining narratives and preoccupations to emerge.

I was introduced to, and inspired by, Transactional Analysis (TA) in 1982 when working for Hounslow Social Services, London, with "at risk" adolescents. Here, I was fortunate to get input on transactional analysis, group work training and supervision from Petrūska Clarkson, one of the founders of metanoia Psychotherapy Training Institute. I completed my first year of transactional analysis training at Metanoia during 1983/1984 and then, encouraged by Petrūska, studied psychology at Brunel University. I continued to employ transactional analysis in my work with children and adolescents in various educational and clinical settings and to benefit from diverse theoretical and supervisory perspectives.

I re-entered formal transactional analysis training in 1987 and here I reconnected with Keith. Alongside our theoretical conversations we also designed and delivered psycho-educational children's workshops for Metanoia and ran an emotional literacy workshop for children at several national and international TA conferences (see Tudor, 1991).

In the following years we prepared for CTA exams together, shared PTSTA supervision sessions, and continued social contact. It was in 1998 that Keith suggested we write together, prompted by one of our many conversations about TA theory and practice. I had started leading a foundation year transactional analysis training group in the previous year. I was therefore immersed in exploring (and re-exploring) the core transactional analysis concepts both in my teaching preparation and dialogues with trainees, colleagues, and supervisors. In doing so, I had become preoccupied with the following three questions.

Can transactional analysis offer models of health as well as pathology?

It appeared to me that games and scripts in particular were pathologically focused. The healthy alternatives were predominantly defined in negative forms such as "game antithesis" or being "script free".

I had been reflecting on Berne's analogy between children's games and psychological games for some time and pondered his statement: "The essential characteristic of human play is not that the emotions are spurious, but that they are regulated" (Berne, 1964/1968a, p. 18). Could healthy affect co-regulation be considered a positive psychological game that underpins or reinforces affirming beliefs about self and others? My thoughts about healthy scripts were less formed.

*What model of ego states (from the many available) makes
most sense to me and what then are the implications for
other core transactional analysis concepts?*

Whilst I could have been satisfied with the multiplicity of ego state models within TA, using each as appeared appropriate, this felt haphazard and created many theoretical inconsistencies. Further, the potential confusion between models is amplified, as they are extrapolated into models of transactions, games, and script.

I was very drawn to Erskine's (1988) formulation of ego states. In picking up and developing Berne's reference to Fairbairn (1952), Erskine rooted ego state development within a relational perspective. Additionally, he equated Fairbairn's terms "Internal Saboteur", "Central Ego" and "Libidinal Ego", which, according to Fairbairn (1952), are "all conceived as inherently dynamic structures resulting from the splitting of an original and single dynamic ego-structure present at the beginning" (p. 148), to Parent, Adult and Child ego states. Erskine later developed the implications of this reformulation for the concept of transactions, particularly in differentiating transference and non-transference transactions (Erskine, 1991). Although I do not subscribe to Erskine's method, I consider that this bold and original reformulation of ego states marked a significant shift from traditional transactional analysis thinking and stands out as a powerful influence.

*How do transactional analysis approaches account
for co-creativity?*

This question was provoked by my parallel immersion in gestalt influences. I was working alongside gestalt therapists, in gestalt personal therapy, and in a gestalt professional development group. The notion of "co-creativity" was often considered and used as a perspective from which to reflect upon interactions.

Other gestalt ideas and practice that influenced me were notions of "interrupting the interruption" (to contact) and the facilitation of novel experience, each designed to encourage the recovery and development of organismic fluidity. A further influence in relation to the co-creation of novelty came from Peter Philippson's idea (personal communication, 1996; see also Philippson, 2009) that the "rule of epoche" (in the phenomenological method), which "urges us to set aside our initial biases and prejudices of things, to suspend our expectations and assumptions" (Spinelli, 1989, p. 17), applies equally to the client as to the practitioner.

My impression was that whilst traditional transactional analysis emphasised the importance of individual autonomy and personal rede-cisions, it largely considered co-creation in pathological terms—that is, symbiosis.

In our conversations, Keith and I found much in common (see Keith's Introduction) and we prompted each other to further reading, reflecting, and talking. Our ideas evolved significantly over the writing process, incorporating many influences. We had an emergent sense of building and articulating the foundational principles of a contempo-rary interpretation on transactional analysis, which we believed were consistent across the four core transactional analysis concepts (i.e., ego stages, transactions, games, and scripts), and dared to propose our work as such.

Three years after our original article was published, Keith's work on the integrating Adult (Tudor, 2003) was published in which he unpacked and significantly developed the implications of our ideas for this core construct. In so doing, he raised the profile of the Adult ego state, now portrayed in a dynamic and far more expansive manner than had pre-viously been described. It was also here that Keith introduced a new graphical notation for the Adult ego state (see Figure 2.4) in the form of several slightly overlapping circles to present the illusion of an oscil-lating, "always in motion" (p. 53) process that is differentiated from fixated Parent and Child defences. We have chosen to adopt this nota-tion in our diagrams throughout this book with exception of Figure 1.2 (where this notation would be difficult to discern given the small size of the circles in these ego state diagrams).

An alternative/additional way to differentiate Adult from Parent and Child graphically is through colour. I often use a green circle to draw Adult and red circles to draw Parent and Child. Clients quickly adopt the idea of avoiding, managing or getting out of the red and going for green in themselves and others. This at least gives a clear, visual map for their aspirations, even if the process of developing the self-awareness and relational skills necessary for achieving them takes time to learn.

What drew me to transactional analysis in the first instance, and still draws me, is the attempt within our community of theorists and prac-titioners to make traditional and contemporary psychology accessible, whilst retaining a depth and sophistication that hopefully can be used to enrich many domains of human interaction. As indicated above, one of my aims in developing co-creative transactional analysis was to create a model that provided theoretical consistency across the four core concepts of transactional analysis. This was partly motivated by my desire to create an accessible, if simplified, version which also made sense to me at deeper levels.

Could I explain co-creative transactional analysis to my (not psychologically minded) parents? Could I explain it to my children, and, if I could, would they find it useful? These questions led me to experiment with ways of presenting and talking about co-creative transactional analysis to different audiences and fed into an introductory article (Summers & Tudor, 2005b) that, significantly, was published on the web, and was expanded upon in a further joint publication (Summers & Tudor, 2007).

In our original work we made two references to Adult–Adult ulterior transactions. In our later more "accessible" articles, we diagrammed the Adult–Adult duplex transaction and described the social level and psychological levels of communication as explicit and implicit, respectively. These were important precursors to my chapter on "Dynamic Ego States" (Summers, 2011; reprinted here as Chapter Four), which explored the significance of unconscious and non-conscious patterns within a co-creative transactional analysis frame. Following Daniel Stern's (2004) distinction between the repressed unconscious and the non-repressed non-conscious, I proposed that the former relates to Parent and Child ego states and the latter to the Adult ego states. My understanding is that Adult–Adult relating may—but does not necessarily or only—imply consciousness. Stern (2004), commenting on a clinical vignette in which a therapeutic rupture between therapist and client has just been successfully navigated, suggested:

> They both are learning (implicitly) that together they can work this kind of situation out. They are cocreating ways-of-being-with-one another. In short, they are implicitly learning ways of regulating their intersubjective field. This delicate choreography goes on mostly outside of consciousness. (p. 167)

I believe unconscious or non-conscious patterns are ever present and have a predominant influence on the co-creation of familiar pathological patterns as well as familiar and novel healthy interactions. This often occurs concurrently in the relational matrix although the relative strength of past and present relating varies.

I consider that progressively "co-creating ways-of-being-with-one another" is the behavioural outcome of the Adult–Adult duplex transaction or transactions, which constitutes changes in implicit relational knowing. This is Berne's (1966) third rule of communication, applied to progressive rather than regressive experience.

Adult consciousness is an ally in monitoring and guiding interactions. Along with Eusden (2011), I consider an important working principle is that of cultivating "curiosity and mindfulness" (p. 107) in relation to emergent relational dynamics. This is consciousness speculatively and respectfully applied to powerful, implicit processes. My Jungian analyst would often embody this by prefixing interpretations with "I wonder if …"

However, attempts at conscious commentary or enquiry by practitioner or client can be used defensively to avoid the deepening of implicit experience. In which case, they would probably not be grounded in conscious or non-conscious Adult and more likely be involved in some form of transferential enactment. Hirsch (2008) has noted that enactments may not necessarily be experienced as disturbing by therapist or client and indeed, more often, may constitute mutual languishing in their respective comfort zones, and that this can occur across the spectrum of therapeutic styles.

It appears that there are no safe or certain conscious methods that can guarantee growth in our clients, since any such method may be hijacked by the implicit agenda. Berne resisted over-structuring groups because he wanted space for the "psychological structure" to emerge. So we can and should expect the implicit agenda to make its presence felt and develop our capacity as practitioners to be therapeutically receptive to it. Our conscious efforts to facilitate growth are subject to inherent limitations, and "the real work" always happens at a deeper level. Nonetheless, we continue to explore, speculate, develop and update our cognitive understanding and relational skills in the service of healing and learning, whilst accepting there is always more to learn and much that can never be known at a conscious level.

The principle method of co-creative transactional analysis is play. This is an intentional—and a playful and provocative—response to Keith's assertion that the principle method of co-creative transactional analysis is empathy (Tudor, 2011a). I think both of these positions are true and that even together they do not exhaust possible methods. In his latest article on this approach, "Empathy: A cocreative perspective" (Tudor, 2011a; reprinted here as Chapter Six), Keith usefully differentiated Adult–Adult empathy from other ways in which empathy can be understood and used. He clearly tracked the development of his thinking from our original co-authored article through to his work on the Adult ego state and this most recent piece, via a review of the concept of empathy (Tudor, 2011d). I do, however, have some concern that empathy may be interpreted by some as the *only* way to practice co-creative TA. I think this concern underpins my own reluctance to describe co-creative transactional analysis method other than through intentionally vague, broad brushstrokes, which allow for, or even encourage, multiple interpretations and forms of application. This fits with my belief that co-creative transactional analysis is best considered as a generative approach designed to facilitate the emergence of new contextually viable possibilities grounded in relational experience—and that this could happen in many ways depending on the practitioner, the client, and the context.

Therefore, I often emphasise "playing" as both a way of being with clients and a way of working and exploring themes together without getting overly anxious about being right or wrong. Winnicott (1967/1971) suggested that mutual play between therapist and client was a precondition for psychotherapy and that, without it, analytic interpretations become a form of indoctrination inviting client compliance and resistance. He stated:

> In this kind of work we know that even the right explanation is ineffectual. The person we are trying to help needs a new experience in a specialized setting. The experience is one of a non-purposive state, as one might say a sort of ticking over of the unintegrated personality. (p. 55)

Of course, play, like empathy, can be used well or badly and this is why flexibility and close attention to the undercurrents and transactional outcomes are essential, whatever method is explicitly adopted.

Having ended my career as a psychotherapist in 2006, I now work as a freelance executive coach. I often work on leadership development programmes delivered by international business schools with people from many different cultures. This has stretched me in new ways and I have engaged in further training including educational and organisational TA, an executive coaching diploma, and psychoanalytic organisational development seminars. I make extensive use of co-creative transactional analysis in my work, principally as an internal guiding framework and sometimes through explicit sharing of concepts about which I continue to ponder, develop, present and discuss in various professional contexts, including my transactional analysis networks.

With accessibility, depth and diversity in mind, I welcome our contributors Helena, Laurie, Marco, Trudi, and Gregor (see Chapter Eight), and appreciate their commitment to share with us aspects of their thinking and practice, which can enrich our exploration and development.

I also, as ever, look forward to my continuing dialogue with Keith, which, here, is interspersed throughout the book as outlined in our Contents page.

I want to thank a number of people with and from whom I continue to enjoy learning through our ongoing, searching and often playful conversations. Thank you to my reading group peers: Jamie Agar, Sue Eusden, Dave Gowling, and Phil Lapworth. Thank you also to my IARTA colleagues: Suzanne Boyd, Mica Douglas, Sue Eusden, Brian Fenton, Heather Fowlie, Ray Little, Carole Shadbolt, Charlotte Sills, and David Tidsall. Finally, thank you to Sue, my partner in love, lust, and adventure, to whom I dedicate this book.

CHAPTER ONE

Co-creative transactional analysis*

Graeme Summers and Keith Tudor

D rawing on field theory and social constructivism, we present a dynamic, co-creative approach to transactional analysis. This approach emphasises the present-centred nature of the therapeutic relationship—or therapeutic relating—and the co-creative nature of transactions, ego states, scripts, and games. We frame this approach within a positive health perspective on transactional analysis (as distinct from an undue emphasis on psychopathology) and argue that co-creative transactional analysis provides a narrative or story about transactional analysis itself, which offers new and contemporary meanings to old transactional truths. The chapter concludes with a series of questions for self-supervision, which may serve as a useful guide to co-creative transactional analysis practice.

There is currently a lively debate in transactional analysis about its present, past, and future. This discussion often becomes polarised in terms of whether transactional analysis is "transactional analysis

*Originally published in the *Transactional Analysis Journal,* 30(1), January 2000, pp. 23–40, © International Transactional Analysis Association (ITAA). Reprinted with permission.

enough" or not. Over the past forty years, transactional analysis has developed in many directions—theoretically, technically, organisationally, and internationally—and in doing so has, in our view, lost some of its radical roots. At the same time, therapy, science and the social/political world have changed at an exponential rate, and transactional analysis needs to account for this.

In the past [then] ten years, a number of writers have argued for what may be characterised as a "back to the future" approach to transactional analysis—that is, returning to its basic concepts [and, in doing so,] discovering new meanings or reaffirming old ones and applying these to a changing and postmodern world. Cornell's (1988) critical review of life script theory, Schmid's (1991) focus on the transactional creation of realities, and Allen and Allen's work on postmodernism (1995) and constructivism (1997) have all been especially influential. It is in this tradition that we locate our work in developing a narrative of transactional analysis that reframes and updates familiar concepts.

The roots of co-creativity

Co-creativity derives principally from two theoretical strands: field theory (Lewin, 1952) and social constructivism (see Gergen, 1985).

Field theory is a general theoretical outlook that emphasises interrelationship. Drawing on the metaphor of an electrical or magnetic field, this holistic approach questions linear causality and suggests that events occur "as a function of the overall properties of the field taken as an interactive dynamic whole" (Parlett, 1991, p. 70). The implication of this approach is that:

> when two people converse or engage with one another in some way, something comes into existence which is a product of neither of them exclusively … There is a shared field, a common communicative home, which is mutually constructed. (p. 75)

This approach has been particularly developed in gestalt theory and therapy. By applying and developing this perspective in relation to transactional analysis, we are emphasising the transactional, the relational and the mutual in the therapeutic relationship.

From social constructivism we derive the perspective that our perceptual and phenomenological experience is an elaboration or construction based on hypothesised cognitive and affective operations—that is, there are many consensual realities, and we organise ourselves and our experiences through the stories or narratives we tell about "reality." Within transactional analysis, Allen and Allen (1997) pointed out that since transactional analysts work with scripts they/[we] are familiar with this narrative view of realities. The principles of constructivism that are relevant to and that inform co-creative transactional analysis may be summarised as follows:

- Meaning constantly evolves through dialogue.
- Discourse creates systems (and not the other way around).
- Therapy is the co-creation, in dialogue, of new narratives, which provide new possibilities.
- The therapist is a participant-observer in this dialogue.

Allen and Allen (1997) summarised and compared the different emphases of constructionist and classical schools of transactional analysis with the following additional implications for co-creative transactional analysis:

- There is an emphasis on continuous self-creation and self-re-creation (in dialogic relationship).
- Ego states and transactions are elicited from meaning (rather than the other way around).
- Script is a story that, like transference, is co-created in an ongoing present process.

Co-creative transactional analysis: guiding principles

The principle of "we"ness

The therapeutic relationship (or relating) is more potent than the potency (or impotency) of the therapist or client alone. It provides a supportive theoretical framework that emphasises the "we"ness (Saner, 1989) of the therapeutic relationship as the medium for human development and change. It also emphasises the cultural context of both individual and field. This is significant given that more cultures in the world are "we" cultures than the individualistic and individualising "me" monocultures of northern and western Europe and non-indigenous North America. These latter cultures have given rise to much monocultural psychology and psychotherapy. For example, "we"ness has generally been discouraged within transactional analysis for fear of inviting symbiosis. The "we"ness of Adult–Adult relating, however, is very different from the "we"ness of Parent–Child, Parent–Parent, or Child–Child relating, all of which constitute transferential or, what we consider, co-transferential processes.

The principle of shared responsibility

Given its emphasis on meaning through dialogue and on multiple meanings and realities, co-creative transactional analysis supports the practical manifestation of interdependence, co-operation and mutuality within the therapeutic relationship by emphasising the shared client–therapist responsibility for the therapeutic process. This is in contrast to traditional transactional analysis, which emphasises the personal responsibility of the client. It also contrasts with more recent integrative transactional analysis approaches, which, in our opinion, tend to over-emphasise the responsibility of the therapist. While the therapist must take a leading role in the creation of therapeutic safety, our emphasis on shared responsibility is intended to provide a conceptual frame for acknowledging and exploring co-created experience.

Berne's (1964/1968a) focus on the advantages of games suggests what, even in apparently negative exchanges, each party contributes to and gains from the relationship between them. The healing aspects of relationship—for example, potency, permission, protection, support, and challenge—are co-created and co-maintained by active contributions from both therapist and client. The therapist's particular contribution is his or her skill in facilitating and using this shared responsibility to promote awareness and development. Shared responsibility is not, however, the same as equal responsibility. Efforts to divide responsibility into a 50:50 or a 60:40 split, for example, are reductionist attempts to define the phenomenon of relationship from an individualistic frame of reference.

The principle of present-centred development

Co-creative transactional analysis emphasises the importance of present-centred human development rather than past-centred child development. Essentially, we view psychotherapy as an Adult–Adult process of learning and healing. Although this process necessitates involvement in, and learning from, positive and negative transference as it is created in the relationship, the therapeutic focus is on supporting the client's here-and-now developmental direction. This reduces the possibility of inappropriate infantilising of adult clients (and trainees), which can develop when growth is predominantly defined within a Parent–Child frame of reference.

Following Bruner's (1986) division of knowledge of the world into the paradigmatic (traditional science and consensual reality) and the narrative (the realm of stories), Allen and Allen (1997) argued that while ego states, transactions and games fit easily into the paradigmatic mode, scripts are more compatible with—and, indeed, *are*—narrative:

> The concepts of ego states and games fit with the modernist's search for "essences." They are conceptualised as "real" and basic … In contrast, at least certain understandings of script fit with the postmodernist position that meanings can emerge and disappear in the context of our interactions. (p. 91)

Although we agree with this reformulation of script theory, we also accept the challenge of the "narrative turn" that philosophy and social science has taken in the last twenty years to deconstruct transactions, ego states and games in order to present a more complete picture of a constructivist, co-creative transactional analysis.

In this chapter we develop co-creative transactional analysis by first discussing the therapeutic relationship, co-created through transactions (or what we term co-creative reality), following which we address the other three main areas or foundations of transactional analysis: ego states (co-creative personality), scripts (co-creative identity), and games (co-creative confirmations).

The therapeutic relationship

It is now widely acknowledged in outcome research on psychotherapy that the therapeutic relationship is the determining factor in successful therapy; for example, Bergin and Lambert (1978), Luborsky, Crits-Christoph, Alexander, Margolis, and Cohen (1983) and Hill (1989) [see also Duncan, Miller, Wampold & Hubble, 2010]. In fact, the relationship is more important in counselling and psychotherapy than is the practitioner's theoretical orientation—see Lambert (1992), Duncan and Moynihan (1994), Kahn (1997). Despite the fact that the therapeutic relationship is presupposed and "a sine qua non of effective therapy" (Stewart, 1996, p. 198), comparatively little has been written explicitly about the therapeutic relationship in transactional analysis—see Berne (1966, 1972/1975b), Barr (1987), Clarkson (1992b), and Erskine (1998b).

Although there are differences between the three so-called traditional "schools" within transactional analysis, all describe the therapeutic relationship in terms of transference (see Tudor, 1999b). Erskine and Trautmann (1996), in particular, emphasise the relationship as central to the integrative approach to transactional analysis (viewed by some as a fourth school within transactional analysis). This approach draws heavily on self psychology and focuses on the importance of the therapist providing empathic attunement to the client. The role of the therapist as provider differs in emphasis from our conceptualisation of psychotherapy based on mutual relationship and shared responsibility.

In a seminal and extended article on the subject, drawing on Greenson's (1967) original work in psychoanalysis, Gelso and Carter (1985) discussed three components of all therapeutic relationships: the working alliance, the transferential or "unreal" relationship, and the "real" relationship. In her model of five relationship modes, Barr (1987) identified a "developmentally needed" (p. 137) relationship. Clarkson (1990, 1995) adopted this and added a fifth component: the transpersonal relationship.

With regard to Gelso and Carter's theorised therapeutic relationships, we agree with Barrett-Lennard's (1985) response to their article:

> No clear-cut grounds are given or evident for distinguishing elements that belong to the real relationship versus the working alliance. The problem may result from these two components being basically different in kind, the former having to do with strength and effectiveness of the relationship ... and the latter referring to a main area of content of the relationship. (p. 287)

Gelso and Carter and those who follow them, then, essentially confuse two forms of knowledge: one defining the content—and, we would add, process—of the relationship; the other evaluating a quality (strength, effectiveness) of the relationship. The working alliance is thus part of making and maintaining an Adult–Adult relationship, not a separate relationship in itself.

On the question of the developmentally needed relationship, it is perhaps significant that Barr (1987), in her brief description of this relationship mode, did not describe or diagram the relationship between client and therapist. We suggest that, in theory and practice, any developmentally needed or reparative transaction is based in a transferential relationship—that is, in some replay of the past in the present (e.g., an "I as I was—You as I would like you to have been" relationship). In our view, the Child developmentally needed relationship is a positive, idealised or idealising version of the transference relationship, whereas age-appropriate Adult developmental needs are a feature of present-centred relating.

Finally, we view Clarkson's addition of the transpersonal as a quality—or moment—in the relationship rather than as a relationship in itself. Thus we consider the notion of a transpersonal relationship to be an over-extrapolation of occasional moments of transcendence that occur within the I–You relationship.

In our view, these three models are overcomplicated both theoretically and from a practical, clinical point of view. A transactional analysis model of therapeutic relationships needs to be based on the analysis of transactions in the therapeutic relationship: a co-creative transactional relationship.

Our simplified proposal is that there are essentially two ways of relating: present-centred Adult–Adult relating and past-centred co-transferential relating (see Figure 1.1). In addition, there are the stepping stones of "partial transferential transactions" by which we move between past- and present-centred relating.

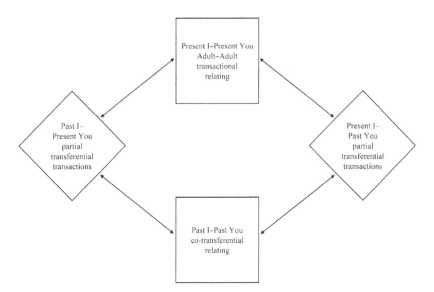

Figure 1.1. Co-creative therapeutic relating.[1]

The process of relating occurs when two or more people engage in a series of transactions. The double-headed arrows in Figure 1.1 represent the equal value we give to both forms of therapeutic relating and the movement between them. Both ways of relating can co-create metanarratives on the therapeutic relationship. However, while co-transference relating creates familiar transferential themes, Adult–Adult relating allows for fresh configurations and meanings to emerge.

This formulation has a number of advantages from a transactional perspective:

1. It names and emphasises the present-centred Adult–Adult therapeutic relationship.
2. It locates and equalises the partial transferential transactions (Past I–Present You and Present I–Past You) in that both client and therapist may be experiencing the past in the present or have what Rogers (1951) referred to as "transferential attitudes" (p. 199). This view suggests that either the therapist or the client can make a therapeutic intervention—that is, can initiate a shift from past- to present-centred relating.
3. It emphasises the shared responsibility of both parties (client and therapist) for creating and maintaining a co-transferential relationship when operating from a Past I–Past You position.
4. It is comprehensive in describing and reflecting therapeutic relationships based on analysis of structural transactions and corresponding rules of communication (Berne, 1966) (see Figure 1.2).

Adult–Adult relating and co-transferential relating are both examples of complementary transactions by which communication can proceed indefinitely (Berne's 1966 first rule of communication). Partial transferential transactions are, of course, crossed transactions whereby "a break in communication results and one or both individuals will need to shift ego-states in order for communication to be re-established" (Stewart & Joines, 1987, p. 65) (Berne's second rule of communication). For this reason we regard the partial transferential transaction as a transitory stepping stone between past- and present-centred ways of relating. Our suggestion is that crossed transactions alone cannot support a sustainable form of relating. If the client is consistently relating transferentially, then it is often useful to assume that the therapist is in some

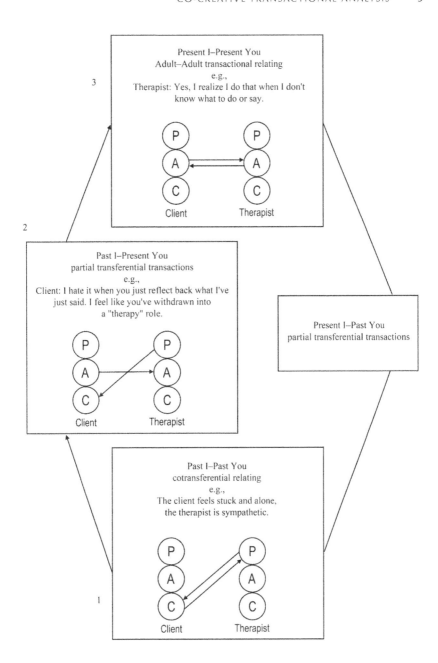

Figure 1.2. Co-creative therapeutic relationships: Mapping a client's crossed transactions.

way contributing to the transferential process. Berne (1966) was clearly suggesting this in his description of ulterior transactions and in his corresponding third rule of communication: "The behavioral outcome of an ulterior transaction is determined at the psychological and not at the social level" (p. 227).

A note on terms

In discussing these therapeutic relationships we use the terms "Adult–Adult" and "co-transferential" rather than "real" and "unreal" (as Gelso and Carter did) because we regard [transference, countertransference and] transferential relating as phenomenologically real. For instance, wanting a therapist to be and seeing her as the independent/loving/responsive mother the client always wanted is no less real a desire for it being projected and transferential. "Transferential" is not "not OK"; it is one way of describing ways of experiencing in therapy (Allen & Allen, 1991).

Ways of relating

In fact, all ways of relating are important; indeed, Berne (1972/1975b) asserted that we often need to play games with clients in order to make a relationship. Also, we prefer to use "past" rather than the possible "not You" because the former emphasises that this relating is transferred from the past rather than implying that it is not real or not really "You." We also recognise—and, along with constructivists, emphasise—that the past is as much affected by the present as the present is influenced by the past. We prefer the term "relating" to the word "relationship" (although we use both interchangeably) since it emphasises a process within the therapeutic relationship rather than a fixed entity. We use structural transactions as the basis for co-creative transactional analysis because they are based on the structural model of ego states, which helps to distinguish between transferential and non-transferential relating (in contrast to functional transactions, based on the functional model of ego states, which is a model for mapping behavioral options). These two approaches to transactions have been well described by Lapworth, Sills, and Fish (1993) [see also the revised edition by Lapworth and Sills (2011)]. Our conceptualisation of ego states is clarified in the subsequent section in this chapter on ego states.

Co-transferential therapeutic relating

Allen and Allen (1997) described a constructivist conceptualisation of transference:

> We create a familiar relationship pattern with the other person in the here and now, and … much of this relationship depends on how we are organised and the stories we and others tell ourselves; that is, we create the relationship based on what we are capable of, our stories, and what others, their stories, and the context allows. (p. 92)

The logic of such a constructivist or co-creative transactional analysis is that transference—and countertransference—are co-created, and thus, along with others, we prefer the term "co-transference":

> This better reflects the reality that meaning is being co-created by both subjectivities … with neither person holding a more objectively "true" version of reality than the other. It reflects an appreciation of the inevitable, moment-by-moment participation of the therapist's subjective organisation of experience in a system of mutual influence. (Sapriel, 1998, p. 42)

Both familiar and fresh meanings are co-created within the relationship. If client and therapist agree to contain the familiar transferential meanings within the therapeutic frame (contracting within the present Adult–Adult therapeutic relationship), then they can enact, explore, clarify, and understand their co-created transference.

The following example is from an initial session with a client who describes how she often feels misunderstood:

CLIENT: I want you to be able to understand me.
THERAPIST: I won't promise to do that. I am willing to explore with you how we create understanding or the lack of it so that we can learn what happens.
CLIENT: That's OK with me.

We either learn more about how we re-enact the past or we learn about how to embrace present possibilities. Co-transference could be considered the manifestation of "co-unconscious states … [that] partners have experienced and produced jointly" (Moreno, 1977, p. vii).

Impasse and impasse resolution may thus be viewed primarily as relational phenomena. Traditionally, transactional analysis theorists have characterised the impasse as an intrapsychic phenomena with Type II and Type III impasses being resolved within the Child ego state (Goulding & Goulding, 1976; Mellor, 1980). Our perspective is that the impasse that was originally co-created within a relationship is now co-maintained through transferential relating, or co-resolved through Adult–Adult contact. For example, a client laments her lack of mothering as she avoids eye contact, sighs deeply, and collapses back into her chair. The therapist feels excluded as he watches her "suffer." They may well be re-enacting past deficits; they are certainly co-creating a deficit of here-and-now contact. The therapist invites reflection on their process:

THERAPIST: You look deprived and I feel excluded. What do you think is happening between us?

CLIENT: I imagined you weren't interested in what I was saying.

THERAPIST: It's true that right now I'm not specifically interested in your relationship with your mother. I'm more interested in you and me, here and now.

CLIENT: Umm … You know, I could feel hurt about that, but, actually, I feel relieved to hear you say that.

In this example the therapist crosses the initial co-transferential transaction by inviting Adult–Adult reflection, which then leads to the co-creation of contact rather than a transferential re-enactment of deficit. [For more on a co-creative approach to impasses see Chapter Ten.]

We now turn to present-centred therapeutic relating before considering the movement between the two (see Figure 1.1).

Present I–Present You: intersubjectivity and therapeutic relating

The present-centred Adult–Adult relationship is the context for learning and healing, including learning from transferential re-enactment. In this regard the Adult–Adult relationship incorporates the I–You relationship as described Buber (1923/1937) in his book entitled *Ich und Du*. This is often translated as "I and Thou", though we prefer the more familiar second person form "you" to the formal "thou" as a more accurate translation of the original German. Buber emphasised the primacy of human relating, mutual confirmation, and healing through meeting.[2]

Similarly, Berne's formulation of the existential life position "I'm OK, You're OK" is significant in that he viewed OKness as existing in a relational context. He did not formulate it simply as "I'm OK," but described it in relation to another. He even extended this in *What Do You Say After You Say Hello?* (Berne, 1972/1975b) in an important and, in our view, often overlooked addition: "I'm OK, You're OK, They're OK" (which he took from Satir, whose formulation was "I count, you count, context counts"). In this regard both Buber and Berne (as well as Satir) predated much modern (and postmodern) concern with intersubjectivity, described by Atwood and Stolorow (1996) as "reciprocal mutual influence" (p. 181) [as well as with the external, social world]. They further described the implications of such reciprocity:

> From this perspective, the observer and his or her language are grasped as intrinsic to the observed, and the impact of the analyst and his or her organising activity on the unfolding of the therapeutic relationship itself becomes the focus of ... investigation and reflection. (p. 181)

One of the implications of Berne's three-handed position in relation to our formulation of a transactional approach to therapeutic relating is, of course, in the context of groups and organisations. If either the client or the therapist is relating from his or her past or "not present" position, and especially if they are both in that position, other group members may not be caught in it or expressing transferential attitudes and will therefore be helpful in being conscious, enlightening witnesses to the co-transference. This configuration can be understood as a manifestation of the following positions: "Past I–Present You–Present Them," "Present I–Past You–Present Them," "Past I–Past You–Present Them." One group therapist became frustrated with a client who kept constantly interrupting her; after a number of such transactions, the therapist raised her voice and said that she was irritated with her client, at which point the client became scared and defensive. The client missed the next group, and at a subsequent group accused the therapist of being abusive toward him. The therapist and a number of group members became involved in an aggressive-defensive game, reminiscent of the client's experience of, and relationship with, his mother. After a number of unsuccessful attempts to communicate with the client, the therapist, using the idea of the Carom transaction (Woollams & Brown, 1978), began to "bounce" her interventions off other group members who had stayed in a present relationship with the client. As a result, the client was helped, albeit only for short periods, to relate in a present-centred way with other group members and, through them, with the group therapist.

Present-centred development

In transactional analysis conceptualisations of depth psychotherapy, there is, in our view, an overemphasis on the Child ego state; we believe that working with the "inner Child" reifies the ego state metaphor (see the section on ego states later in this chapter, pp. 17–21). We therefore question transactional analysis techniques of deconfusion and redecision in the Child when they are based on regression to childhood scenes [see also discussion in Chapter Seven, pp. 152–154]. A person's emotional desire to complete an archaic scene through an exchange with, for example, a parental figure is not an attempt to resolve the transference; it *is* the transference. Our task as therapists is not to facilitate such completion and thereby reinforce the transferential pattern; it is primarily to facilitate suspension of the transferential expectation and to invite co-creation of fresh experience(s): "For the clinician, the developmental literature suggests that the careful, continued attention to the effectiveness of a client's present day functioning is more apt to facilitate self-enhancement than the therapeutic 're-doing' of a specific developmental period" (Cornell, 1988, p. 278). It is this juxtaposition of co-transferential and present-centred relating, developing in parallel, that facilitates the therapeutic emergence of transference. This duality of relating enables transferential phenomena to be experienced, compassionately identified and contained in the relationship. Integration then occurs as the client gradually embodies and re-owns previously fixated aspects of his or her experience in the context of freshly co-created support that was originally absent in childhood.

What differentiates Adult contact from the re-enactment of archaic, fixated experience (i.e., Parent or Child ego states) is not the source or intensity of feelings, but the incorporation of self and relational support.

When a client reaches for, and co-creates, contactful engagement in a manner that is new, he or she has, by definition, moved out of an archaic ego state. Our view is that archaic ego states are defences to be deconstructed rather than deconfused or redecided. The only purpose of "working with the Child ego state" is, in our view, to identify fixated, and therefore alienated, aspects of experience; aspects that can then be assimilated [or integrated] through present-centred relating. We thus prefer to conceptualise the sharing and integration of previously withheld feelings, needs and desires as the expansion of the Adult rather than the deconfusion of the Child [see Chapters Two and Four]. Depth psychotherapy is the process by which fixated, archaic experience is transformed into an extended range of Adult relational capacity.

Recent developmental theorists such as Stern (1985) have considered developmental phases as ongoing processes throughout the life cycle, with such phases not attached to childhood or any other specific life stage (see the section on script later in this chapter, pp. 21–24). Stern's suggestion that four senses of self (emergent, core, intersubjective, and verbal) develop in parallel throughout adult life supports the possibility of working at non-verbal levels of self-development within an Adult frame of reference. This contrasts with defining such work as preverbal along with the associated regressive implications. Similarly, developments in attachment theory conceptualise attachment as a life-cycle issue. As Holmes (1993) summarised it:

> Bowlby's conviction that attachment needs continue throughout life and are not outgrown has important implications for psychotherapy. It means that the therapist inevitably becomes an important attachment figure for the client and that this is not necessarily best seen as a "regression" to infantile dependence but rather the re-activation of attachment needs that have been previously suppressed. (p. 143)

In transactional terms, psychotherapy enables clients to explore how they create re-enactments of insecure attachments in the co-transferential relationship as well as how to develop a secure attachment within Adult–Adult relating. Berne's second rule of communication, which states that communication is (at least temporarily) broken following a crossed transaction, helps us to appreciate the perceived risk for clients and therapists in making the transition between co-transferential and Adult–Adult relating. Such a move may break the attachment, and an insecure attachment (symbiosis) may be seen as better than no attachment at all.

These perspectives on human development support present-centred diagnosis, contracting, and treatment planning.

Partial transferential transactions

Partial transferential transactions are transactions in which one party is in Adult and the other is not (see Figures 1.1 and 1.2). These transactions provide the link between the co-transferential relationship and the Present I–Present You relationship, and thus the map of co-creative therapeutic relationships (Figure 1.1) forms a chart by which we may navigate—or narrate—our way to present-centred Adult–Adult therapeutic relating (see Figure 1.2, to be read from the bottom up).

The example in Figure 1.2 reflects the point that the client may equally raise awareness of co-transferential relating. Another example, this time of the therapist inviting Present I–Present You relating, goes as follows:

CLIENT: I must change. I haven't got time to stay like this.
THERAPIST: You sound harsh.
CLIENT: Life is harsh.
THERAPIST: I understand you experience life as harsh and I'm interested in whether you want to experiment with creating other kinds of life experience here.
CLIENT: (Looks startled.) Yes.

This begins (from the therapist) with an empathic transaction; the therapist then acknowledges the client's frame of reference in experiencing life as harsh *and* (rather than "but") invites the client to create a different experience "here" (i.e., in the present). An implication of the constructivist perspective is that the therapist does not have to confront the validity of the client's frame of reference (only its uniqueness) as a way of experiencing life.

In cases of recurring crossed transactions, the analysis of ulterior transactions may reveal underlying co-transference. For example, a client repeatedly complains that the therapist is not listening to him. The therapist suggests that this is the client's projection. The therapist's defensiveness and subsequent defining of the client could indeed constitute "not listening." An exploration of the co-transference would involve a careful investigation as to the subtle ways in which the client's perception might be true. The shared exploration of ulterior transactions in therapy or supervision may therefore reveal instances in which an apparently present-centred communication has a past-centred transferential dynamic embedded within it. Conversely, analysis of apparent transferential process may reveal ulterior Adult–Adult dynamics.

Having offered this new narrative about therapeutic relationships or relating based on transactions or co-creative reality, we now turn our attention to examining the other foundations of transactional analysis from a co-creative perspective. We begin with ego states, followed by script theory. Traditional transactional analysis theory offers us an outstanding and elegant system for understanding transferential phenomena. However, as Cornell (1988) observed, "Like many clinicians, Berne became possessed by the effort to understand pathology. He lost track of health" (p. 274). The narrative theme throughout this revision of major transactional analysis concepts acknowledges the contribution of transactional analysis to healthy as well as pathological processes. This balanced interest in health as well as pathology reflects current developments in health psychology, mental health (meaning *health*) and "salutogenesis" (i.e., the origin of health) (Antonovsky, 1979, 1987), and mental health promotion (see Tudor, 1996a).

Ego states: co-creative personality

The notion of an Integrated Adult ego state was first suggested by Berne (1961/1975a):

> Anyone functioning as an Adult should ideally exhibit three kinds of tendencies: personal attractiveness and responsiveness [pathos], objective data-processing [logos], and ethical responsibility [ethos]; representing respectively archaeopsyche, neopsyche, and exteropsyche elements "integrated" into the neopsyche ego state, perhaps as "influences." (p. 195)

This idea is developed in the structural model of ego states based on [James and Jongeward's (1971) and] Erskine's (1988) interpretation of Berne. This model serves as a useful basis for a co-creative approach because of its clear distinction between Adult integration and fixated archaic responses; thus, the Integrated Adult is distinguished from introjected Parent states and fixated archaic Child ego states. Parent and Child ego states are patterns of relating employed in and out of awareness as defences against Adult integration. We therefore consider Parent and Child ego states to represent fixated creative adjustments that have been developed earlier in life and that are pathological in so far as they are compulsively used in the here and now at the expense of excluding other choices. We agree with Erskine's view that the "Adult ego state consists of current age-related motor behavior; emotional, cognitive and moral development; the ability to be creative; and the capacity for full contactful engagement in meaningful relationships" (p. 16). Having adopted this model as the basis for a co-creative approach, we suggest several modifications to support the transition from a modernist to a postmodern basis for a co-creative transactional analysis.

- First, we question the notion that the Adult ego state is the basis for objective processing and suggest that the ego state model may be used as a way of describing different kinds of subjective experience. Moving away from modernist conceptions of a definable, objective reality, we embrace the perspective of intersubjectivity and the postmodern notion of coexisting alternative realities. We believe that this perspective helps to highlight the cultural context of embedded assumptions, which could otherwise be dangerously and blindly defined as objective. Matze (1991) argued that the distinction between transferential and non-transferential transactions is itself "grounded in a myth of objectivity" (p. 142) and that therapists should treat all transactions as transferential so that the therapist "minimizes the possibility of a major error in empathic attunement" (p. 142). We consider this to be throwing the Adult out with the bath water. In contrast, we believe it is possible to disregard the myth of objectivity and to maintain the transference/non-transference distinction through a framework of systematic, intersubjective phenomenology. This view is based on Berne's (1961/1975a) conceptualisation of structural analysis as a systematic phenomenology. It suggests that different kinds of reality can be experienced by an individual: some are based on past experience of self (Child), others are based on past experience of others (Parent), and still others are present-centred (Adult). We believe it is Berne's articulation of the phenomenological experience of shifts in patterns of perception, thought, feeling and behaviour that makes intuitive sense to so many people.

Many psychodynamic writers, such as Matze (1991), have argued that therapy is solely about the transference relationship. However, we believe that the systematic phenomenology of transactional analysis supports the notion of non-transferential Adult–Adult relating. Of course, this does not mean that therapist and client are objectively free from the influence of past experience. We remain embedded in matrices of our culture (see section on script, pp. 21–24). We continually co-influence each other and negotiate the unknown, partly based on previous experience. However, we can experience ourselves as present-centred or past-centred and as progressive or regressive in relation to the world. These shifts in experience of self remain discernible and usable within an intersubjective and postmodern frame of reference.

• The second alteration we make to the ego state model is to move away from the structural metaphor in which it has been cast. The mechanical metaphor of "personality structure" has been popular throughout this [last] century. It has invited questions such as: "What is the structure?" "What is wrong with it?" and "How can it be fixed?" This mechanistic metaphor is based on modernist principles of objective reality and truth. Berne suggested that transactional analysis works most effectively when we behave as though this metaphor were reality and when we talk to the "inner Child" or "Parent" as though they actually exist: "The trichotomy must be taken quite literally. It is just as if each patient were three different people. Until the therapist can perceive it this way, he is not ready to use this system effectively" (Berne, 1961/1975a, p. 235).

This has led to many transactional analytic techniques that suggest ways of working with the inner Parent; for example, Schiff (1969), McNeel (1976). Dashiell (1978), and Mellor and Andrewartha (1980), and/or the inner Child, e.g., Berne (1966), Erskine (1974), and Clarkson and Fish (1988). We suggest a move away from this structural metaphor and a movement toward the metaphor of possibility. Considering the ego state model as a system of relational possibilities (and even probabilities) rather than structures invites different questions, such as: "Why this possibility at this point in time?" "What other possibilities are there?" and "What needs to happen now to generate and support new possibilities?"

This perspective shifts the therapeutic emphasis away from the treatment of ego state structures and toward an exploration of how relational possibilities are co-created on a moment-to-moment basis. We shift the therapeutic focus away from work with the metaphorical inner Child or Parent and instead explore the process through which Child or Parent ego states are co-created within the co-transference of the therapeutic relationship/relating. We learn how we co-create regressive experience(s) by attending to the co-transference as it emerges and unfolds in the relationship. Clarification of the co-transference [between client and therapist] then supports our experimentation with the co-creation of progressive rather than regressive experience(s). The therapeutic focus is not on changing prior ego states but on recognising that we do not have to continue creating ego states based on the old models. It is possible—and possibly OK—to do something different. It is possible to make meaning of our experience outside of the Parent–Child frame of reference. It is possible to invent and use imagination to co-create different realities and meanings that enhance our life experience.

An excellent visual representation of this perspective is Escher's "Drawing Hands," in which two hands are drawing each other: each is bringing the other into existence. The South African word ubuntu (translated or interpreted as "I am because we are") also echoes this approach. The postmodern perspective suggests that ego state structures do not pre-exist prior to transactions but are co-created within and elicited through our transactions. They only pre-exist as possible or probable ways of relating. The structural metaphor reifies these possibilities, creating the illusion of a structural entity (see Loria, 1990). We suggest that the structural perspective paradoxically reinforces archaic possibilities in an attempt to "fix" them. In contrast, we prefer to emphasise the inextricable link between ego states and transactions by viewing the ego state model as a way of describing "co-created personality."

Finally, whilst we note that this shift can still accommodate Berne's (1961/1975a) four criteria for the recognition/diagnosis of ego states (behavioral, social, historical, and phenomenological), we incorporate a significant development. The intersubjective exploration and classification of ego states (or relational possibilities) can now be extended to include intuition of the possible and not just the probable (based on past experience). We find Schmid's (1991) ideas about intuition particularly useful in support of this approach. He pointed out that Berne focused on using intuition to diagnose or analyse archaic ego states by intuiting the represented archaic realities of the client's presentation (Schmid, 1991). He further suggested developing our capacity to intuit new, possible ways of relating. We believe Schmid has counterbalanced Berne's intuition for archaic possibilities with an emphasis on intuiting future possibilities. Perhaps we need to see ourselves as transactional *designers* as well as transactional analysts: what possibilities can we intuit for, and with, our clients and our relationship with them, and how can we support the exploration and development of these possibilities? [For further discussion of intuition, see Chapter Ten, pp. 215–218.].

Script: co-creative identity

In a critical review of script theory, Cornell (1988) suggested that script, as presented in most transactional analysis literature, is "overly reductionistic and insufficiently attentive to the formative factors in healthy psychological development" (p. 270). From a philosophical point of view, this is especially ironic given the potential compatibility of script theory with constructivism (Allen & Allen, 1997). However, if, with Allen and Allen (1995), we are to view scripts as constructive narratives that, like memories, are co-created in the present and projected into the past, then we need to reformulate much of our present understanding of script and script theory. Several points inform this critique:

- That traditional, linear, stage theories of (child) development have been challenged by writers such as Stern (1985): "It, therefore, cannot be known, in advance, on theoretical grounds, at what point in life a particular traditional clinical–developmental issue will receive its pathogenic origin" (p. 256).
- That script theory does not account for temperament and the interplay between this and attachment theory.
- That scripts are co-created; Cornell (1988) referred to the (then) current developmental research, which suggests that infants influence and shape their parents as much as they are shaped by their parents [and such research has continued to demonstrate this].
- That injunctions, programmes, and drivers/counterinjunctions are, equally, co-created and decided [in the way in which "decision" is

viewed within transactional analysis i.e., not simply cognitively] and only become part of a person's script if accepted and "fixed" as such.

• That despite the concept of cultural scripting (White & White, 1975), the script, in one of its most popular and most-often used manifestations, (the script matrix) is, in its reference only to the heterosexual nuclear family, deeply culturally determined.

• That a postmodern script theory suggests that we can have several stories about our lives running in parallel—and that we can choose between them. Allen and Allen (1995) stated that "each person is entitled to more than one story" (p. 329). The stories we write may be based on motives combining survival, compliance, rebellion, resilience, aspiration, self-assertion, loyalty, revenge, and love.

Cornell (1988) acknowledged that English (1977) has stood virtually alone in acknowledging scripts as valuable assets. We adopt Cornell's (1988) definition of script because of its applicability to both healthy and pathological process and its recognition of the significance of meaning:

> Life script is the ongoing process of a self-defining and sometimes self-limiting psychological construction of reality. Script formation is the process by which the individual attempts to make sense of family and social environments, to establish meaning in life, and to predict and manage life's problems in the hope of realising one's dreams and desires. (p. 281)

As regards the script matrix, we suggest taking the logic of Cornell's (1988) arguments further in developing a narrative map of the influences on co-creative identity:

1. We agree with Cornell in drawing the script matrix horizontally, bringing the "parental" influences into a mutual relationship with the "child" or subject.
2. We extend the mutuality of vectors to include the Parent vector.
3. Perhaps most significantly and radically, we replace "Mother" and "Father" with any polarity (or continuum) that is significant to the subject based on his or her own construction(s) of reality (see Figure 1.3).

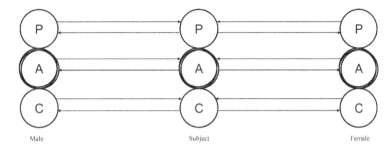

Figure 1.3 Co-creative script matrix (developed from Cornell, 1988).

Thus, the injunctions, programmes and drivers of the script cut both ways. A child telling her parent to "Go away" may be both receiving and responding to *and* conveying a Don't Exist injunction. Of course, the relative impact on the parent, who usually has more power than the child, will vary according to his or her own development, history, experiences, pathology, present support, and so on. The child who models his or her parents' various behaviours, for example, by succeeding at school, also perpetuates the family/cultural "success" story and this again impacts the parents. Similarly, the driver messages are equally mutual: "Pull yourself together, son" (from a father) may be matched by a "Hold me and be there for me always" (from the son), which may represent mutual drives to "Be strong."

Our horizontal diagram does not represent equality of power in parent–child relationships. It is intended to emphasise our ongoing capacity to influence and be influenced [for further discussion of which, see Chapter Ten]. The matrix can be used to map mutual influences at any stage in the life cycle and may be applied to various situations in which we may be more or less powerful than others by virtue of status, knowledge, financial resources, age, or discrimination based on class, disability, gender, race, sexual orientation, and so on.

We can also consider script influences in terms of other polarities and the continua between them. For example, an important polarity in the identity development of a black child brought up in a predominantly white culture is likely to be black minority home culture and white dominant school culture.[3] Indeed, there are a number of models of minority identity development (e.g., Atkinson, Morton & Sue, 1989)—as well as models that describe the development of white racial consciousness (Helms, 1984)—that could be represented by, and within, the context of the co-creative script matrix. Similarly, the predominant polarity that influences the experiences of a child brought up by gay, lesbian or bisexual parents, *depending on their circumstances*, at *certain points in their life*, *may* be a gay–straight polarity. The italics represent the fact that such influences are not determined, as is implied by traditional conceptualisations of script, but, rather, in our view, *constructed*; in other words, the construction of the script matrix is itself a personal construct. Thus, the script matrix becomes a co-created series of matrices, rather like a constantly changing helix of relational atoms, spinning around us, by which we tell, retell and reformulate the stories of different influences on our continuing development (see Figure 1.4).

In this model, scripts as co-creative identity are, as Allen and Allen (1997) observed, clearly compatible with our postmodernist project of retelling transactional analysis—and, indeed, they are the precursor of present notions of narrative in (formed) therapy.

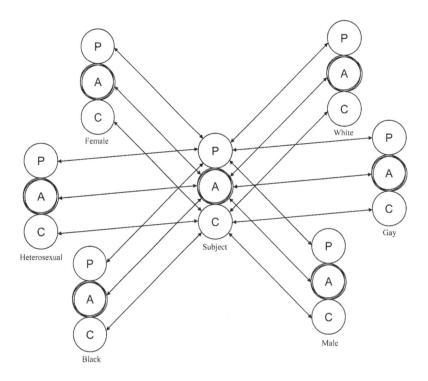

Figure 1.4. A script helix.

Games: co-creative confirmations

Consistent with developing transactional analysis as a theoretical model of psychological health, an approach that may be described as "psycho-sanology" as well as one of psychopathology, we envisage that game theory can describe both healthy and pathological processes. Berne's (1964/1968a) definition of a game as "an ongoing series of complementary ulterior transactions progressing to a well-defined, predictable outcome" (p. 44) provides us with a neutral, non-pathological formulation that later definitions restrict. We choose this definition precisely because it allows us to describe both healthy and satisfying patterns as well as the pathological repetition and re-enactment of traumatic experience.

The application of game theory to pathological process is well described in the transactional analysis literature: for example, degrees of game (Berne, 1964/1968a), the drama triangle (Karpman, 1968), Formula G (Berne, 1972/1975b), the Goulding-Kupfer game diagram (Goulding & Goulding, 1979), and the bystander role (Clarkson, 1987). In addition, the almost exclusively pathological focus of game theory implies that ulterior transactions are exchanged between archaic ego states communicating contaminated negative beliefs about self, others, and the world. The undeveloped exception to this pathological focus is Berne's concept of the "good" game—that is, "one whose social contribution outweighs the complexity of its motivations … one which contributes both to the well-being of the other players and to the unfolding of the one who is 'it'" (Berne, 1964/1968a, p. 143). This is similar to the concept of "growth vitality games" developed by Satir (1967/1978, p. 186).

To illustrate the possibility of the game as a healthy process, we suggest a particular application of James' (1973) game plan (with Laurence Collinson's addition of the two mystery questions, cited in Stewart & Joines, 1987, p. 261):

1. What keeps happening to me over and over again?
2. How does it start?
3. What happens next?
4. (Mystery question)
5. And then?
6. (Mystery question)
7. How does it end?

8a. How do I feel?
8b. How do I think the other person feels?

Consider a relationship with someone you know that is consistently satisfying. Now use the above game plan to map out the sequence of the pattern you manage to co-create with this person over and over again. Finally consider the mystery questions:

4. What is my secret message to the other person?
6. What is the other person's secret message to me?

Typical responses to this approach are that such patterns start with a sense of anticipation, welcoming, and reconnection. The middle phase often involves sharing, recognition, openness, and acceptance. Such patterns often end with satisfaction, confirmation, and well-being. Common ulterior messages include "I like you," "I love you," and "I respect you." In satisfying relationships, such patterns create a framework within which intimacy can be risked.

These healthy patterns fit the definition of a game we have adopted from Berne. From a postmodern perspective we suggest that games are patterns we engage in, and through which we co-create confirmation of versions of reality [for further elaboration of which see Chapter Ten]. These versions of reality may be past- or present-centred and can incorporate either discounting or, importantly, accounting and, therefore, non-exploitative ulterior transactions. In many ways, game theory is the aspect of transactional analysis in which Berne particularly emphasised the co-created nature of relationship patterns.

Conclusion

For the practitioner, the value of theory is in how useful it is in informing practice. By way of concluding, and in the spirit of the narrative turn of postmodern, constructivist enquiry, we offer a number of questions that arise from the ideas presented in this chapter. The first comes from Berne himself, who wrote only briefly about the therapeutic relationship as such (see Berne, 1966). In doing so he suggested that before and in the first few minutes of each session or meeting with a client(s), the therapist should ask himself or herself "some fundamental questions about the real meaning of the therapeutic relationship" (pp. 63–64). He viewed this first with regard to the therapist's own development: "'Why am I sitting in this room? Why am I not at home with my children? … What will this hour contribute to my unfolding?'" (p. 64). Second, Berne suggested reflecting on the client and his or her motivations:

> Why are they here? Why are they not at home with their children or doing what their fancy dictates? Why did they choose psychotherapy as a solution? Why not religion, alcohol, drugs, crime, gambling? … What will this hour contribute to their unfolding? (p. 64)

To these questions we add further self-supervision questions for the transactional analysis practitioner, questions that are derived from a co-creative approach to the four main areas of transactional analysis discussed in this chapter:

- What patterns emerge between us?
- How are we presently making sense of these patterns?
- What are we each contributing to these patterns?
- What happens if we create different meanings for the same patterns?
- What happens if we do something different?
- How do we make sense of different patterns that we co-create?
- What ego states are we evoking and co-creating in each other?
- Why are we creating these ego states at this point in time?
- What else may be possible?
- What version of reality might we (have we) been confirming?
- How can we explore, acknowledge and choose between different realities?
- What constructs are we using to define self and other?
- How do these constructs support or limit us?

Notes

1. We are pleased to have this opportunity to reproduce this diagram correctly as, unforntunately, in an earlier publication (Summers & Tudor, 2005a), it was misprinted with two "Present I–Present You" boxes, top (correct) and left (incorrect), and two "Present I–Past You" boxes, right (correct) and bottom (incorrect). We are grateful to John Savage for alerting us to this.

2. Drawing on the work of Emmanuel Lévinas (1906–1995) on the other/ Other, Schmid (2006) has made the point that as it is the other that calls us, the "I", into service, this therapeutic or helping relationship should, more accurately, be described as "Thou–I".

3. Here we use "black" in the political sense of the word. As Brah (1992) noted:

> The term "black" was adopted by the emerging coalitions amongst African-Caribbean and South Asian organisations and activists in the late 1960s and 1970s. They were influenced by the way the Black Power movement in the USA, which had turned the concept of Black on its head, divested it of its pejorative connotations in radicalised discourses, and transformed it into a confident expression of an assertive group identity. (p. 127)

> In other countries, such as Aotearoa New Zealand, the term "brown" is used in a similar way, although, as Brah acknowledged, whilst black activism aimed to generate solidarity, it did not necessarily assume "that all members of the diverse black communities inevitably identify with the concept." (p. 129)

CHAPTER TWO

The neopsyche: the integrating Adult ego state*

Keith Tudor

In transactional analysis literature, of the three ego states the Adult ego state is the least developed. In 1977 Krumper commented that "the Adult ego state seems to get little attention in transactional analysis theory" (p. 299), an observation that is as true today as then. [A survey of articles published in the *Transactional Analysis Journal* (*TAJ*) over four decades (1971–2012)[1] reveals only twenty-one articles specifically on the Adult ego state, only one of which is about working with the Adult ego state, compared with a total of thirty-five on the Child and sixty-six on the Parent, figures that represent, respectively, 17.21%, 28.69% and 54.09% of the total articles on ego states published in the *TAJ* in this period. A summary of this survey is presented in Table 2.1, which distinguishes in each category between those articles that deal with the theory of the particular ego states and the application of "working with" the respective ego state.

*Originally published in 2003 in *Ego States: Key Concepts in Transactional Analysis*, edited by Charlotte Sills and Helena Hargaden, published by Worth, London. Reproduced here by kind permission of Worth Publishing.

Table 2.1. Articles on ego states published in the *Transactional Analysis Journal* 1971–2012.

Years	Parent ego state(s)			Child ego state(s)			Adult ego state(s)		
	Ego state	Working with	Total	Ego state	Working with	Total	Ego state	Working with	Total
1971–1979	18	13	31	8	4	12	9	1	10
1980–1989	7	13	20	6	3	9	9	0	9
1990–1999	6	7	13	6	2	8	0	0	0
2000–2009	1	0	1	2	3	5	1	0	1
2010–2012	1	0	1	1	0	1	1	0	1
Totals[2]	29⅔	30	66	21½	10⅓	35	18⅔	1	21
Percentages			54.09%			28.69%			17.21%

Apart from the obvious predominance of interest in the Parent ego state, the total number of articles on which is more than those on both the Child and the Adult, this survey also reflects changing interests over the decades, with a declining interest in the Parent, and, indeed, a declining interest in the structure of ego states (see Figure 2.1).

In *Transactional Analysis in Psychotherapy* Berne (1961/1975a) commented on the features of the ego state model as presented in the two-dimensional medium of diagrams on paper, reflecting that "the Parent was put at the top and the Child at the bottom intuitively" (p. 60). Assuming that Berne himself wrote that sentence "in Adult", it is interesting that the Adult ego state appears to attract less of his intuition. Here, in Berne, as elsewhere in transactional analysis theory and practice, the Adult ego state is a residual state left over after all the elements of Child and Parent have been detected, and reduced to "the earthly realities of objective living" (ibid., p. 60). It is as if the symptomatology of transactional analysis itself excludes the Adult from its full analysis, design, or consideration.

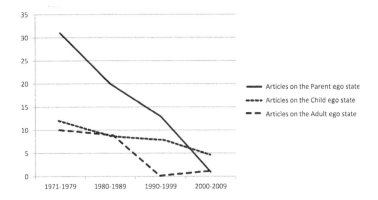

Figure 2.1. Articles on ego states published in the *Transactional Analysis Journal* 1971–2009.

During the course of writing the [original] chapter I asked a number of transactional analysis practitioners what their view of the Adult ego state was. Responses included: "There's nothing in it", "It's empty", "It's separate", "Who wants to be a computer?", "Adult is boring. It just does things", "It's here today, gone tomorrow: today's Adult is tomorrow's Child", even "Does the Adult exist?" These comments and questions reflect not only the responses or reactions of particular practitioners, but also, more broadly, reflect the Adult as portrayed in transactional analysis literature. Despite more recent work developing Berne's (1961/1975a) incipient notion of the Integrated Adult, such as James and Jongeward (1971), Erskine (1988), Erskine and Moursund (1988), and Lapworth, Sills, and Fish (1993), Berne's description of the Adult as a data processor still haunts transactional analysis. Even the "Integrated Adult" appears a somewhat dull and static entity. In this chapter I aim to lay this particular ghost by describing and developing an expansive Adult ego state that characterises a pulsating personality, processing and integrating feelings, attitudes, thoughts and behaviours appropriate to the here-and-now—at all ages from conception to death. This present-centred state of the ego has the ability and capacity to act autonomously (with awareness, spontaneity, and intimacy), to laugh, have fun and be silly, to learn, to develop and maintain a critical consciousness, to aspire, to express ambivalence and disappointment, to have a sense of community feeling, social justice, spirituality, and much, much more. The Integrated—or, more accurately, *integrating*—Adult describes the individual's capacity to reflect upon and integrate their own archaic states as well as past introjects, and to draw on them in the service of present-centred relating—in life as well as in the therapeutic milieu, whether as therapist or client.

In arguing the case for this expansive and integrating Adult, this chapter is divided, like the courses of a substantial Italian meal (to be digested over time), into five parts. Before offering a critical review of the literature on, and models of, the Adult ego state from Berne (1961/1975a) onwards, I first locate these discussions in the context of debates about ego states in general. In doing so, I discuss the implications of the meta-phor of "ego states" and lay the theoretical foundations for the inte-grating Adult by considering transactional analysis as an organismic psychology. Following this (in the third part of the chapter), I present a revised model of the Adult, based on constructivist approaches to transactional analysis and, specifically, co-creative transactional analy-sis (Summers & Tudor, 2000). This provides a methodology for the prac-tice of expanding the Adult ego state. Given my constructivist reading both of transactional analysis as well as the therapeutic field in general, I emphasise the social/cultural context of such theory and practice and development as well as its relation to health psychology. The chapter concludes with a reflection on the implications of an expanded notion of Adult ego states for transactional analysis itself. Whilst the chapter is written in a certain, linear and logical order, the reader, depending on their interest and appetite, may of course skip the *antipasto* (ego states) and even the *primo piatto* (on the Adult ego state in transactional analy-sis literature), preferring instead to address the *secondo* or main course (on the integrating Adult) first: in other words, each part is designed to read independently—and, of course, interdependently!

Ego states

Ego states are fundamental to transactional analysis, indeed it may be said that they define this modality or branch of psychology. As Berne (1970/1973) put it: "Parent, Adult, and Child ego states were first sys-tematically studied by transactional analysis, and they're its founda-tion stones and its mark. Whatever deals with ego states is transactional analysis, and whatever overlooks them is not" (p. 223). Since Berne's original work, notably Berne (1961/1975a), the definitions, diagnoses, structures and functions of ego states have been much debated—see particularly Novey, Porter-Steele, Gobes, and Massey (1993), as well as other references in this [the original] chapter and other chapters in the book [Sills & Hargaden, 2003a]. No conceptual or clinical deconstruction, reconstruction or expansion of the Adult ego state can take place in isolation from the Parent and Child ego states and current considerations of their nature, structure, and function. Thus, in this first part, I refer to some discussions on ego state theory, following which I discuss the implications of the ego state metaphor, and the value of meta perspectives on ego state theory and models.

Ego states—States of the ego

Drawing originally on a biological metaphor, Berne (1961/1975a) described aspects of human mental activity as "organs" or, more precisely, "psychic organs" whose function is to organise external and internal material. Drawing on Federn's (1952a) work identifying states of the ego, Berne (1961/1975a) defined these "phenomenologically as a coherent system of feelings related to a given subject, and operationally as a set of coherent behavior patterns, or pragmatically, as a system of feelings which motivates a related set of behavior patterns" (p. 17). Berne viewed the personality as a complex system *that may be thought of as* being organised into three structures:

- An elaborative system connected to the mental-emotional analysis of the here-and-now (the *neopsyche*).
- A system aimed at organising introjected psychic material (the *exteropsyche*).
- A system linked to the organisation of instinctual drives, basic needs, and primary emotional experiences (the *archaeopsyche*).

These systems form the basis of three discrete mental, emotional and behavioural organisations that Berne referred to as *ego states*, naming these "psychic organs" and their activities as the Parent ego state (exteropsyche), Adult ego state (neopsyche), and the Child ego state (archaeopsyche) (see Figure 2.2).

However, as Jacobs (2000) pointed out: "the relationship between the psychic organs archaeopsyche, neopsyche, and exteropsyche …

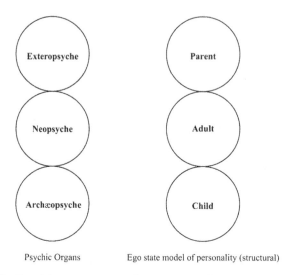

Psychic Organs   Ego state model of personality (structural)

Figure 2.2. Psychic organs and corresponding ego states (Berne, 1961/1975a).

and the ego states Parent, Adult, and Child ... is a distinction between an *imagined framework* and the identification and naming of behaviors into *generalized categories*" (p. 12, my emphasis). Furthermore, following Holloway (1977) and Ohlsson (1988), Jacobs argued that there are many states of the ego in relation to each psychic organ, the implication of which is that the familiar structural diagram does not reflect the myriad functional manifestations of these three psychic absolutes. Whilst I agree with Jacobs on this as regards the Parent and Child—and that it is more accurate to use the terms Parent ego states and Child ego states—I do not agree with regard to the Adult manifestation of the neopsyche (an argument developed below). In any case, it was unfortunate that Berne chose to represent psychic organs and ego states by means of identical diagrams that reflect correspondence.

Moreover, once Berne moved beyond this original (first order) structure of the personality, matters became more complex. Indeed, Berne's (1961/1975a) original second order structural analysis ego diagram, in which he labelled the original ego states P_1, A_1 and C_1 and then subdivided them (to include P_2, A_2 and C_2), has subsequently been renamed P_2, A_2 and C_2 with the subdivisions—within the Child ego state only—carrying the nomenclature P_1, A_1 and C_1! A second complexity (and confusion) concerns different understandings (and ego state diagrams) about human (child and later adult) development. A number of transactional analysis authors—Levin (1974), Schiff et al. (1975), Woollams and Brown (1978), Klein (1980), Levin-Landheer (1982), Novey (in Novey, Porter-Steele, Gobes, & Massey, 1993) and Hine (1997)—propose an unfolding, epigenetic development of ego states, broadly, Child, then Adult, and then Parent. (For a comparison of the theories of Levin, 1974; Schiff et al., 1975; and Klein, 1980, see Magner, 1985 [and also Tudor, 2010b]). However, these views are based on a conflation and confusion of metaphors: on the one hand, ego states as an image and representation of the structure of personality and, on the other, ego states as a metaphor for stages of development. Assertions that the Adult ego state (A_2) does not begin to develop until twelve months (Levin, 1974; Schiff et al., 1975; Woollams & Brown, 1978), eighteen months (Klein, 1980) or "a later stage of cognitive development" (Hine, 1997, p. 285) are not based on a structural definition of ego states. If the Adult ego state is defined as "characterized by an autonomous set of feelings, attitudes, and behavior patterns which are adapted to the current reality" (Berne, 1961/1975a, p. 76), it follows that the neonate has an Adult ego state (see Gobes in Novey Porter-Steele, Gobes, & Massey, 1993) or, as Sprietsma (1982) put it: "a person is actually 'Born Adult'" (p. 228). In the spirit of James and Jongeward's (1971) comment that "the Adult ego state is ageless" (p. 277), and taking this logic one step further (back), I suggest that a person is conceived Adult or, more accurately, that the foetus, developing autonomous sets of feelings, attitudes and behaviour patterns, adapting to its reality *in utero*, may be thought of as having a neopsyche or an Adult ego state—and, of course, depending on its experience in the uterine environment and that of its mother, may also develop an archaeopsyche and exteropsyche with their respective Child and Parent ego states (see Figure 2.4 below; and Bale, 1999). This view is also consistent with developmental theorists as diverse as Lake (1980), Stern (1985), and Piontelli (1992)—and represented in part three of this chapter (pp. 45–58).

One of the great problems in discussing ego states within (let alone outside) transactional analysis is the different—and *differing*—views and models of ego states. This confusion dates back to Berne himself, who defined ego states in contradictory ways (Berne, 1961/1975a) [for an analysis of which see Tudor, 2010b]. Central to our current concern is the issue as to whether the Child ego state is defined as comprising fixated material only and the Parent as comprising introjected material only, or whether both Child and Parent also "contain" archaic experiences and introjects that are script free. As Stewart (2001) has pointed out, one's view of cure is dependent on which of these two definitions is adopted—that is, whether the "totally cured person" may be characterised as having only an Integrated or integrating Adult or whether she or he has all three ego states: "it's purely from this difference in definition that the difference between the two models arises" (p. 144). In the absence of standard nomenclature and agreed definitions (and unlike Stewart I think this is no bad thing), in the interests of open (and clear) communication, I think it *is* incumbent on authors and practitioners, supervisors and trainers to be clear about the models and definitions they use—and in this I agree with some of Stewart's "call to action". In using and discussing definitions, I find the "if ... then" formulation of philosophical logic consistent with constructivist philosophy, accurate and useful, thus: "*If* we define Adult in such a way, *then* we may consider this quality or experience as Adult—and, by implication, not Child or Parent".

The matter of metaphor

In referring to Berne's view of personality (p. 33 above), I emphasised the phrase "*that may be thought of as*" to reflect and represent the metaphorical "as if" nature of "ego states". In this I am with Loria (1990), Allen and Allen (1991, 1995), Schmidt (1991) and Jacobs (2000) in viewing ego states as useful metaphors for understanding personality, rather than "realities" in themselves. However, from Berne (1961/1975a) onwards, a number of theoreticians and practitioners within transactional analysis have argued that—and from the basis that—ego states are real (see Jacobs, 2000 for a useful review of these different traditions). However, although, following Federn (1952a), Berne (1961/1975a) claimed that Parent, Adult and Child are "phenomenological realities" (p. 24), he did not claim the ego state *model* as "real": "hence a set of circles ... *may be taken as a fair way of representing* the structure of personality" (p. 40, my emphasis).

One of the problems with ego states and the ego state model is, as Loria (1990) observed, that they (and it) have become reified:

> the concept *ego state* that was used originally by Berne in a
> figurative or illustrative manner has taken on the characteristics
> of a *thing* with its own constitution and existence—the metaphor
> has become reified. Like Berne's mythical "psychic organs"...
> an ego state cannot be abstracted from a person like a gall stone.
> (p. 154)

As Jacobs (2000) commented: "at this point it is doubtful if psychic organs will ever be identified with actual neurological sites" (p. 12), although Drego (2000) appeared to find a way of squaring these particular circles by emphasising the *phenomenological* nature of psychological realities. Notwithstanding this, the general reification of ego states as absolute realities misunderstands the nature and use of metaphor.

Kopp (1971) defined metaphor "as a way of speaking in which one thing is expressed in terms of another, whereby this bringing together throws new light on the character of what is being described" (p. 17). Thus metaphor is, as Gordon (1978) put it, a "novel representation" of something. It is not the reality or the referent object; neither is it the only way of representing and describing the referent (in this case human personality); and it needs refreshing. In this sense "ego states" and "ego state diagrams" are merely metaphors that may be assessed by their accuracy in offering a representative description of personality and their usefulness in facilitating clinical (educational and organisational) practice—and social change. After all, transactional analysis *is* a social psychiatry. Discussing the person-centred approach, a colleague said: "The reason I like the [person-centred] approach is because it's got the best metaphors" (P. Sanders, personal communication, January 2001)—"best" in this sense meaning the most useful, philosophically coherent, personally compatible, etc. In many ways choosing a particular theoretical orientation may be viewed as: "You pays your money, and you buys your metaphor!" Three implications follow from this perspective on metaphor and are briefly elaborated with regard to TA.

i. A metaphor is a metaphor is a metaphor

Transactional analysts along with other therapists and practitioners involved in "talking therapy" clearly need to mind their language—that is, to mind about language, and to pay attention to and to have a view about the nature of metaphor as well as the metaphors they and their clients use. Viewing and talking about the Adult as an objective data processor clearly influences the way we think about ourselves and others, what it means to be Adult (and adult), the nature of therapy, cure, etc.

ii. The metaphor that is the metaphor is not the metaphor

This echo of Taoist philosophy—the way that is (presented as) *the* way is not the way, encapsulated in such sayings as "If you meet the Buddha on the road, kill him!" (Kopp, 1971)—reminds us to stay awake to the dangers of standardisation and regulation, whether theoretical, intellectual, professional, or organisational. The reification and objectification of ego states and the ego state model itself and the over-detailed concern (even obsession) with what's "in" particular ego states (the answer to which is, of course, nothing) contradicts Berne's original contribution of structural analysis as a "systematic *phenomenology*", especially in his, and its, attention to detail regarding the requirements for diagnosis (Berne, 1961/1975a).

iii. Metaphors are mutable

Metaphors need to be renewed in a continual process of novel re-presentation. The problem with the ego state model of transactional analysis is, in this respect, the problem of inaccurate, unhelpful and outmoded metaphors such as the data processing, computer-like Adult. Also, as the metaphorical frameworks of therapy are influenced by the *zeitgeist* (see Sanders & Tudor, 2001)—and vice versa—it is important that metaphors and the language of therapy also reflect and represent the zeitgeist and, of course, people's constructions of it:

> we prefer to think of human psychology in terms of a different, more enduring—and, for us, a more satisfactory—metaphor, namely an ecological one. The person-as-biological-system is best understood as a complex micro-system within and connected to a complex macro-system. Psycho-technology, then, is of no more use in human healing than technology has been in taming the forces of nature. (p. 149)

Furthermore, as Jacobs (2000) put it: "creating alternative metaphors will develop a more personal, *mutually constructed relationship* between helper and helped" (p. 21, my emphasis). If we argue (as I do) that the foetus has an "Adult", this may be the point at which the Parent/Adult/Child metaphor breaks down and we need to represent new metaphors by means of new nomenclature such as "past self" or "fixated (experienced) self" (Child); "other self" or "fixated (introjected) self" (Parent); and "present self", "fluid self" or, if I am nail my colours to an organismic mast, more accurately and simply, "organism" (i.e., integrating Adult).

From metaphor to metatheory

If the critiques offered in this first part of the chapter thus far may be characterised as from *within* (concerning ego state theory and models) and from *alongside* (regarding metaphor), then this section offers a critique from *above*—that is, from a metatheoretical perspective.

Pine (1990) identified four psychologies based on four different views of human nature: drive theory, ego psychology, object relations and self theory. As Sills and Hargaden [2003b] pointed out in their Introduction [to the volume in which this chapter first appeared], this taxonomy offers a useful metatheory for understanding the different (and differing) theories and models of ego states within TA. What Pine omitted, however, is organismic psychology, based on organismic motivation—see Woodworth with Sheehan (1931/1965), Goldstein (1934/1995), and Hall and Lindzey (1978). With the exception of its influence on the person-centred approach and, to a certain extent, on gestalt psychology and psychotherapy, organismic psychology is one of the lost traditions in the history of twentieth-century psychology—although, interestingly (and significantly for my present purpose), Hagehülsmann (1984) suggested that most schools or traditions within transactional analysis rest on assumptions that represent an organismic model of human nature. Taking Hall and Lindzey's (1978) summary of organismic theory, Table 2.2 compares this with aspects of transactional analysis as a way of setting out the theoretical foundations for a more organismic view of the neopsyche.

Table 2.2. Locating transactional analysis as an organismic psychology.

Organismic theory	*Transactional analysis*
Organismic theory is integrative	
"Organismic theory emphasises the unity, integration, consistency, and coherence of the normal personality. Organisation is the natural state of the organism; disorganisation is pathological and is usually brought about by the impact of an oppressive or threatening environment." (Hall & Lindzey, 1978, p. 298)	There is an increasing interest in integrative transactional analysis and transactional analysis as an integrative psychotherapy (see Erskine & Moursund, 1988; Clarkson, 1992b). The implications of health psychology and "normal personality" have been explored by Cornell (1988) and Summers and Tudor (2000) amongst others.
	In this sense, organisation may be viewed as integrating Adult (A_2) and "disorganisation" as Child and Parent [for further discussion of which, see Chapter Five].
Organismic theory is holistic	
Thus, whilst its constituent parts may be differentiated for analysis, *any such part is not abstracted in principle from the whole.*	This argues for a more holistic view of the personality (than is generally current in TA) in which ego states are seen as a useful atomistic abstraction (or not) only in the context of the organismic, holistic organisation of such "parts".
Organismic theory is based on a unitary drive theory	
In the more general field of humanistic psychology, this is usually conceptualised as the drive of self-actualisation (see Maslow, 1967/1993).	This is not prominent in TA. Berne refers only occasionally to drive theory in his writings. The influence of Freudian ideas on drive appears in Berne's references to *eros* and *mortido* (Berne, 1957/1981). The nearest Berne came to a "drive theory" was

(Continued)

Table 2.2. Continued.

Organismic theory	Transactional analysis
	his thinking on human hungers (Berne, 1970/1973). Interestingly, Hine (1997) viewed ego state theory as "an early integration of drive theory (wired-in networks), and self-schema theory (networks developed mainly in the self-other relationship)." (p. 284)
Organismic theory emphasises the inherent potentiality of the organism for growth	
This refers to the actualising *tendency* to be found in all organisms and in nature itself (see Rogers, 1959, 1978, 1980a).	This was recognised by Berne in his references to *physis* (see Berne, 1957/1981, 1963, 1972/1975b).
Organismic theory is all-encompassing	
This refers to the broad theoretical base offered by organismic theory for understanding the total organism.	TA is generally viewed by its proponents as offering a broad understanding of the total organism/person in their context, especially given its fields of application. Berne's (1961/1975a) outline of the significant properties of the ego states/psychic organs involves reference to a wide-ranging multi-disciplinary knowledge base.
Organismic theory takes a holistic approach to the study of the person	
This follows on from the previous point and emphasises heuristic research methodology.	TA approach to research over the years has tended to be more empirical than heuristic.

Within transactional analysis and based on Berne's (1961/1975a) own criteria for ego state diagnosis, Drego (2000) identified four ego state models: the phenomenological, the historical, the behavioural, and the social, [each of which] have what Drego referred to as "socioethical aspects", which affect the quality of human life. She presented this overview of ego states from a multidimensional perspective on science, one in which ego states are both metaphorical and real, intrapsychic and transactional, and archaic and contemporary [– and, for this reason, what Drego has referred to as "models", I would say are more accurately described as] meta models or paradigms.

Having reviewed the context or ground in which Adult ego states are located, I now turn my attention to the figure of the Adult ego state itself. In the next part/course of the chapter (a more substantial *primo piatto*), the transactional analysis literature on the Adult is reviewed; this is followed, in the third part (the main, *secondo piatto*), by an elaboration of the integrating Adult ego state.

The Adult ego state in transactional analysis

Whilst numerous contributions and models over the past forty years have developed the structural analysis of Parent and Child ego states at a second and even third order level, the Adult remains largely blank. This is, in part, due to Berne's (1961/1975a) [ambiguity and perhaps] ambivalence about the Adult; indeed, he himself described this as "the most obscure area in structural analysis" (p. 195). In a short passage on the Adult in a chapter on the "Finer Structure of the Personality" (Berne, 1961/1975a), three important points concerning Berne's thinking about the Adult may be discerned.

1. Berne placed "ethos" (moral qualities) and "pathos" (responsible feelings) within the Adult (see Figure 2.3)

    The A_2 between ethos and pathos was later referred to as "technics" (Kertesz & Savorgnan, cited in James & Jongeward, 1971), and is sometimes referred to as "logos". In his article on ego structure, Erskine (1988) suggested that, along with ethos and pathos, logos (the ability to use logic and abstract reasoning) and technos (the ability to create) "describe the full neopsychic capacity of the Adult ego state to integrate values, process information, respond to emotions and sensations, and be creative and contactful" (p. 16).

2. Berne presented a second order structural analysis of the Adult

    Although Berne represented these qualities and feelings as a second order structural analysis of the Adult, it is not clear precisely what is "second order" about this incipient and somewhat speculative analysis. Also, it is not clear what the remaining A_2 (sic) (the Adult

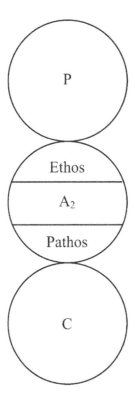

Figure 2.3. Second order structure of the Adult (Berne, 1961).

in the Adult) represents. Although this finer structure is sometimes referred to as Berne's embryonic "Integrated Adult", he himself acknowledged that "the mechanism of this 'integration' remains to be elucidated" (Berne, 1961/1975a, p. 194). It is indeed a "tentative formulation" (ibid., p. 195).

3. Berne advanced a view of the epigenetic origins of the Adult Third, and perhaps most importantly for my current concern:

> it appears that in many cases certain child-like qualities become integrated into the Adult ego state in a manner different from the contamination process … it can be observed that certain people when functioning *qua* Adult have a charm and openness of nature which is reminiscent of that exhibited by children. (pp. 194–195)

This is a significant passage, which hints at the integrative process (or "mechanism") whereby qualities, attitudes, feelings, behaviours and thoughts that are integrated into the Adult are uncontaminated and unproblematic. [James and Jongeward (1971) also quote this passage in support of their concept of the Integrated Adult.] At the same it infantilises the Adult by suggesting that Adult qualities are "child like" in origin, not only metaphorically ("as if") but structurally. This is itself a serious contamination of what it means to be Adult (also see Gobes in Novey Porter-Steele, Gobes, & Massey, 1993). Lest this be viewed as a momentary slip, a few sentences later, Berne (ibid.) elaborated:

> transactionally ... anyone functioning as an Adult should ide-
> ally exhibit three kinds of tendencies: personal attractiveness and
> responsiveness, objective data processing, and ethical responsibility;
> representing respectively archaeopsychic, neopsychic and extero-
> psychic elements "integrated" into the neopsychic ego state. (p. 195)

There are two principal implications—and objections—to this view:

1. That the Adult in the Adult is (only) an objective data processor. This view is contradicted by human Adult experience, by much subsequent thinking in transactional analysis, including this present work, and by developments in neuroscience.
2. That the origins of these qualities of attractiveness and responsiveness and ethical responsibility lie necessarily in archaic or introjected material. Given Erikson's influence on Berne (see Stewart, 1992), this view is presumably based on an epigenetic formulation of child development (e.g., Erikson, 1950/1965) and is contradicted by research in the field of child development over the past fifteen years (see, for instance, Stern, 1985).

Other models of the Adult ego state in transactional analysis

The problem inherent in these implications is, again, based on a confusion of models and undeclared differences of definition, and specifically a conflation of the structural and functional models of ego states. In the above passage from Berne, the key lies in the words, "anyone *functioning* as an Adult ...". This is not only prescriptive and somewhat grandiose ("anyone"), it is partial as it is concerned only with functioning.

As regards the functioning of the Adult, there has been some considerable debate over the years as to whether the Adult "contains" feelings. Eminent transactional analysts such as Steiner, James and

Harris have [separately] asserted that the Adult is "impassionate", without feeling, unemotional, etc. Developing the ubiquitous computer analogy, Krumper (1977) suggested that like any other computer the Adult may be divided into subsystems representing: the function of memory (content) (Ac) (analogous to recording tape), and the function of associative processes (Aa) (analogous to the central processor). In an attempt to complement the existing theory of the functioning of the Adult ego state, Phelan and Phelan (1978) introduced the concept of the "fully functioning Adult" with functional subdivisions, which, drawing on research on the characteristics of left and right brain hemispheres, accounts for the "Rational Adult" and the integrated behaviour alluded to by Berne—referred to as the "Poetic Adult", a term the authors chose to emphasise the "non linear and creative dimension of thinking" (p. 123). In a similar vein, Kujit (1980) distinguished between two Adult "categories": the Analytical Adult and the Experiencing Adult.

Whilst these terms and concepts have contributed to our understanding of the Adult ego state, they have largely done so by means of an implicit functional model of ego states. Describing particular functions of the Adult by use of terms such as the "Poetic Adult" (a compound noun) implies that it is a particular state of the ego. As Erskine (1988) pointed out, when Berne (1961/1975a, 1964/1968a) used the terms "adapted" and "natural" in relation to the Child ego state, he used them as modifying adjectives referring to manifestations of intrapsychic dynamics. Terms such as "Free Child" and "Critical Parent" are problematic as such descriptions are nominalisations ultimately based on assumptions about the nature of social science—concerned with realism as an approach to ontology (concerning the essence of things); positivism in epistemology (concerning the grounds of knowledge); and determinism regarding human nature—all of which are at odds with a constructivist philosophy and its method of enquiry and practice. In order to elaborate this, it is now time to proceed to the main course (part three) concerning the neopsychic integrating Adult.

The integrating Adult

C.1 ALF

(CLIENT):   (Withdrawn, sitting hunched up, head down on one side.) I'm not sure what I'm doing here. (Pauses, sighs …) I'm not sure there's any point … if you can help …

T.1 BEA
(THERAPIST):   (Sighs.) You're not sure if I can help you and if there's any point …

C.2 ALF: (Interrupting, looks up.) That's right (said with some energy), I'm not worth it.

T.2 BEA: You said that with some energy.

C.3 ALF: (Aggressively.) So?

T.3 BEA: So … you made contact with me, with some energy, when you said, "I'm not worth it". It's as if …

C.4 ALF: Yeah, well, I'm not worth it.

T.4 BEA: (Pause.) It seems that you maintain your view that you're not worth it by interrupting me.

C.5 ALF: (Head down.) I'm sorry.

T.5 BEA: I didn't say that for you to be sorry.

C.6 ALF: (Silent for some time.)

T.6 BEA: Did you get it wrong again?

C.7 ALF: (Nods.)

T.7 BEA: Well, maybe I got it wrong too.

C.8. ALF: (Looks up.) What do you mean?

T.8 BEA: Well, the way I put it, about you interrupting me, may have sounded like I was blaming you.

C.9 ALF: (Nods.) Yeah.

T.9 BEA: What I was observing was that you seemed to be judging yourself ("I'm not worth it") and closing the door on what I might say.

C.10 ALF: (Long pause … begins to cry, softly, moving in and out of contact, looking up at Bea and then looking away.)

T.10 BEA: (Maintains eye contact with Alf when he looks away.) I'm still here.

C.11 ALF: When I was naughty my mum used to shut me in the toy cupboard. In the end I used to go there first before she could get me.

T.11 BEA: So you used to close the door before she could get you.

C.12 ALF: (Nods.)

T.12 BEA: That sounds like a good way of protecting yourself then … (pause) … and now, here, with me?

C.13 ALF: Well I guess I don't have to shut you out … (Continued below on pp. 58–59.)

By now it will be clear to the reader that this author favours a definition of the neopsyche as the congruent, expansive and expanding aspect of the individual's personality, which may be expressed in many ways. However, it is precisely because of constructivist objections to realism, positivism and determinism in social science and associated "objectivist" methodology, that this present contribution seeks to develop a systematic *intersubjective* phenomenology of the Adult. It does not, therefore, seek to offer another "objective" (and ultimately functional) view of the Adult ego state. In developing and describing the "integrating Adult", the properties of the neopsyche are explored as is the nature of its organising principle: integration. This is followed by some concluding observations about the structure of the Adult ego state and the implications of this constructivist perspective for present-centred human development.

Properties

In an important but rarely quoted passage in *Transactional Analysis in Psychotherapy*, Berne (1961/1975a) discussed the four significant properties of ego states (and psychic organs) (see Table 2.3).

Table 2.3. The properties, description, and associated disciplines of psychic organs (summarised from Berne, 1961/1975a).

Properties	Description	Disciplines
Executive power	"each gives rise to its own idiosyncratic patterns of organised behavior." (Berne, 1961/1975, p. 75)	Psycho-physiology, physiology, psychopathology, neurophysiology
Adaptability	to the immediate social situation	Social sciences
Biological fluidity	"in the sense that responses are modified as a result of natural growth and previous experiences." (ibid., p. 75)	Psychoanalysis
Mentality	mediating the phenomena of experience	Psychology, especially introspective, phenomenological, structural and existential psychologies

Moreover, "the complete diagnosis of an ego state requires that all four of these aspects are available for consideration and the final validity of such a diagnosis is not established until all four have been correlated" (p. 75). These properties are briefly elaborated here as regards the Adult ego state.

The *executive power* of the Adult has been discussed more in relation to other ego states than to, and of, itself; for example: "the Adult is the only force which can effectively intervene between the Parent and Child, and all therapeutic interventions must take account of that" (Berne, ibid., p. 373). From a constructivist point of view, the transactional analyst is more interested in the "power 'in'" the client's Adult as distinct from the Adult's "power over" other ego states or other people. This also offers an empowering Adult–Adult alternative to the Parental (Parent–Child) permission transaction, which is, essentially, about "giving power to" an alternative that facilitates people's personal power (see Rogers, 1978).

Adaptability to the environment (uterus, family, community, workplace, etc.) is an important feature of organismic development and of being human and, inevitably, a social being whether child or adult—or Adult; clearly it is important not to confuse Adult with being "grown up". This is not to suggest that we simply accept, assimilate and adapt to our environment (which may be thought of in terms of passivity, discounting, symbiosis, script and game theory); it *is* to acknowledge that adaptability concerns taking account of others, of limitations, and of consequences—tasks that are not only social but also existential. Given constructivist sensibilities to the *inter*subjective and to *shared* responsibility (see Summers & Tudor, 2000), the emphasis here is on *inter*-adaptability.

The "natural growth" inherent in *biological fluidity* reminds us that ongoing adult development (as with child development) includes maturation, learning, and socialisation, and that alongside continuity in development (from child to adult) there is also discontinuity and even a reversal of patterned interactions (see Neugarten, 1968). Similarly, personality development may be continuous, discontinuous, or interrupted. The notion of fluidity in growth (and personality) echoes Rogers' (1961) process conception of psychotherapy in which he proposes a movement from fixity (and rigidity) to one of fluidity, at which point "the person becomes a unity of flow, of motion … he has become an integrated process of changingness" (p. 158) [for further elaboration of which see Tudor & Worrall, 2006)].

All aspects of the human psyche mediate the phenomena of experience (*mentality*). In stating this, Berne clearly defined transactional analysis as a "systematic phenomenology"—and transactional analysts, therefore, as systematic phenomenologists. What distinguishes the current, present-centred *neo*psyche from its *archaeo*psyche (archaic, experienced) and *extero*psyche (archaic, introjected) counterparts is precisely its integrated and integrating process of changingness: experiencing, reflecting, mediating, and integrating.

Clarkson and Gilbert (1988) used these properties to argue that the Parent and Child (as well as Adult) are open to growth, development, and change. However, whilst the properties of executive power, adaptability and mentality clearly apply to all psychic organs and ego states, it does not make sense that the exteropsyche or the archaeopsyche have biological fluidity as they are fixed states: how can you have a Child ego state that "grows up"?

Whilst these Bernean properties of psychic organs are consistent with Hall and Lindzey's (1978) summary of principles of organismic theory (see Table 2.3 above), they do not carry the sense of movement and aspiration inherent in the concept of *physis* (Berne, 1957/1981) or more elaborated in the concept of the "actualising tendency" (Rogers, 1959, 1978, 1980a), the characteristics of which, are found in all forms of organic life, are that:

- It provides the sole motivation for human development and behaviour.
- It is both individual and universal, holistic, ubiquitous and constant; this is similar to Drego's (2000) view of the wholeness of the Adult.
- It changes in tension.
- It is a constructive, directional process, which is both organisational and aspirational, towards autonomy.
- It is reflective of pro-social human nature.
- Reflective consciousness is its salient human channel (Brodley, 1999).

Berne himself demonstrated an early interest in science and neuroscience (specifically the experimental work of the neurosurgeon Penfield) and would certainly appreciate the current interest in the psychotherapeutic implications of research in this field [see Gildebrand, 2003]. Recent research in neuroscience on the architecture and evolution of the brain demonstrates that it retains features of our ancestors: reptiles, lower mammals and primates, respectively:

- The striatum (also referred to as the basal ganglia), which is responsible for motor routines, including automatic ones.
- The paleomammalian brain (or limbic system), which is associated with emotion and behaviour as well as uniquely mammalian behaviours such as nursing, parental care, play, and the infant distress cry; thus, primal yearnings, which Hargaden and Sills (2002) located in C_0, are viewed here as age-appropriate "properties" of the [integrating] Adult/neopsyche.
- The cortex (or neomammalian brain), the greatest degree of development of which in humans is the prefrontal cortex, which is responsible for planning, directed attention, delay of gratification, affect regulation, etc. (see Pally, 2000).

Furthermore, and again consistent with organismic psychology, rather than these functions being located in a particular brain region, the brain operates as a dynamic integrated whole (Edelman, 1989). This research is highly significant for discussions about the neopsyche as it is clear that such brain functions are organic and organismic, integrated, Adult and present-centred. In this context it is clearly more relevant to help people acknowledge their "inner reptile" or "somatic simian" than it is to help people get in touch with their "Inner Child"!

Having discussed the properties of the Adult ego state, I now turn to the meaning of integration and integrating—which is core to our understanding of the neopsychic integrating Adult.

Integration, integrating

It is no coincidence that this current work has evolved in the context within the broader psychotherapeutic field of great interest in integrative psychotherapy. Such interest is itself no coincidence given that "integration", the capacity to reflect upon and make sense of our worlds, lies at the heart of what it is to be human—and at the centre of our current concern. In her major work on concepts of mental health, Jahoda (1958) viewed integration, specifically of our attitudes towards ourselves and our style and degree of growth and development, as a key concept in mental health. Other writers view integration as criterial to psychological health and maturity. In this section I elaborate some of the features of the neopsyche (see Figure 2.4) and of integration [which is further elaborated in Chapter Four].

- **Autonomy** Citing Berne's (1961/1975a) definition of the Adult ego state as "autonomous", Erskine (1988) suggested that this referred to "the neopsychic state of the ego functioning without intrapsychic

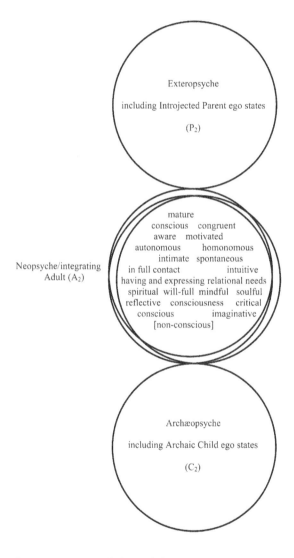

Figure 2.4. The integrating Adult model.[3]

control by an introjected or archaic ego" (p. 16). The capacity for integration requires freedom as well as separateness from external constraint. Drawing on the work of the German philosopher Immanuel Kant (1724–1804), and specifically his concept of practical Reason, Brady (1980) argued that autonomy and Reason are virtually synonymous. Significantly, Jahoda's (1958) review suggested that mental health is based on the individual's relation to reality in terms of autonomy, their perception of reality, and environmental mastery, and from Berne (1964/1968a) we derive the definition of autonomy as the release of the human capacities of awareness and for spontaneity and intimacy—and responsibility (see van Beekum & Krijgsman, 2000).

- **Relational needs** Present-centred, age-appropriate relational needs—and the impetus or tendency to meet them and have them met—are central to the neopsyche (and to an understanding of it). Following Kohut (1971, 1977), relational needs are viewed as healthy and developmental and not necessarily pathological. Although, emerging in a study of transference, the eight relational needs identified by Erskine (1998a)—for security; to feel validated, affirmed, and significant; for acceptance by a stable, dependable and protective other person; for confirmation of personal experience; for self-definition; to have an impact on others; to have another initiate; and to express love—as well as others may also be taken as essential inter-human needs.
- **Consciousness** The neopsyche is the seat of consciousness: experience that arises as a result of the workings of each individual brain and mind in relation to its environment. Precisely how consciousness arises as a result of particular neural processes and interactions, (with the brain, body, and the world) and how we can understand different subjective states (referred to as "qualia"), is the business not only of neuroscience but also of psychology and, indeed, transactional analysis.
- **Reflective consciousness** Being able to reflect on oneself, on the content and process of life, is an essential part of being human or "person" (Harré, 1983), and is crucial for the "reflective practitioner" (Schon, 1983). This, of course, includes the ability to reflect on different aspects of ourselves including the past and archaic and introjected ego states; as Erskine (1988) put it: "the healthy ego is one in which the Adult ego state, with full neopsychic functioning, is in charge and has integrated (assimilated) archeopsychic and exteropsychic

content and experiences" (p. 19). It is this capacity to reflect on ourselves and others, to spit out those experiences or introjections that are or are no longer relevant, and to assimilate the past in the service of the present, that defines the "integrating Adult"—which, as a noun, *describes the process of the neopsyche* and not simply one of its functions.

- **Critical consciousness** One of the problems with functional terms such as "Critical Parent" and "Rebellious Child" is they label critical, [criticality and, by implication, critique] and rebellion as negative, problematic and ultimately pathological. In my view an essential quality of the "integrating Adult" is, precisely, a critical consciousness that is alert and that does not accept what is assumed, given, or received.[4] It is no accident that in addition to such qualities as openness, caring, having a desire for authenticity, wholeness and intimacy, a yearning for the spiritual, and, significantly, being a "process person", Rogers' (1980a) view of "the person of tomorrow" also includes the qualities of scepticism, having an authority within, and even being anti-institutional. In expanding the Adult—and our concept of Adult and what it means to be adult—I am reclaiming critical consciousness, disobedience (Steiner, 1981), dissent, and deviance. As Samuels wryly put it:

> what interests me about the therapists is how conventional they are! They are happier with straight people. They are happier with nuclear families. It is a very odd thing that we deal so much with the unconscious—we deal with the kinky—and yet we are a very conventional group of people. (Samuels & Williams, 2001, p. 3)

- **Maturity and motivation** The neopsyche is the mature psyche (given that "maturity" is understood in terms of being age-appropriate). It is "fully functioning" in the Rogerian sense of the concept—that is, synonymous with optimal psychological adjustment and complete congruence, and characterised by openness to, and trust in, experience, and the ability to live attentively in the present (Rogers, 1961). Sharing a unified and integrative concept of human motivation, the neopsyche is synonymous with the organism, behaving as an organised whole; interacting with perceived outer and inner realities in the service of the actualising tendency; engaging in an organismic valuing process; constantly differentiating; and always in motion (as suggested by its representation in Figure 2.4). As Rogers (1951) put it: the human species (as with other species) "has one basic tendency and striving—to actualize, maintain and enhance the experiencing organism" (p. 487). Drawing on Rank's view of will as a positive guiding organisation and integration of the self, Amundson and Parry (1979) paid attention to the will as "the directing dimension of the personality" (p. 20). Amundson and Parry have also made the case that Berne brought to fruition many of Rank's proposals.[5]

• **Imagination** There is, certainly in this constructivist conceptualisation, a sense of liberation about the neopsyche. Free from the contaminations of archaic, fixated and introjected material, the mature organism/person is curious; open to contact and relationship—not only with people but also with things—through ideas, aesthetics, and the arts [and the environment]. It/she/he is playful and sensual. Just as this is the ego state of pure Reason, it is also the location of sheer intuition (which some may define as extremely rapid reasoning). Alongside the reflective and critical consciousness lies the state of unconsciousness [and/or non-consciousness], re-membered through dreams and the imagination, for, as Shakespeare's Hamlet observed: "There are more things in heaven and earth, Horatio/ Than are dreamt of in your philosophy" (Shakespeare, 1603, *Hamlet*, I.v.166).

Whilst I believe that these are key features of the neopsyche (and in this context it behoves me to advance them), of course there are others [see discussions in Chapters Three and Five and Žvelc's contribution in Chapter Eight]. Spirituality or spiritual aspirations may be viewed as essentially neopsychic—and, of course, depending on an ego state diagnosis, also archeopsychic or exteropsychic. The present-centred nature of the Adult is compatible, for instance, with Buddhist teaching on philosophy, psychology, and practice in everyday living. It is clear, however, that any description of properties, feature or qualities would not be sufficiently organismic, constructivist, co-creative, dialogic or simply comprehensive. Any qualities of an organismic, evolutionary neopsyche, as expressed by the name "Adult ego state", must necessarily be described in relation to a particular individual in terms of a full ego state diagnosis—that is, behavioural, social, historical, and phenomenological, as Berne (1961/1975a) outlined.

Before discussing the methodology of expanding the Adult, some of the theoretical implications of the argument thus far are summarised.

(Readers who are enjoying the gastronomic metaphor may consider this insertion as a cleansing and clarifying sorbet before the fourth course!)

Integrating Adult—A structural summary of a state of process

A number of theoretical points follow from the arguments advanced so far:

1. Regarding ego states

    As "Ego states and transactions are elicited from meaning (rather than the other way round)" (Summers & Tudor, 2000, present p. 3), the Adult ego state is (literally and visually) deconstructed in favour of a process conception of the neopsychic integrating Adult (see Figure 2.4).

2. Regarding the Adult

    As a present-centred, processing state of the ego, the integrating Adult is not subdivided along preconceived or functional lines—as did Berne (1961/1975a), Krumper (1977), Phelan and Phelan (1978), and Kujit (1980).

    As the neopsyche/integrating Adult is conceptually different from the archaeopsyche and exteropsyche, [it is named as such, and is thus distinguished from the exteropsyche and archaeopsyche] which are defined, respectively, by their archaic and introjected nature, within each of which are posited a number of distinct ego states that describe specific archaic, fixated, and introjected states of the ego.

3. Regarding *physis* or *phusis*

    As Berne (1957/1981) described this as "the force for Nature, which eternally strives to make things grow and to make growing things more perfect" (p. 98), in this model, it only makes sense to diagram this in and from the neopsyche/integrating Adult and not in the (Archaic) Child (as Berne did, 1972/1975b) (see Figure 2.5).

    The single-headed arrows going in to and out from the integrating Adult represent physis, which is not only a quality of an individual neopsyche but is found in others and in "Nature" (for more about integration and the environment, see Chapter Five, pp. 107–110 below).[6] [The double-headed arrows represent physis extending into the Introjected Parent and the Archaic Child ego states and, thus, represents the force, urge or motivation for health and resolving ill-health and illness.] Summers (personal communication,

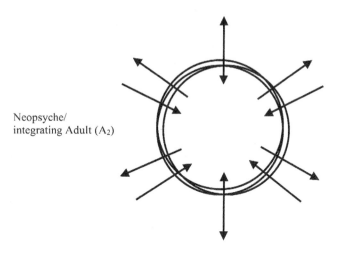

Neopsyche/
integrating Adult (A_2)

Figure 2.5. Physis and integration.

February 2002) distinguished between this mature physis and "pseudo physis", which he views as "a narcissistic, archaic Child or Parent defence".

4. Regarding development

As people are conceived Adult, Gobes' (1993) model of ego state development (in Novey, Porter-Steele, Gobes, & Massey, 1993) is more consistent with the present view of the neopsyche/integrating Adult and is thus preferred to that of other transactional analysis developmental theorists (from Schiff et al., 1975, to Hine, 1997).

[The last figure in Figure 2.6 is reminiscent of James and Jongeward's (1971) ego state analysis of the "integration process" (p. 298).]

5. Regarding the designation of certain attributes and qualities

As the Adult develops from conception, the organismic processes and qualities hitherto associated with the "Little Professor" (A_1), such as intuition, creativity, etc.—see, for example, Woollams and Brown (1978), and Hine (1997)—are conceptually relocated in the developing and evolving integrating Adult (A_2). As the archaeopsyche describes that archaic (experienced) part of the psyche, which encompasses a number of archaic, fixated states, then the name "Little Professor" or designation A_1 refers to a pseudo "adult-in-the-Child" whose consistent patterns of behaviour and experiencing are characterised by a "smartness" that is learned as

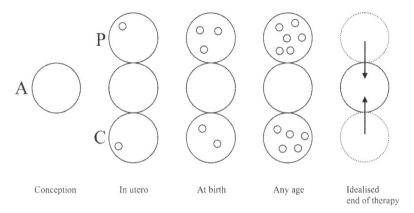

Figure 2.6. Ego state development in the integrating Adult model (developed from Gobes in Novey, Porter-Steele, Gobes, & Massey, 1993).

an adaptation and that may be distinguished from an organismic, neopsychic intelligence and intuition—that is, integrating Adult. To view A_1 [as the site of intuition]is to confuse a particular description of the *structure* [and content] of personality at any one time with an epigenetic, *developmental* model of personality. Similarly, present-centred emotions, such as those yearnings that Hargaden and Sills (2002) identify as C_0 are conceptualised as within the neopsychic integrating Adult.

Functional nomenclature such as "Critical Parent" and "Adapted Child" are not considered helpful to a constructivist understanding of the individual or to such conceptualisations of personality and ego states. Terms that describe a "critical Adult", "rebellious Adult" or even "revolutionary Adult" may help both therapist and client (and theorist) in a process of *metanoia* (change), expansion, and liberation. The key question is whether such qualities are *integrated* and form a present-centred sense of self [and self-with-other]—or not. In short, if, for example, nurturing and caring are integrated then they are "Adult" (i.e., a quality of the evolving neopsyche); if they are not, they may be understood as an Introjected Parent ego state or an Archaic Child ego state—depending, of course, on the diagnosis. In the absence of specific diagnosis and in the endeavour of promoting a systematic phenomenology (i.e., transactional analysis), it is both inaccurate and confusing simply to name these qualities as "Nurturing Parent", and so forth.

This present work in effect criticises the reification of both Child and Parent ego states in transactional analysis theory and practice, the objection to which extends to include the possible reification of the integrating Adult. The difference is that, with regard to the integrating Adult, there is no end to integration: as the neopsychic Adult is in constant process, it may not be fixed either clinically or conceptually.

Having laid the conceptual and theoretical foundations of a new view of the neopsyche, it is time to turn to the methodological implications of this perspective for clinical practice.

Expanding Adult

In this fourth part (we are now on to the sweet course or *i dolci*) there is a selection of "sweets"; in other words, whilst some practice and methodology is presented it is by no means comprehensive. Ultimately it is for the individual practitioner to develop their own practice and method of expanding Adult. In Italy there is a tradition of guests bringing their own selection of sweets to a meal; it is in such sharing, sampling and experimentation that co-creative transactional analysis practice will evolve [as evidenced, for example, in Chapter Eight]. With reference to clinical psychotherapeutic practice, I elaborate some of the implications of the previous theoretical discussion of the neopsychic integrating Adult for both practice and method, beginning with a continuation of the previous vignette (from above, pp. 45–46).

c.13 ALF: Well I guess I don't have to shut you out.

T.13 BEA: (Nodding.) Umm … and an important part of the therapy here is to play with what you're guessing and what you know about you and me.

c.14 ALF: (Smiling.) Playing sounds good …

T.14 BEA: (Smiles.)

c.15 ALF: (Pause.) You mean guessing is OK?

T.15 BEA: In the absence of knowing, guessing sounds pretty good to me.

c.16 ALF: (Throws his head back, laughs and lets out a huge breath.) What a relief. I feel lighter … better … like I'm not wrong.

T.16 BEA: So now you have the possibility of being lighter, better, right, of breathing easily.

C.17 ALF: (Sitting forward, taking big breaths.) That's right. It's like I was only seeing through a mist, having a film over my eyes. Now I can see you and see that you care, that you're not being critical, that you don't think I'm wrong and that you're going to shut me in the cupboard, I guess.

T.17 BEA: So you're still guessing on that one!

C.18 ALF: (Smiles.) No … and, yes, I guess sometimes yes.

T.18 BEA: That's the play: the interplay between knowing here and now that you're OK and worth it and sometimes not knowing that about yourself and not knowing that about me in relation to you.

C.19 ALF: That's about it.

Assuming health (alongside illness)

As did our original article (Summers & Tudor, 2000), this present constructivist contribution draws on a tradition of health psychology. In this frame of reference we may be ill and well at the same time: alongside psychopathology, however we describe, define and categorise it there is a "psycho*sanology*" (Antonovsky, 1979, 1987); alongside mental illness is mental health or well-being (see Tudor, 1996a)—and, indeed, I argued for the addition of a sixth "health" axis to the [then] current *DSM-IV* multi-axial diagnosis (see Tudor, 2004). More subtly, our "illness" may be part of a health crisis in the organism. What this means in practice is that what many clients present as illness, a crisis or a problem is simply a part of life [see Mazzetti's contribution in Chapter Eight]. In my initial transactions with a client (and supervisee or trainee), I am often concerned both to understand and to deconstruct the present "problem", usually by means of specifying, and confrontational transactions. Often I say something along the lines of, "So that's the problem. What's the matter?" This both acknowledges that there is a perceived problem but that there is not necessarily anything the matter. Either it has literally little or no "matter" (as in substance), or having a problem is *in itself* not necessarily a problem. This is informed in part by Freire's (1972) "problem-posing" pedagogy of the oppressed, which welcomes and, moreover, poses problems to the student and through which the discussion and resolving of learning (in Freire's context, literacy) develops. Interestingly, James and Jongeward (1971) suggested that "raising the right question" activates—and strengthens—the Adult. In the vignette above, the therapist's assumption of health alongside pathology may be seen in her acknowledging the client's creative adaptation in the past (T.12) and in his present "guessing" (T.13). Following phenomenological method—after all, as has been noted, transactional analysis is a "systematic phenomenology" (Berne, 1961/1975a)—the therapist also challenges the client's self-judgement (see C.2 in the vignette).

Assuming neopsychic integrating Adult functioning (alongside Introjected Parent and Archaic Child ego states)

One therapeutic slogan of a constructivist, co-creative transactional analysis might well be: "Assume Adult—until proved otherwise". Building on the assumption of health, and the co-existence of health and illness, this therapeutic assumption and attitude supports the neopsychic integrating Adult functioning of the client. As above, some of what is presented as archaic and/or introjected may well not be, and, at this stage, decontamination work may be useful to clarify the phenomenological difference between archaeopsyche and exteropsyche on the one hand and the neopsyche on the other—and it is worth noting that "decontamination" is, in effect, therapeutic work with the Adult ego state [for further discussion of which see Chapter Seven]. However, the word and the concept is problematic in that it implies a notion of cure as a fixed, uncontaminated, descaled, barnacle-free Adult ego state. *Expanding* the Adult takes this process a step further in inviting the client, literally, to expand their consciousness, autonomy, homonomy, etc. As noted earlier, critical consciousness requires and, indeed, contributes to an evolving Adult definition of what it is to be adult/Adult. Again, more subtly, given the different nature of the neopsyche on the one hand and the archaeopsyche and exteropsyche on the other (see above, p. 33), it follows that we can be "in" Adult and Child or Parent *at the same time*. Similarly, we can co-create present-centred non-transferential Adult–Adult relating at the same time as we co-create transferential (or partially transferential) relating (see Summers & Tudor, 2000). In the vignette above the therapist assumes Adult functioning alongside transferential relating (T.3), in acknowledging her "mistake" (T.7), and in inviting the client to focus on present relating (T.12, T.13 onwards).

Making contact

Rogers (1957, 1959) described contact or "psychological contact" as the precondition for therapy. With the exception of Erskine's (1988, 1993) work on contact, enquiry, and attunement, and some recent work (van Beekum & Krijgsman, 2000; White, 2001), transactional analysis, certainly compared with gestalt and person-centred psychologies and therapies, has underemphasised this necessary condition of the therapeutic relationship. In this present work, contact is viewed as a consistent attitude and endeavour embodied by the therapist, which conveys an acceptance of, and empathy for, the client. Such attitudes, of unconditional positive regard and empathic understanding, if received by the client resonate at many levels, especially in the limbic system as well as in the imagination, and encourage the client's self-acceptance and self-understanding. In expanding the Adult, such contact is present-centred, focusing on what is happening here-and-now rather than what was happening there-and-then; on what *is* happening rather than on what isn't happening. This focus and emphasis may be seen in the vignettes (above, pp. 45–46, 58–59). In many ways the whole piece is concerned with making and maintaining contact, including non-verbal contact (e.g., T.10) and acknowledging the break or rupture in the contact (T.4 to C.9). In this sense, transactional analysis "proper"—that is, the analysis of transactions, may be viewed and experienced as the moment-by-moment analysis of contact between therapist and client: both when contact is full and ongoing and when it is ruptured. Acknowledging and working through ruptures is an essential part of the therapeutic process and promotes an expansive and contactful relationship. Put another way: "ruptures in the empathic process, perceived or real, offer opportunities for the therapist to facilitate the client to integrate previously disassociated ego states" (Hargaden & Sills, 2002, pp. 57–58).

Diagnosing psyche and ego states

With its plethora of diagnostic theory, formulations and even formulae, transactional analysis is open to the criticism that it has simply introjected the medical model of diagnosis → treatment → cure. Steiner's (1971a) caution about diagnosis as a form of alienation remains largely lost in the mists of a once radical time in transactional analysis. The word diagnosis is derived, through Latin, from the Greek word διαγιγνώσκει, meaning to discern or distinguish, and in itself does not carry the more pejorative overtones of its close association with the more deleterious aspects of the allopathic medical model. At best, diagnosis is based on, and in, ongoing enquiry in the therapeutic relationship, with a view to enhancing the understanding of both client and therapist [see Rogers, 1951; also Chapter Seven]. In terms of the accuracy of diagnosis or discernment—of ego states—Berne (1961/1975a) offered a (usually) sequential outline of a clinical procedure for correlating four requirements for a full diagnosis, based on:

- *Behavioural* diagnosis—usually made on the basis of clinical experience, taking account of demeanours, gestures, voice, vocabulary, and other characteristics (see C.2, C.5 in the vignette above).
- *Social* or *operational* diagnosis—the response of someone else in the environment of the subject concerned (see T.4).
- The *historical* diagnosis—the subject's internal corroboration of the original prototype for the behaviour, attitude, thinking, feeling, etc. (e.g., C.11).
- The *phenomenological* diagnosis—based on the subject being able to re-experience in the present, "in full intensity, with little weathering" (ibid., p. 76), the earlier, historical moment or epoch (see C.1 to C.7).

All too often ego state diagnosis is based on the viewer's reading of the external manifestation of a particular behaviour, based on a crude classification of associations: critical (Parent), rebellious (Child), etc. Unfortunately, as noted above (p. 44), Berne (1961/1975a) fell into the same trap, associating attractiveness/responsiveness with Child, and ethical responsibility with Parent. Another pitfall in clinical practice is diagnosis based on the social/operational reaction of the practitioner without sufficient reflection in terms of their own cultural frame of reference, countertransference, etc., which, if unchecked, untrained, or unsupervised, can lead to defining and blaming transactions. What was radical about Berne's contribution was giving equal weight to the internal, phenomenological experiencing of the client (the historical and phenomenological criteria), as well as providing theory, which encourages the practitioner to be both thorough in checking out the *properties* of a person's ego state, as well as cautious and exploratory in offering all this to the client as (only) one way of describing and understanding themselves and their world. One of the implications of this present work is that the therapist needs to know and to be able to distinguish and discern in relation to each client what is Adult and what is not—by means of a full ego state diagnosis.

If this is the enquiring approach to diagnosis, then the necessary attunement is in how this is delivered, mediated, and processed. Just as there are process contracts (see Lee, 1997), so diagnosis needs to be held as a process—and, indeed, is formulated *in* the process, for example, through analysis of the therapist's countertransference or through reflection on, and acknowledgement of, co-created co-transferential relating. There are several points in the vignettes (above, pp. 45–46, 58–59) when the therapist might have been tempted to interpret what the client was saying and to make the link to a diagnostic formulation; note the "the" as in "to make *the* link", as if there is only one. Instead, she reflected on the rupture in the relationship, and acknowledged the part she played in it. To paraphrase Berne's (1966) comment that "visual observation is the basis of all good clinical work and takes precedence even over technique" (pp. 65–66): contact, enquiry and attunement is the basis of a good therapeutic relationship and takes precedence over diagnosis.

Working in relationship to support integration

The emphasis in clinical practice in expanding the Adult is on the co-creation of the therapeutic relationship, both tranferential and present-centred (see Summers & Tudor, 2000). Both therapist and client bring to therapy ideas, both contaminated and expansive, about what it means to be adult: "If I were really grown up I wouldn't be feeling this hurt"; "If I were really grown up I wouldn't need to see a therapist"—and, perhaps, "If I were really grown up I wouldn't need to *be* a therapist!"; "Now I'm adult I can laugh and cry, sing and weep"; and "Part of being adult and having a place in the world is being a therapist"; etc. Therapist and client, as any parties in any relationship, are always co-creating something. Therapy is attending to what we co-create. In this frame of reference, therapy is:

1. First, the co-creation of new (neo)psychic relational possibilities, played out, tried and tested in the therapeutic relationship and milieu (for example, the possibility of "guessing" in the vignette above); and

2. Second, concerned with dealing with the grief of past traumas, deficits and limitations—and in this, therapy is essentially a phenomenological and existential process.

The approach promoted in this chapter does not ignore transactional analysis therapeutic work with Archaic Child ego states (such as deconfusion) or with Introjected Parent ego states (such as the Parent interview); rather it offers a reframing of such therapeutic work through its focus on the neopsychic Adult. It does generally confront an overemphasis on the "Inner Child" and "Inner Child work": it *is* too late to have a happy childhood; it's not too late to be happy now [to grieve the loss of what was—and what wasn't –] and to review and reframe that unhappy childhood. Thus, regressive therapy is generally eschewed in favour of integrating, strengthening and expanding present-centred Adult functioning. This is the task of a genuinely integrative—or integrating psychotherapy. In similar vein, what are diagnosed as "personality disorders" are viewed, within this present frame of reference, as personality *processes* [see Tudor & Widdowson, 2008], in response to which the work and the healing lies in the therapeutic relationship [– or therapeutic relating and different ways-of-being-with –] and especially the observance, maintenance and negotiation of boundaries.

Organisational implications of the integrating Adult

In this brief concluding part, some organisational implications for transactional analysis of this present view of the neopsychic integrating Adult are briefly considered.

If "ego states" are reified then the structure of personality becomes reified and potentially ossified. People talk about being "in my Child" and, worse, "my Child is feeling ..." etc. So too, at an organisational level, there is a danger that the structure of the "personality" of transactional analysis in its ethos, values and organisation becomes fixed, rigid, obsessive, and conservative. Offering an organismic and process view of the mature and evolving personality, the theory of the integrating Adult, and the methodology of expanding the Adult, supports those transactional analysts who are reflective, critical, imaginative, and embracing of diversity, including criticism. This is particularly important as "rebellion" (especially in clients and trainees) is often pathologised. Unlike Moiso and Novellino (2000), I do not see the "rebellious aspect" of transactional analysis stressed at all. Far from it: the radical and critical spirit of the early years of transactional analysis has been all but lost.

The integrating Adult brings—indeed, insists on bringing—a reflective and critical consciousness to bear on all aspects of life, including the organisation of transactional analysis and transactional analysis organisations. For example, one of the principles that informs therapeutic communities (TCs) is that there is a "culture of enquiry" in which:

> all members … can question managerial issues, psychological processes, group and institutional dynamics … discussion is regarded as a learning experience … everything within the community is available for discussion … [and] managerial information and issues which affect the community are shared with the whole community. (Kennard & Lees, 2001, p. 148)

These principles, which are entirely consistent with the commitment in transactional analysis to open communication, may be useful in offering support for the broader therapeutic community of transactional analysis at all levels and, within it, training institutes to promote open communication, including criticism, and mutual learning through dialogue.

Specific concerns about the state of transactional analysis include:

- Pressure to conform to traditional views of theory—for instance, regarding contracts and escape hatch closure, which, together with a "You can't quote it if it's not published" attitude to the development of theory and ideas, generally encourages conformity and discourages exploration.
- Pressure to complete training at one training institute—which may suit the trainer/institute financially and psychologically, but equally may not suit the trainee. This is particularly ironic given the centrality of autonomy in transactional analysis; its history in terms of the (original) mentoring model of training whereby, before the comparatively recent advent of training institutes, student/practitioners, attending particular workshops, events, and short courses, put together their own package of training towards certification; and the fact that the current organisational structure and examination requirements within transactional analysis still allow for such a

portfolio approach: all of which leaves more freedom of choice and personal power with the student.[7]

• Certain structures and attitudes that serve to protect a professional hierarchy:

1. The accreditation of trainers within transactional analysis can appear, and be experienced, as a kind of pyramid selling of training, which, in promoting a closed shop attitude to training, excludes and discounts the experience of others, including some trainees who are themselves experienced educators and trainers.

2. The notion that the transactional analysis practitioner cannot say or do something publically about transactional analysis until they are qualified—that is, as a certified transactional analyst.[8]

These concerns could be viewed as evidence of a heavy, institutional "Be Strong" and "Be Perfect" transactional analysis Parent (with hints of "Please Me"), which would suggest that, as a community, we need to be mindful of the obsessive-compulsive traits, adaptations or even disorders of transactional analysis as well as the adaptations it engenders. In this sense this present contribution may be seen as an intervention (or interposition) designed to confront organisational atrophy, and to support script prevention and autonomy and homonomy.

As with any good meal, taking in a number of courses over a number of hours, ending with a plate of cheeses (*i formaggi*), and preferably accompanied by a robust red wine, this chapter is offered in the spirit not only of satisfying a certain hunger but also of stimulating the senses, to be sampled, chewed over, and some even spat out; to be reflected upon with good colleagues and friends; to be the subject of discernment; and, of course, to be expanded. If this helps you, the reader—and, ultimately, your clients—to make more sense of themselves, others, and your and their worlds, and to be able to impact on them with a sense of social responsibility and citizenship, as autonomous, homonomous, conscious as well as non-conscious, imaginative and free-thinking human beings, then this chapter has been worth preparing and offering [and, for this present version, revisiting and revising].

Notes

1. This research and Table has been updated and revised for this publication (to October 2012).

2. Articles that deal with more than one ego state are counted in each column but, in terms of the percentages, are counted as a proportion—that is, a half or a third of the particular article.

3. This is a simplified version of the figure in the original chapter; see also Figure 2.5.

4. I think about the development of such conditions or conditionality in terms of Steiner's (1971b) stroke economy, based on the following rules: don't give strokes when we have them to give; don't ask for strokes when we need them; don't accept strokes if we want them; don't reject strokes when we don't want them; and don't give ourselves strokes—and the development of critical facilities as, in part, based on a rejection of such self-limiting rules.

5. Interestingly, Rank also influenced Rogers, especially through the person and work of Jessie Taft (1882–1960), who coined the term "relationship therapy" (Taft, 1933), a term that Rogers (1942) adopted.

6. Berne (1957/1981) referred to *physis* as a "growth force" (pp. 142, 216, 228) and as an "urge" (p. 114). In her article on the subject, Clarkson (1992a) suggested that as this concept appeared in Berne's work from 1947 to 1972 "physis was one of the most enduring concepts accompanying Berne's theoretical and practical developments in transactional analysis" (p. 202).

7. In the context of debates about the statutory regulation of professions and the state registration of the title "psychotherapist", and the rejection of this by the psychotherapy profession in the UK, I was dismayed to discover recently that the UK ITA had instituted a scheme whereby the training hours of psychotherapy trainees would only be recognised and "counted" towards their CTA if they have undertaken them at a registered training establishment (RTE); and that a transactional analysis trainer who is already accredited by virtue of being a TSTA, TTA, STA or PTSTA, and who teaches at an RTE has also to be registered with the ITA (see ITA, 2013). In the context of UK psychotherapists having moved away from statutory regulation, the ITA's decision to impose such requirements appears a clear case of societal or, more specifically, organisational regression in the face of professional progression (see Smith, 2011; Tudor, 2011c)—and appears to run counter to valuing autonomy.

8. I was again dismayed to learn that the ITA has recently introduced the requirement that transactional analysis trainees who submit an article for consideration for publication in its magazine, *The Transactional Analyst*, have to obtain the support of their supervisor, who, in effect, has to endorse their article, a decision that, again, appears to compromise autonomy and the human right of the freedom of expression.

CHAPTER THREE

Response to "The neopsyche: the integrating Adult ego state", and rejoinder

Graeme Summers and Keith Tudor

T his chapter comprises a response to Keith's original chapter on the neopsyche/integrating Adult (Tudor, 2003; present Chapter Two) written by Graeme, in which he also takes the opportunity to reflect on our original article. It is followed by a rejoinder from Keith.

Response from Graeme

In general, I am satisfied that much of our original article remains coherent and meaningful to me. There are, however, some clarifications and developments I would like to share and discuss, stimulated by your chapter on the Neopsyche. I follow the structure that you provide in your chapter above.

The use of metaphor

Your discussion on this theme resonates with me at philosophical, interpersonal and theoretical levels. At a macro level, consistent with social constructivist perspectives, I consider that all of our perceptions are metaphors and stories about reality—including, of course, this one!

To import a metaphor from behavioural economics, the notion of "coherent arbitrariness" (Ariely, Loewenstein, & Prelec, 2003) has interesting applications to psychological life in general. This idea originated in relation to studying the perceived monetary value of goods or services and shows that we tend to construct arbitrary amounts that "feel" right. The "feeling" of rightness is intuited from other contextual inputs, which give us a guide price; for example, looking at pricing of vaguely similar products or other precedents, which can give us "coherence" in the midst of uncertainty regarding the monetary value of something. The point here is that we tend not to think in terms of fundamental values; rather, the monetary value we attribute to many things are arbitrary social constructions, and coherence is often created through comparison with other (also arbitrary) prices. What happens if we apply this idea to other areas of our lives, perhaps even to our deepest feelings about what is meaningful and valuable? In a shame experience we might think of ourselves as "unworthy", or, in a narcissistic moment, consider ourselves especially "entitled". What contextual inputs do we draw upon to assess our own self-worth?

Therapists using eye movement desensitisation and reprocessing (EMDR) ask the client "What would you prefer to believe about yourself?" and use the answer to construct a subjective scale of validity to assess progress. I love the sense of possibilities implied by this question, which can often elude us when in a negative mindset.

Our orientation towards the world as well as ourselves is also variable. I have often considered it curious that a feature of depressive mood is that someone becomes concerned with meaning or, rather, the lack of it, and asks, "What is the point?", as if seeking an absolute answer. On a better day, it appears to me that this same question does not become answered but becomes irrelevant. Instead of pursuing the elusive absolute, we get on with our lives: satisfied to engage with the coherent enough arbitrary meanings and metaphors we find and construct within ourselves and with others along the way.

More significantly, perhaps when we look for cognitive meaning, we may be looking in the wrong place to satisfy the urge that drives the seeking. As Stern (2004) put it:

> in most psychodynamic treatments there is a rush toward meaning, leaving the present moment behind. We forget that there is a difference between meaning, in the sense of understanding enough

to explain it, and experiencing something more and more deeply.
(p. 128)

So, in addition to cognitive metaphors, it also makes sense for us to speak of "implicit metaphors" as expectations about how we might be in the world with ourselves and with others, which expand or limit our felt experience. I think this is the level at which the Boston Change Process Study Group (BCPSG) aimed to address when they suggested that psychotherapy be directed at changing "implicit relational knowing" (Lyons-Ruth et al., 1998, p. 282) rather than conscious insight; as Stern (2004) put it: "Lived stories are experiences that are narratively formatted in the mind but not verbalized or told" (p. 47). Modell (2003) thought of these relational schemas as "wordless affective metaphors" (p. 45). Furthermore, he placed metaphors at the heart of psychotherapeutic transformation since "they transfer meaning between dissimilar domains", which leads to "new combinations of thought", but argued that, if no transformation takes place, "the metaphoric process was foreclosed or frozen" (p. 41).

Novelty

If we are inclusive of implicit process, then I agree with your suggestion that metaphor can both illuminate and deepen our experience and that: "Metaphors need to be renewed in a continual process of novel re-presentation" (p. 38). This emphasis on novelty and the "neo" echoes our original proposition (Summers & Tudor, 2000) that the role of the therapist "is primarily to facilitate suspension of the transferential expectation and to invite co-creation of fresh experience(s)" (p. 14).

I no longer work as a therapist, but the principle still applies to my coaching work. I led a coaching group in which a participant cynically declared that our group work was "OK, but hardly life changing". In response I mimicked his words and tone, reflecting his hostility and defensiveness and probably adding some of my own. He then said: "I didn't say it like that, did I?" The other group members gently nodded. He softened—and so did I. He subsequently became more open about what he really wanted, and, through his vulnerability and excitement, engaged myself and others creatively to support his aspirations. He later stated that he had found the robust and yet supportive nature of the group to be "unusual".

Ego states

In relation to transactional analysis theory, I appreciate the way you develop our emphasis on ego states as metaphor, particularly in clarifying the "conflation and confusion of metaphors: on the one hand, ego states as an image and representation of the structure of personality and, on the other, ego states as a metaphor for stages of development" (p. 35).

I wonder, however, if it is the "conflation" of these metaphors that is part of the appeal of the three ego state model of health (Novey in Novey, Porter-Steele, Gobes, & Massey, 1993), since it has been, and remains, the dominant model of ego states in the transactional analysis literature. Whilst speaking of the infant, neonate or even foetus as having Adult capacities is, as you clearly articulate, entirely consistent with our terms of reference, it is an emotionally counter-intuitive suggestion. However, alongside ourselves, several transactional analysis authors—Little (2001), Žvelc (2002), Fowlie (2005), and Wells (2012)—are developing and utilising variants of the one ego state model of health pioneered by Erskine. I would even consider articles by Novellino (1993) and Hargaden and Fenton (2005) on non-verbal Adult transactions to be moving in this direction.

Like you, I welcome this theoretical diversity and vitality and have no wish to subscribe to, or promote, standard imperial units of transactional analysis theory. I am left with appreciation for Berne's intuitive grasp of the colloquial power of the terms he adopted in the first instance as we build upon his legacy in our different ways.

Your description of the subjectivity of "best" prompts me to say something about my preference for the one ego state model of health. I think it holds the "best" theoretical consistency with Fairbairn's (1952) model of the ego, and Berne's descriptions of transference and countertransference transactions (Berne, 1972/1975b), and his three rules of communication (Berne, 1966). Our subsequent theoretical adaptations to ego states, transactions, games and scripts offer me an internal coherence with respect to these core transactional analysis concepts and also provide coherence with developments in related disciplines. Additionally, our suggestion that the ego state model be considered as "systematic, intersubjective phenomenology" (Summers & Tudor, 2000, p. 18) continues to resonate with me at psychological, philosophical and political levels. Stern (2004) put it like this: "Together, you cocreate experiences.

Your phenomenal experience includes your direct experience of the other's phenomenal experience. The setting is not only social, it is quintessentially intersubjective" (p. 118).

Metatheory

You provide an interesting overview in terms of broader paradigms and I welcome you positioning a humanistic paradigm (i.e., organismic psychology) alongside the psychoanalytic paradigms proposed by Pine (1990)—that is, drive, ego, object, self.

Having said that, there are ways in which organismic psychology doesn't appeal to me as a paradigm. The notion of universality and integration feels somewhat idealistic. I think, at root, I do have faith in self-actualising tendencies but I think we sometimes choose, in or out of awareness, to stagnate or implode. I actually think that ambivalence about growing/learning is natural, and that we learn, individually and collectively, to manage/co-regulate all sorts of experiences and mixed motivations. For example, my partner has a text message ringtone of Yoda (from *Star Wars*) announcing "a message from the dark side there is"! Humour is one of many ways to acknowledge and regulate our negative impulses.

I do however lean towards holistic appreciation of interconnected phenomena, as suggested by field theory, and evolutionary and intersubjective psychology. For me it is a given that we impact and are impacted by our local and global environments. This includes our social culture(s) and intimate relationships—the intersubjective fields—which provide a "contextual precondition for having any experience at all" (Orange, Atwood, & Stolorow, 1997, cited in Stolorow, Orange, & Atwood, 2002, p. 371).

The Adult ego state

Your reference to Berne (1961/1975a) describing the Adult as "the most obscure area in structural analysis" (p. 195) sets the opening frame for this section in which you propose a vibrant alternative to this theoretical void.

Perhaps pathological patterns were a better subject matter for Berne's obsessive tendencies, since they provide a range of classifiable but predictable sequences. In contrast, health is less predictable and harder to describe or define. It's great to see you employ your own obsessive tendencies in service of describing health, beginning with a sharp analysis and critique of Berne's epigenetic assumptions of how integration occurs, namely via movement from archaic ego states into Adult. A similar view from contemporary transactional analysis is expressed by Stuthridge (2010):

> There are two key outcomes, then, of early interaction between the infant and care-giver: a shifting matrix of multiple Child and Parent ego states representing self–other experiences and a process of integration which can be conceived as a function of the Adult ego. (p. 77)

Here, Stuthridge considered integrating Adult to be a developmental achievement and that "Infants are not born with a unitary subjective sense of self" (p. 78). However, I consider "Adult" as a metaphor for any experience that is not defensively organised—that is, defensively split off. So, where Stuthridge would classify early representations of self or other to be Child and Parent, which are then integrated, I would consider them to be Adult in the first instance only to become Child or Parent ego states in response to unbearable experience that cannot be (co)regulated. Whilst a coherent subjective sense of self develops over time with appropriate relational care, I would see this as the healthy development of Adult, not the starting point. Here I would use the term "unitary" to mean "not defensively split" and to be inclusive of fragments of emergent experience that have not yet coalesced into core or intersubjective senses of self (Stern, 1998). As indicated in our original article, this process of self-development applies throughout the life cycle and not just in infancy.

This epigenetic debate echoes Fairbairn's (1952) differentiation from Freud:

> all the ego-structures are conceived as inherently dynamic; and the central ego represents the central portion of an original unitary, dynamic ego-structure, from which the subsidiary egos come to be subsequently split off. Thus, whilst Freud regards the structural "ego" as a derivative of the structureless "id", I regard the libidinal ego (which corresponds to the "id") as a split off portion of the original, dynamic ego. (p. 148)

From our perspective, then, Parent–Child dynamics represent defensive attempts to regulate internally what we feel we cannot tolerate more openly. So, we adopt archaic strategies in our attempt to manage what feels unmanageable even though the outcome may be predictably poor. The notion that we "split" ourselves to manage unbearable affect in response to relational yearning, frustration and consequent ambivalence lies at the heart of Fairbairn's work.

In discussing ego state properties, I agree with you about the importance of creating Adult–Adult alternatives to the Parent–Child permission transaction. This metaphorical shift feels right both clinically and, again, politically.

Adaptability is a feature of archaic states within our model in the sense that we can make situations fit our familiar negative expectations, even in favourable circumstances, in order to defend against the de-stabilisation that novelty might engender. The notion of "inter-adaptability" is perhaps most evident in complementary transactions through which we might adapt to each other as partners in the co-creation of familiar or novel experiences.

Regarding biological fluidity, I would add emphasis to your statement that ongoing human "personality development may be continuous, discontinuous or interrupted" (p. 48) by suggesting that some discontinuity is necessary for growth and that non-linear progression and disturbance is also a normal part of change. I think this is where my critique of your "integrating" prefix for Adult surfaces because I think dis-integrating and non-integrating are also important aspects of Adult experience even though I much prefer the feeling of "flow" (Csikszentmihalyi, 1990), the felt sense of integration and fluidity that accompanies peak experiences. Nevertheless, your "integrating" prefix is a powerful metaphor that emphasises ongoing process and I find much agreement with your account.

Finally, you rightly link the capacity to mentalise to systemic phenomenology and note that we have this capacity across all three types of ego states. We (Summers & Tudor, 2000) originally postulated that even discarding the "myth of objectivity", these "shifts in experience of self remain discernible and usable within an intersubjective and postmodern frame of reference" (p. 19). I further suggest (Summers, 2011; present Chapter Four) that this means different levels of conscious, preconscious and non-conscious/unconscious experience are possible across this "systematic" trio.

I understand Berne's reference to structural analysis as a systematic phenomenology to mean that the metaphors of Parent, Adult and Child can be used systematically to classify experience. Given our emphasis on relating as both the context and the medium for the formation and development of personality, it made sense for us (Summers & Tudor, 2000) to reconsider the ego state model as a "systematic, intersubjective phenomenology" (p. 18).

Your analysis of Berne's (1961/1975a) ego state properties is useful in clarifying our co-creative approach to personality and the Adult ego state whilst maintaining conceptual linkage to the original concepts.

Integration, integrating

Here you propose several features of integrating Adult. I think your suggestion that autonomy requires "freedom as well as separateness from external constraint" (p. 52) is more compatible with the "myth of the isolated mind" (Stolorow & Atwood, 1992, p. 7) than our co-creative proposition, though I think you redress this by giving weight to "essential inter-human needs" (p. 52).

Your classifications of consciousness are clarifying, but, as I argue in my chapter (Summers, 2011), not applicable to all stages of development.

I enjoyed your lively description of the Adult as the mature psyche and have been reflecting on your suggestion that it behaves as "an organised whole"—which is a controversial notion within the field of psychology. For example, Schore (2010) has described the notion of a unitary self as misleading, stating that: "Over the life span the early-forming unconscious implicit self continues to develop to more complexity, and it operates in qualitatively different ways from the later-forming conscious explicit self" (p. 178).

Within transactional analysis, and consistent with the dominant three ego state model of health, the "implicit" domain has largely been associated with Child ego states (Cornell, 2003; Gildebrand, 2003). Whilst the implicit domain has always been implicitly included in Parent, Adult and Child within our model of ego states, I think that we have made this more explicit in more recent publications (Summers & Tudor, 2005b, 2007; Summers, 2011; and in this present work, see especially Chapters Five and Seven).

Both the three ego state and the one ego state models of health propose that it can be useful to think of the healthy self as being divided as well as being integrated/integrating. The challenge here is to hold both views as plausible constructions or metaphors, each illuminating the nature of being human in different ways. This parallels the wave–particle paradox in physics and the difficulty of holding different paradigms simultaneously, due, respectively, to the inherent nature of matter itself or the inherent limitations of observation.

In the search for organising or integrating processes, Modell (2003) used metaphor to bridge implicit/explicit realms; Bucci (1997) proposed that "The referential process is the operation that connects the multiple representational formats of the non verbal systems to one another and to words" (p. 13); and Stern (2004) suggested that in narratives there is a "two-way traffic between the implicit and explicit" (p. 175). Fosshage (2010) differentiated between "explicit learning" and "implicit procedural learning" and considered the implications for practice:

> In clinical situations when procedural knowledge is not accessible to consciousness, emphasis on "interactive intersubjective processes" or "non-interpretive processes" will be more productive. However, if procedural knowledge can come into consciousness, via an explicit declarative focus, increased awareness gradually contributes to a capacity to suspend momentarily intractable mental models to enable the registration and establishment of new models, based on co-creation of new relational experience within the analytic relationship, into long-term memory. (p. 247)

These authors engage with questions of self and self-other processes, which attempt to account for different types of experience. Variously, implicit and explicit domains are acknowledged as being different and yet often deeply interwoven. Although you have chosen to emphasis "integrating" in this account, I think that our co-creative Adult incorporates both explicit and implicit domains and the interweaving between them in relation to ongoing well-being.

Expanding the Adult

Here you discuss implications for practice in terms of underlying assumptions, contact, diagnosis, and working relationally.

One of the aims of co-creative transactional analysis is to offer psychological models of health alongside pathology. Your proposed assumptions of health (alongside illness) and Adult (alongside Parent and Child) convey this well. My general approach is to assume the co-existence of health and pathology within and between myself and my client(s) without prioritising either. Health provides opportunities for further growth and development through optimising challenge, whilst pathology provides opportunities for healing. Both learning and healing can happen in many ordinary ways as well as in specific learning/healing contexts, and I agree that the explicit and implicit assumptions we bring to these situations is strongly influential. I further suggest that it is through facilitating changes in implicit relational knowing that practitioners help clients expand their non-consciousness as well as consciousness. In this sense, as Stern (2004) described it: "verbal interpretations and implicit expansions of the intersubjective field are complementary acts" (p. 178).

I also agree that making contact is essential to healing and learning but would not define this only in terms of empathy, awareness, or consciousness. Gestalt theorists have proposed a process-orientated view that "self is the system of present contacts and the agent of growth" (Perls, Hefferline, & Goodman, 1951/1996, p. 372) and that:

> Contacting is, in general, the growing of the organism. By contacting we mean food-getting and eating, loving and making love, aggressing, conflicting, communicating, perceiving, learning, locomotion, technique, and in general every function that must be primarily considered as occurring at the boundary in an organism/environment field. (ibid., p. 427)

Regarding the recognition of ego states you state that: "the therapist needs to know and to be able to distinguish and discern in relation to each client what is Adult and what is not—by means of a full ego state diagnosis" (p. 63). I think that this diagnostic approach is also relevant to the *practitioner's* shifts in ego states, together with an appreciation that practitioner and client are continually influencing each other. This diagnostic ideal needs to be tempered with an equal appreciation that there is no such thing as immaculate perception and that any form of diagnosis is constructed within, and influenced by, cultural context. The importance of uniqueness that you emphasise, therefore, applies to the situation and the practitioner as well as the client, and echoes a phenomenological rather than modernist world view.

The co-creation of relational possibilities, both transferential and novel, lies at the heart of our conceptualisation of relational therapeutic work. I appreciate your distilled articulation of therapy as: a) creating something new, and b) grieving for what has been lost. Erskine (1993) has pointed out that grief is often stimulated following the "juxtaposition" (p. 184), which the novelty creates alongside previous experience. In the coaching world Kohlrieser (2006) has applied the same principle to leadership development through the bonding cycle. He proposed that good people-leaders need to bond effectively with others and can only do so if they have the capacity to grieve past losses and therefore be able to engage openly in new and existing working relationships.

Organisational implications of the integrating Adult

I think this aspirational perspective reflects your personal and professional values and, as you suggest, reflects some of the values already expressed in transactional analysis codes of ethics, specifically: autonomy, open communication, and mutual respect. To this, I would add my own values of curiosity, creativity, and compassion. The first two of these values reflect an appreciation of uncertainty, and yet support the risk-taking necessary for growth and vitality. The last value helps manage anger and disappointment when I or others succumb to not infrequent fallibility in the rough and tumble of relational and organisational life. I also consider that there is much that cannot be consciously or critically reflected upon due to the limitations of consciousness. I do not view this as a failure of Adult ability, but an appreciation that "Adult" experience is much more than conscious awareness and, therefore, provides the larger context within which we take conscious steps to learn and improve, individually and collectively.

Rejoinder from Keith

Thank you, Graeme, for your response to my original chapter. In terms of our process, for me, yours stands not only as a considered commentary on and, in some ways, a development of the chapter, but also, as I wrote the chapter on my own, as something of a completion of a conversation about this aspect of co-creative transactional analysis—that is, ego state theory and, specifically, the integrating Adult ego state. I agree with most of your comments and additions, and appreciate the way you've woven in references to economics and coaching; I also loved your comment about "standard imperial units" (p. 72), with its hints of a political, anti-imperialist critique. Here I rejoinder your response with regard to two concepts: the organism and, briefly here, integrating (for more on which, see Chapter Five), and, returning to a debate we had when we were writing the original article, raise the issue of the value— or otherwise—of the three ego state model. With respect to some possible further differences with regard to human development, which you outlined in your chapter on dynamic ego states (Summers, 2011), as this appears here in the next chapter (Chapter Four), I pick this up in my rejoinder to it in Chapter Five.

Organism

As you know, I have been researching organismic psychology for some time, especially as a significant influence on person-centred psychology. As Mike Worrall and I put it: "At the heart of the person-centred approach and the theory and practice of person-centred therapy lies the organism, a pulsing biological entity and a significant and enduring image" (Tudor & Worrall, 2006, p. 45). The tradition of organismic psychology dates back to the work of Kantor (1924a, 1924b), and included, notably, Goldstein (1934/1995), who wrote a book *The Organism*, but also Wheeler (1940), Murphy (1947), and Werner (1948), all of whom were hugely influenced by the work of the philosopher Alfred North Whitehead (1861–1947) and his process philosophy (see, especially, Whitehead, 1920, 1929/1978). Although, nowadays, in the person-centred and experiential tradition, and, more broadly, in humanistic psychology, there is more talk and writing about the self, and the human being as a self (even a reified "Self"), or as selves or configurations of selves, I argue that as the self is a differentiated portion of the greater perceptual field—that is, the organism (Rogers, 1951), it follows that the organism is conceptually and developmentally prior to self (for further elaboration of which see Tudor & Worrall, 2006). I am increasingly viewing this as not only describing an ontological reality, but also acknowledging an inextricably social, cultural and environmental perspective about the human condition.

Interestingly, in their major work *Theories of Personality*, Hall and Lindzey (1970) acknowledged Rogers as adopting an "organismic orientation", although they did not categorise him as an organismic theorist until the third edition of their work (published in 1978) when they significantly revised their appraisal:

> In previous editions, we called Rogers' viewpoint "self theory"
> but that no longer seems to us to characterize accurately Rogers'
> position. It is clear from his recent writings that the emphasis
> should fall on the organism, not the self. Indeed the self or self-
> concept … is apt to be a distorted picture of the person's authentic
> nature. (Hall & Lindzey, 1978, p. 279)

In our book *Person-Centred Theory: A Clinical Philosophy*, I and Worrall (2006) identified and elaborated a number of qualities of the organism, which include: being holistic, experiential, concrescent (growing together), differentiating, co-regulatory, interdependent, and directional. Whilst I appreciate that the entity/image/metaphor of the organism doesn't necessarily appeal to you (or others), I do want to take up your association of the organism with universality and integration and your feeling that this or these notions are idealistic. Here I address universalism and pick the point about integration in a subsequent section.

As I understand it, universalism refers to the condition of being universal and the idea that there is a universal explanation for everything. Interestingly, in theology, universalism refers to the doctrine of universal salvation or reconciliation. I think we would agree that the notion that a piece of theory can provide a complete understanding of everything, or even anything, is a myth. Mark Widdowson and I made this point in our critique of the process model in transactional analysis and what we view as the universal theory of personality adaptations (Tudor & Widdowson, 2008). The search for universal laws that explain *the* "reality" represent objectivist approaches to social science which are, at best, partial, definitely outmoded, and, at worst, grandiose and dangerous. I don't have a problem with your concern about universalism; it's just that I simply don't think that either the concept of the organism or organismic psychology itself claims to be universal. What organismic psychology does propose is a unity of the organism, within which there are, of course, differentiated aspects, such as the self; it also proposes and, indeed, is predicated upon, holism—see Smuts (1926/1987), and Angyal (1939, 1941)—on the principle of which (if you'll forgive the pun) I think we are united, if not whole!

This brings me to the question of the organism behaving as "an organised whole", which may—or may not—be a controversial concept within psychology; in any case, I don't think that Schore (2010), whom you cite, is critiquing organismic organisation so much as a fixed view of self, even an unconscious self. I think it's possible to hold that the organism is "organised" in the sense that it has an inherent directionality and that it tends to actualise both towards autonomy and homonomy, and that it is coherent. I think this is a more accurate and process-oriented way to describe "the actualising tendency" (for a critique of which see Tudor & Worrall, 2006)—and I think this is more a matter of fact than of faith. Of course, as we develop and grow, we become more complex, and our "organisation" will take and manifest in different forms and ways: and in this I agree with both Stern (1985, 1998) and Schore (2010). Of course we fall over, are mistrustful, feel ashamed and have doubts, feel guilty, inferior, confused, and isolated, as you say, stagnate or implode, and despair. The point—or, at least, my point—is that it is the "organisation" of the organism that helps us to pick ourselves up, make sense of our stagnation or implosion, and move on. I loved your reference to your partner's ringtone, as I used to think that all texting (txting) was from the "dark side"—but, then, I do acknowledge my Luddite inclinations! More seriously, the message of the "dark side" is, also, one of hope: when Luke Skywalker confronts Darth Vader in *The Empire Strikes Back* (Kirsher, 1980), he (Luke) says, "I know there is good in you." Interestingly, with regard to the discussion of the self, this comment is preceded by the following dialogue:

DARTH VADER: The Emperor has been expecting you.
LUKE SKYWALKER: I know, father.
DARTH VADER: So, you have accepted the truth.
LUKE SKYWALKER: I've accepted the truth that you were once Anakin Skywalker, my father.
DARTH VADER: That name no longer has any meaning for me.
LUKE SKYWALKER: It is the name of your true self, you've only forgotten. I know there is good in you; the Emperor hasn't driven it from you fully.

I don't think that there is a true self, only a "true" organism or, better, an organism with the qualities that I and others have described, and, which, for me, encompasses the things you're saying about the more difficult stuff: ambivalence, mixed emotions, disintegration, etc. We may not agree on this but I hope, at least, that our differences are clearer.

Before I leave the organism (at least for now!), I do want to link this entity and image to the concept of "flow" (Csikszentmihalyi, 1990), which you cite. One of the reasons I like the entity and metaphor of the organism is that, given that it tends to actualise and is, therefore, directional, moving, differentiating, etc., it seems to me to describe the flow or fluidity of the human being, *being* human. Indeed, "fluidity" is, if generally unacknowledged, a key value of person-centred therapy and, I would suggest, more broadly, of humanistic psychology. In describing his process conception of therapy, Rogers (1958/1967a) himself was clear that he valued fluidity but that others may not: "This", he wrote, "is one of the social value judgements which individuals and cultures will have to make" (p. 135). Elsewhere (Rogers, 1953/1967b), he described one of the fundamental directions taken by the process of therapy as:

> the free experiencing of the actual sensory and visceral reactions of the organism *without too much of an attempt to relate these experiences to the self.* This is usually accompanied by the conviction that this material does not belong to, and cannot be organised into, the self. The end point of this process is that the client discovers that he can be his experience, with all of its variety and surface contradiction; that he can formulate himself out of his experience, instead of trying to impose a formulation of self upon his experiences, denying to awareness those elements which do not fit. (p. 80, my emphasis)

I think that Rogers' commitment to free experiencing—one might also say, free associating—and his concern that such experiencing is not "formulated" by "self" or, importantly, the therapist, supports our interest in co-creative relating. Personally, I think that we offer a more relational—or, perhaps, a more interrelational—perspective than Rogers, in that we would also promote an engagement and dialogue with "those elements which do not fit"—and, indeed, an aspect of the critique that I and Worrall advanced in our work was that Rogers did not take his relational theory to its logical conclusion. This may also address your concern that my requirement for autonomy was too isolationist or individualistic. Nowadays, I don't tend to use the concept of autonomy much, and, if and when I do, drawing on Angyal's (1941) work, I tend to say or write "and homonomy", thereby emphasising the sense of, and trend to, belonging alongside that of, and to, self-determination. Oh dear, there's that word "self" again!

A note on health

I agree with your general approach: "to assume the co-existence of health and pathology within and between myself and my client(s) without prioritising either" (p. 78), and I particularly like your summary: "Health provides opportunities for further growth and development through optimising challenge, whilst pathology provides opportunities for healing" (p. 78). However, as Winnicott observed, "Health is much more difficult to deal with than disease" (quoted by Phillips, 1988, p. 1) and, as I have discovered in my work on this subject over some years (Tudor, 1996a, 2004, 2008a), health is a disputed concept and, in some quarters, seen as a self-deceptive "flight". My own interest in and focus on health, growth and growth models, *psychosanology* alongside psychopathology, and salutogenesis alongside pathogenesis, has, at times, involved struggle and conflict. In 2010 I completed my PhD on the subject, published as *The Fight for Health* (Tudor, 2010a); the "fight" of the title acknowledging both a critical theoretical perspective as well as particular personal, professional and political experiences in the field of health and, specifically, mental health. If I emphasise and perhaps at times overemphasise health, I do so for strategic reasons—one might say "to bring balance to the force!"

Integration and integrating

In the sense that "integration" and especially "Integrated", as in "the Integrated Adult", sounds like a fixed end point, and that that represents an ideal such as "cure", I agree that integration is idealistic. To the extent that integration and, more clearly, *integrating* describes a process, I don't agree that this is idealistic; rather, I view this as realistic in that it describes the experiencing and integrating organism (as above). I agree with your sense of the power of the prefix and the metaphor and, in that we are both trying to describe, an integrating, flowing process, which, of course, can be disintegrating and stuck, I think we're pretty close on this. Nevertheless, I appreciate what I take as a reminder to be cautious about idealising or reifying anything.

I address the other, developmental aspects of the critique of integration in Chapter Five.

Three, one or two ego states?

Three ego states and one ego state

Given that the main focus of the original chapter (Tudor, 2003; present Chapter Three) is on ego states, and as this is a response and rejoinder, I want to take this opportunity to clarify a common misconception about what has come to be referred to as the "one ego state model", and to pick up a conversation we had, mostly, as I remember it, walking on the beach at Arnside in Cumbria in the UK on visits in the mid to late 1990s, about the three ego state model.

As you know, my research into the Adult ego state in transactional analysis led me to develop the idea of the integrating Adult, the origins of which I found in Berne's (1961/1975a) seminal work, *Transactional Analysis in Psychotherapy* (see Figure I.1). In 2005 I met Claude Steiner at the ITAA Conference in Edinburgh where we began to have some discussions about radical psychiatry (about which we agree) and about ego state theory (about which we disagree). Some years later (in 2008) I invited him over from the United States to do a workshop in Sheffield, UK where we had the opportunity to get to know each other further and to discuss aspects of transactional analysis theory and practice. During this visit, I also had the good fortune to see him working in a group with the concept of the stroke economy and facilitating participants to identify the introjected Critical Parent messages, which interrupt the acceptance and rejection of, and requests for, strokes. In the course of our time together, in response to him questioning me as to where I had got this idea of the "integrative" nature of the Adult, I said, "It's in Berne." He replied, "No, it isn't." I responded, "Yes, it is. It's in *Transactional Analysis in Psychotherapy*." To cut a long story short, this exchange was the inspiration for me doing the research and textual analysis of *Transactional Analysis in Psychotherapy*, which resulted in the article on "The State of the Ego: Then and Now" (Tudor, 2010b). In the article, I identified two sets of ego state models in transactional analysis: those based on a view of three ego states and those based on the Integrated or integrating Adult. One of the differences between these two sets of models is that "cure", health or the hypothesised end of therapy is viewed as, respectively, a "complete" set of three ego states (what I referred to as the "set 1 model of ego states"), or an Integrated/integrating Adult (the "set 2 model of ego states"). This has led some people to refer to the latter as a "one ego state model". My problem with this—and, I think, you'd agree—is not only that this is unrealistic (in that I am sure that people will always have unresolved introjected or archaic material), but also that it discounts the reality and, as you acknowledge, the opportunity of those introjected and archaic experiences and schemas. Although I do advocate the neopsychic integrating Adult, I do not wish to discount exteropsyche Parent ego states or archaeopsyche Child ego states and, therefore, do not view the integrating Adult as a "one ego state model".

Two ego states?

We both were clearly convinced by James and Jongeward's (1971) Integrated Adult and Erskine's (1988) Integrated Adult model—with the subsequent modification of using the term "integrating" (as discussed elsewhere and above). Further, I remember presenting something of this logic: that if, in effect, we are distinguishing between health and pathology, present-centred relating and past-centred relating, then:

1. Why would we not promote a two ego state model of present-centred integrating Adult and past-centred aspects of the personality that is Parent and Child ego states?
2. Why would we particularly want to distinguish, or to continue to distinguish, between introjected (Parent) messages and archaic (Child) experiences.

I note that in 1988 Tony White proposed a "two ego state model" but that his proposed two ego states were Parent and Adult, with the Adult (A_2) "in" the Parent (P_2), but that this clearly is based on a very different view of the developmental history of the Adult than ours. I envisage that this neo–archaeopsyche, two ego state model would or could be represented as in Figure 3.1.

This model represents a present-centred and past-centred view of the personality, a personality that is in transaction with others and

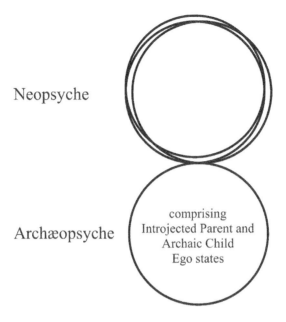

Neopsyche

Archæopsyche

comprising
Introjected Parent and
Archaic Child
Ego states

Figure 3.1. The neo–archaeopsyche, two ego state model.

the environment—and a model that is consistent with our original work (Summers & Tudor, 2000) regarding transactions. In this conceptualisation:

1. The term "archaeopsyche" is used to encompass both the archae-opsyche and the exteropsyche on the basis that introjected Parent messages are also experienced by the person/subject and thus, phe-nomenologically, are not "extero" or external to the person.
2. The circles remain stacked for reason of familiarity and for ease of diagramming transactions.
3. The Adult is placed on top, somewhat "intuitively" (echoing Berne), but also strategically, with regard both to acknowledging health, and to recognise that introjected and archaic material often feels like it's "underneath".
4. Whereas the neopsyche would not be divided (as I argued in my original chapter; present Chapter Two), the archaeopsyche may be subject to second and third order structural analysis but not with any named adult states—that is, A_1, A_0, etc.

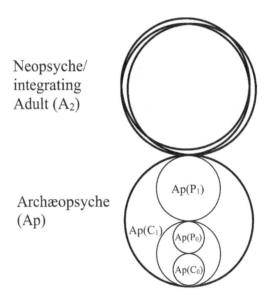

Figure 3.2. The neo–archaeopsyche, two ego state model, including second and third order analysis.

Whilst I appreciate—as you represented so well in our discussions—that both the nomenclature "Parent, Adult, Child" and the PAC model of ego states to which they refer hold a familiarity, merit, and resonance, I offer this alternative model as a logical extension of our thinking on ego states.

CHAPTER FOUR

Dynamic ego states: the significance of non-conscious and unconscious patterns, as well as conscious patterns*

Graeme Summers

Introduction

In this chapter I explore the significance of levels of consciousness with particular reference to ego state theory (Berne, 1961/1975a). In doing so I also describe a dynamic ego state model developed specifically to account for non-conscious as well as unconscious, preconscious and conscious patterns of experience.

Dynamic ego states

Inspired by the work of Daniel Stern (2004) and the Boston Change Process Study Group (BCPSG) (2010), the dynamic ego state model is my attempt to account for some recent developments in developmental psychology, neuroscience, and positive psychology, within a transactional analysis theoretical frame (Figure 4.1).

*Originally published in 2011 in *Relational Transactional Analysis*, edited by Heather Fowlie and Charlotte Sills (Fowlie & Sills, 2011), Karnac, London. Reprinted with permission of the publisher.

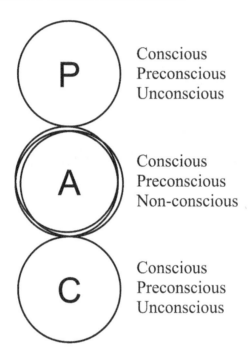

Figure 4.1. Dynamic ego states (Summers, 2008).

The dynamic ego state model builds upon the foundations of co-creative transactional analysis (Summers & Tudor, 2000) to propose:

- That ego states are "patterns" of experience; they are relational possibilities and probabilities.
- That Adult ego state represents our flexible, creative and resourceful self or sense of self.
- That Parent and Child ego states represent our rigid or compulsive psychological defensive patterns, most often used in times of stress.
- That personal development is a process of expanding Adult relational capacity and reducing Parent and Child probabilities.

I have chosen the term "dynamic" for two reasons. First, it echoes Freud's (1915e) use of this adjective to describe the unconscious when referring to active repression from conscious awareness, and so accurately reflects its usage in relation to Child and Parent ego states within this model. Second, it helps the consideration of personality in terms of ongoing vitality, both within and between people, rather than reified personality structure, and, therefore, reflects the phenomenological, field theoretical and social constructivist basis of co-creative transactional analysis. I do not use the term to denote affinity with Blackstone's (1993) idea of the dynamic Child, especially since my conceptualisation of the Child ego state is radically different from her formulation.

The unconscious and the non-conscious

I was introduced to the distinction between non-conscious and unconscious through Stern's (2004) writing, which helped both clarify and develop my thinking in relation to co-creative transactional analysis. I resonated with his suggestion that we consider aspects of implicit relationship that are *not conscious but also not defensive or pathological* as non-conscious, while reserving the term unconscious for that which is dynamically and defensively repressed. This useful distinction helps account for non-verbal health, healing, and creativity, which may or may not become verbalised by therapist or client. Stern's proposition is that interpersonal experiences may be transformative, in therapy or otherwise, without ever being named or made explicit.

Applying this to co-creative transactional analysis, I think of Parent and Child ego states as largely implicit unconscious processes in which the deepest unresolved transferential dramas unfold within the therapeutic dyad. Through unconscious co-transferential enactments the therapist becomes part of the problem with the client in order to become part of the solution. The heart of the transformational process, however, takes place within implicit non-conscious interrelations through the co-creative, but not necessarily conscious, verbal or explicit Adult–Adult "moments of meeting" (Stern, 2004, p. 165) and new ways of being with another that develop in parallel with co-transferential replays.

I draw on Little's (2006) use of "structuring" and "non-structuring" internalisations to distinguish between Child–Parent and Adult ego states, respectively. In this formulation Child–Parent relational units that develop defensively in response to (inevitable) unbearable or unmanageable experience are differentiated from good enough self-other interactions that are generalised and represented internally. I build upon this conceptual frame to locate the Child–Parent ego states and Adult ego states, each underpinned by "Representations of Interactions that have been Generalized" (RIGs) (Stern, 1985, p. 97) within implicit memory in the unconscious and non-conscious, respectively. Using this theoretical base I consider "working in the relationship" to mean that therapist and client work together at the intimate edge of bearable and unbearable experiences. Therapeutic work involves co-creating viable experiential alternatives to co-transferential defensive transactions to enable the client to be more fully present in relationship with himself/ herself and with the therapist. These therapeutic experiences may or may not become explicit: "It is more likely that the majority of all we know about how to be with others resides in implicit knowing and will remain there" (Stern, 2004, p. 115).

I remember a moment in my own therapy when I talked about a painful experience in a somewhat stereotypical northern English, working-class male, matter-of-fact way. In response, my therapist visibly softened, showing subtle signs of sadness in her face, which, in turn, helped me soften. Although this interaction was not explicitly discussed, in hindsight I believe it helped me feel recognised at an emotional level, and yet the absence of explicit discussion of the experience respectfully echoed my allegiance to my culture of origin. Such refined choices of interaction, assuming they are even available to consciousness, concur with Stern's caution that "an attempt to make this moment of meeting explicit, especially immediately after it occurred, could undo some of its effect" (ibid., p. 191).

In its publication *Change Process in Psychotherapy*, the BCPSG (2010) wrote: "The task of therapy is to change implicit relational knowing" (p. 193). It viewed the development of the implicit relationship between therapist and client as the medium to "make more of the patient's world relationable … [and to] create new relational possibilities" (p. 194).

As I have already noted, this does not necessarily imply that previously repressed unconscious experiences were once conscious or that they become conscious in the therapeutic journey. I consider that repression has different meanings depending on whether we use Freud's (1923b) or Fairbairn's (1952) conceptualisation of the ego. Within a Freudian frame, repression means active repression from consciousness; however, within a Fairbairnian frame, we can also understand repression as meaning repression from relationship. This latter conceptual frame helps distinguish between levels of unconsciously repressed experience that may be consciously recoverable, and those that may be relationally recoverable through change in implicit relational knowing, but which are still unavailable to explicit consciousness.

The additional significance of acknowledging a non-conscious implicit realm of experience and relating is that it supports the conceptualisation of the expanded/expanding Adult ego state and further differentiates it from restricted notions that Adult ego state is merely to do with consciousness.

In his chapter on the neopsyche/integrating Adult, Tudor (2003) built creatively upon the one ego state model of health as pioneered by Erskine (1988), and as adapted within co-creative transactional analysis (Summers & Tudor, 2000). I agree with much of his chapter, especially his articulation of the implication (within this model) that we are "conceived Adult". Tudor (2003) has stated that his reference to conception more accurately refers to the notion that the foetus "adapting to its reality *in utero*, may be thought of as having a neopsyche or Adult ego state" (p. 35), and has acknowledged that "this may be the point at which the Parent, Adult, Child metaphor breaks down and we need to present new metaphors by means of new nomenclature" (ibid., p. 39).

I do, however, think he created some confusion when he subsequently described integration as "the capacity to reflect upon and make sense of our worlds" (p. 50). He further stated:

> It is this capacity to reflect on ourselves and others, to spit out those experiences or introjections that are no longer relevant, and to assimilate the past in service of the present, that defines the "integrating Adult" … [and] In my view an essential quality of the "integrating Adult" is, precisely, a critical consciousness that is alert and does not accept what is assumed given or received." (p. 53)

All of this makes sense in relation to reasonably well-functioning, chronological adults, but seems a tall order for a foetus! In the main, Tudor's descriptions of "integrating" lean heavily towards explicit consciousness and necessitate a level of developmental achievement way beyond that of a foetus or neonate.

This contrasts with the co-creative transactional analysis assertion that Stern's (1985) description of four senses of self "supports the possibility of working at non-verbal levels of self-development within an Adult frame of reference" (Summers & Tudor, 2000, p. 15). So, while Tudor usefully builds on the co-creative ego state model, especially in terms of discussing the importance of Adult reflective and critical consciousness in later human development, I think the non-verbal and implicit aspects of the original co-creative transactional analysis formulation of ego states need to be re-asserted.

My interpretation of integrating incorporates much less developmentally sophisticated processes. I think in terms of biological notions of organism–environment co-regulation, which is more of a gestalt formulation: "We cannot do anything to take into our bodies those necessary things we require, whether it is affection, knowledge, or air without interacting with the environment" (Wallen, 1970, p. 10). From this perspective, I think the foetus example holds true and that human co-regulation then takes on more sophisticated forms from birth onwards.

On further reflection, however, I am less inclined to use the prefix integrated or integrating in relation to Adult. I think it is important to account for experiences, relational or otherwise, that we hold as somewhat unintegrated fragments but are not defensively organised. In the ongoing process of lifelong learning we hold many fragments of experience (ideas, feelings, images) at different levels (conscious/preconscious/non-conscious), which we may or not be able to integrate, but we are nonetheless able to tolerate the fragmentation, not knowing, and uncertainty. In contrast, I think that certainty is often an expression of a Parent ego state used to defend against the experience of the unknown. In everyday learning we often need to dis-integrate our familiar ways of meaning-making to create an "open space". Such familiar ways may be habitual preferences of thought, feeling or behaviour that we need to deconstruct in order to learn something new. Incorporating the concept of non-conscious processes within the Adult, I therefore propose that dynamic Adult ego states can be considered to have integrating, disintegrating, and non-integrating capacities, which play a pivotal role in healing, learning, and living—in and out of awareness.

Conscious and preconscious

The conscious/preconscious distinction, like the dynamic unconscious, also dates back to Freud's dynamic model of the psyche. In *The Interpretation of Dreams*, Freud (1900a) saw the preconscious as a screen lying between the unconscious and conscious systems. He proposed that the unconscious can only reach consciousness via the preconscious system and that it is this, therefore, that is the main domain of psychotherapeutic work. The preconscious is often used to refer to experiences, thoughts, or memories that while not in present consciousness are readily accessible through an introspective search and then available for conscious attention.

Tudor (2003) suggested that "the neopsyche is the seat of consciousness" (p. 52). Whilst I think this is true in terms of deeper reflective consciousness, I also think that a person can be conscious in a more limited way when using Parent or Child ego states. For example, I may well be conscious that I am being critically condemning of another person. However, I may not be conscious of the way in which I am unthinkingly copying the attitudes of an authority figure, or that I am adopting this attitude as a psychological defence. I could also scan my preconscious experiences whilst using a Parent or Child ego state to gather evidence in support of my defensive position.

I recall an executive coaching client whose direct reports were telling him via a process of 360 degree feedback (that is, a process of getting performance feedback from different perspectives e.g., bosses, peers, direct reports, customers, etc.) that "He wasn't there much and when he was there he was critical". This feedback was not surprising to him—he was already conscious that he related in this way. What he realised through our coaching work was that he was re-enacting a relational pattern he had experienced many times with his own father. Not only was this a useful cognitive insight, it was also painful for him to remember this aspect of his childhood and to recognise that his archaic experience of his father was now strongly echoed by the people who presently worked for him. This illustrates that the conscious/preconscious distinction is particularly relevant to the transactional analysis concept of contamination (Berne, 1961/1975a). Contamination occurs when an individual mistakes their Parent or Child for Adult. Decontamination involves the process by which Parent and Child patterns of experience become consciously differentiated from Adult and, therefore, available for reflective consideration. Eusden (2011) has suggested that it is at this point that a person can develop the capacity to have "one foot in and one foot out" (p. 107) and to "mind the gap" (p. 101) between deeply felt co-existing psychological realities [for further discussion of which, see Chapter Seven].

[This involves understanding both our archaic and our present-centred attempts to regulate emotions in response to which] Eusden and Summers (2008) proposed the concept of "Vital Rhythms". Here we related Panksepp's (1998) classification of emotional systems to ego states and hypothesised that each system can be regulated within

Adult or within the archaic Child–Parent relational units—the former being more functional than the latter. Glynn Hudson-Allez (2008) also referred to Panksepp when she linked the capacity to use secure attachment (which I consider an Adult capacity) to the effective co-regulation of panic states.

As the client's unconscious/preconscious archaic strategies for managing emotions become apparent within the unfolding co-transference, opportunities emerge to co-regulate these affect states within the developing Adult–Adult attachment of the therapeutic relationship. Note that one of the strengths of Berne's (1961/1975a) "PAC" (Parent, Adult, Child) model is accessibility. I have witnessed many people make important insights about their own patterns as they use this deceptively simple model to recognise how problematic patterns in the present have meaningful roots in earlier experiences. Such insights can provide the basis for immediate changes and/or serve as a prompt to further personal development.

Equally, the move from preconscious to conscious awareness may be the consequence of deeper emotional work:

> It is noteworthy that in the field of psychotherapy, the focus of therapeutic action has begun to shift from models favoring cognition to models which emphasise the primacy of interpersonal factors and bodily-rooted affect. These models suggest that insight is the result not the agent of change. This gives a new meaning to Berne's recommendation first to change then to analyse. (Allen, 2010, p. 44)

In this case, cognitive insight, and the conscious Adult re-working of personal narratives can serve to reinforce personal transformation that has already been made at deeper experiential levels.

The conscious/preconscious distinction within Adult has particular significance in relation to the recent explosive emergence of positive psychology (Seligman, 2003). Here we move our focus away from problematic experiences that may require healing or transformation in order to unlock creative potential towards patterns that are already functional and creative. Within the terms of the [original] chapter, the emphasis here is on bringing preconscious competence into awareness. Fredrickson (2009) found that when people experience positive affect; for example, joy, interest, happiness, and anticipation, their peripheral vision expands. She linked this and other empirical findings to the "broaden and build" strategy, which suggests that positive emotions encourage exploratory thought and behaviours that, in turn, build new skills and resources. The metaphor of building suggests a pro-active, skill-based process that is prompted by, and reinforcing of, positive affect. Fredrickson also reported that positive affect is generally experienced with significantly less intensity than negative affect; for example, anger and fear. Whilst I do not necessarily regard anger and fear as negative, this does remind us, as practitioners and clients, also to attend to the flow of possibly less intense yet positively experienced emotions that can support personal development.

Numerous strengths inventories have been developed in recent years with the intention of helping people discover and clarify what is right with them, rather than what is wrong with them. Again, the intention here is to invite preconscious health into consciousness.

Within my coaching practice, solutions-focused enquiry (Jackson & McKergow, 2007) often proves useful. A female senior manager wanted to raise the profile of herself and her department. She identified that she needed to make more connections with key people operating at the executive level above her, but felt repulsed at the idea of politically motivated "schmoozing". I asked about the good relationships she already had with some of her seniors and how they had come about. She realised that they had all developed through collaborative cross-functional projects, where, together, they had made genuine contributions to the work of the organisation. Following on from this insight she was able to develop a viable strategy for raising her and her department's profile in a way that felt congruent with her values and natural ways of being.

Positive psychology has many overlaps with transactional analysis (see, for example, Napper, 2009), both in the affirmation of human well-being and the encouragement to act and not just to think or feel. From a psycho-educational perspective, there is congruence here with Temple's (1999, 2004) work on functional fluency, a term she uses to describe "the behavioural manifestations of the integrating Adult ego state" (1999, p. 164). Temple has devised research-based classifications for identifying a range of social behaviours, an approach that offers a method for expanding Adult flexibility at a conscious behavioural level.

Conclusion

There are many ways in which people heal, learn, and develop, within which "The explicit and implicit intermingle at many points" (Stern, 2004, p. 187). As I consider this in relation to ego states my main proposition is that, while Parent and Child ego states are relational possibilities experienced, expressed and maintained largely through unconscious implicit interactions, it is non-conscious implicit processes that form the ongoing experiential basis for Adult ego states.

My secondary proposition is that preconscious searching for meaningful connections can be made with respect to our healthy functioning as well as our troubles. As Damasio (2010) stated:

> Mind is a most natural result of evolution, and it is mostly non conscious, internal, and unrevealed. It comes to be known through the narrow window of consciousness … which is an internal and imperfectly constructed informer rather than an external, reliable observer. (p. 117)

With this thought in mind I conclude, as ever, with great respect for the unknown that lies within and between us, despite our earnest attempts to understand and make use of the aspects of our experience that we are able to perceive.

CHAPTER FIVE

Response to "Dynamic ego states", and rejoinder

Keith Tudor and Graeme Summers

This chapter comprises a response to Graeme's paper on "Dynamic Ego States" (Summers, 2011; present Chapter Four) written by Keith; this is followed by a rejoinder from Graeme. As we have acknowledged in our respective Introductions, Keith's chapter on the neopsyche/integrating Adult (Tudor, 2003; present Chapter Two) was an outcome of our earlier collaboration (Summers & Tudor, 2000), and, specifically, an elaboration of the Adult ego state in the context of Berne's (1961/1975a) theory—or theories—of ego states (see also Tudor, 2010b). Graeme's (2011) chapter on dynamic ego states was a separate and further elaboration of ego states and included some critiques of Keith's chapter.

Response from Keith

When Heather (Fowlie) and Charlotte (Sills) asked me to provide an endorsement of their book (Fowlie & Sills, 2011), and I received an electronic version of it, I, of course, read your chapter first! I liked it, especially as it gave me an insight into the development of your thinking in recent years, including some differences between us, which you highlighted. I am therefore particularly glad that we have created this opportunity not only to publish our original work and ideas, but also to draw out and clarify differences, and to develop our ideas—each and both—and to do so in a co-creative way. Here, I have organised my response to your chapter under four headings: dynamics; different consciousness; integration; and integrating.

Dynamics

I am curious as to your choice of this word to describe your model of ego states as, to my mind and ear, its provenance is more psychoanalytic than anything else, and not from the traditions—phenomenological, existential, humanistic—on which we originally drew. Although you are clear that you wanted to echo Freud's (1923b) use of the term in his description of the unconscious and repression, I'm not clear why you wanted to have that particular echo or resonance. I agree that the word "dynamic", which, in its meaning, suggests energy or effective action, vigour, activity, force and energy, refers to active repression from conscious awareness; indeed, it is for that very reason and association that the word or term seems less appropriate to describe a—or the—process in Child and Parent ego states within the co-creative model. Finally, on this, even if "dynamic" is a useful word to describe psychodynamics *within* the individual, it seems less than useful to describe emergent and possible processes *between* individuals. I and my psyche may be worthy of some analysis or interpretation on the basis of psychodynamic principles (or not!), but is our *relationship* best described as psycho-*dynamic*? I don't think so.

Interestingly, as I was writing this paragraph, I was distracted by a thought about a case study I need to write for full membership of a professional association. One of the requirements is to write a "dynamic formulation". I get what it means and what it is asking for, but it annoys me that, for membership of a generic psychotherapy organisation, there is a requirement that is so clearly based on a concept and, beyond that, a language that is both particular—and, I would argue—partial. Language matters (see also Chapter Ten).

Different consciousness

I like the fact that in your diagram of the ego state model, you name different domains of consciousness.

I, too, liked our original emphasis on the conscious and the non-conscious in addition to the unconscious and agree, as you put it (Summers, 2011), that this emphasis: "supports the conceptualisation of the expanded/expanding Adult ego state and further differentiates it from restricted notions that Adult ego state is merely to do with consciousness" (p. 93). I also agree with you that I have tended to emphasise "explicit consciousness" and thus the conscious functioning of the neopsychic integrating Adult perhaps at the expense of developing a co-creative perspective on the unconscious. In your chapter you quote me (Tudor, 2003):

> It is this capacity to reflect on ourselves and others, to spit out those experiences or introjections that are no longer relevant, and to assimilate the past in service of the present, that defines the "integrating Adult" … [and] In my view an essential quality of the "integrating Adult" is, precisely, a critical consciousness that is alert and does not accept what is assumed given or received."
> (present p. 53)

In response, you wrote (Summers, 2011): "All of this makes sense in relation to reasonably well-functioning, chronological adults, but seems a tall order for a foetus!" (present p. 93) Interestingly—and, in the light of your critique, perhaps ironically—when I wrote that passage, I was thinking not so much about a chronological adult but rather about an infant spitting out her or his food. On reflection, I think that I might have added (to that passage) after "a critical conscious-ness", "and non-consciousness"; nevertheless, I stand by my think-ing that integration is "the capacity to reflect upon and make sense of our worlds" (p. 216)—at whatever age and in whatever way we (as adults) conceptualise and language the infant's capacity to "reflect on" and "make sense". To some extent this is a problem of trying to verbalise experiences that are preverbal—which Stern did brilliantly in his *Diary of a Baby* (Stern, 1992). Notwithstanding this, I accept that I may have caused confusion by not giving necessary detail to what this might look like at different stages or phases of development. In response, I wonder if it would be useful to think about different forms of conscious/ness (as above) in terms of Stern's (1998) domains of self, a theory on which we both draw (see Table 5.1; to be read from the bottom up).

In terms of elaborating the "non-verbal and implicit aspects of the original co-creative transactional analysis formulation of ego

Table 5.1. Senses of self and domains of relatedness and consciousness (based on Stern, 1998).

Age				Domain of consciousness	
0–2 months Onwards	9 months Onwards	18 months Onwards	3 years Onwards		
			Narrative	Conscious	
				Preconscious	Non-conscious
				Unconscious	
		Verbal		Conscious	
				Preconscious	Non-conscious
				Unconscious	
	Intersubjective			Conscious	
				Preconscious	Non-conscious
				Unconscious	
Core-self-with-another	Self-with-a-self-regulating other Self-resonating-with-another Self-in-the-presence-of-another Self-with-others			Conscious Preconscious Unconscious	Non-conscious
Core	Self-agency Self-coherence Self-continuity			Conscious Preconscious Unconscious	Non-conscious
Emergent				Conscious Preconscious Unconscious	Non-conscious

states" (p. 93), I offer some thoughts that have been (re)stimulated by your chapter.

Non-verbal

We know, of course, the impact of the non-verbal and of non-verbal communication: facial expression, gestures, paralinguistics, body language and posture, personal space (proxemics), eye gaze, touch (haptics), and appearance. Some research, notably Mehrabian's (1981) study, put the impact of wordless communication as high as ninety-three per cent of all communication; this statistic is based on his research that seven per cent of meaning is in the words spoken; thirty-eight per cent of meaning is paralinguistic—that is, the way that the words are said; and fifty-five per cent of meaning is in facial expression. This has huge implications for our work. I was reminded of this the other day when I was presenting a paper I had written, which the participants had read as preparation for the session. One participant commented that she hadn't liked it as much as some of my other writing that she'd read. I was genuinely surprised at this as I thought I had put myself in the article. I acknowledged this and, unselfconsciously, began flicking through the article to see if I had missed something—myself perhaps! We continued with the session and discussed some theory; later, a couple of the participants came back to this earlier exchange, and one in particular commented on how touched she'd been by my genuine acceptance of her criticism and my curiosity. My genuineness had been judged not only by what I'd *said* (which was very little), but more by my gesture, the flicking through of the article, which was seen as a spontaneous sign of openness and enquiry.

Implicit—and tacit—knowing

I agree that implicit knowing is important and, indeed, I included a reference to this in my article on a co-creative perspective on empathy (Tudor, 2011a; present Chapter Six) in which (to preview a passage) I quote Bohart and Tallman (1999), who suggested that: "the therapist's empathic attempts may be particularly useful, as therapist and client together 'co-create' an articulation of implicit or unconscious experience" (p. 403).

Such knowing is based on aspects of perception that enter into conscious awareness through skills such as fine observation skills (in which I think, at best, transactional analysis offers a particularly good foundation), but also by means of speculative skills such as observing patterns and configurations (gestalt); working with dreams; attending to the body; and intuition—interestingly, the subject of Berne's early interest (Berne, 1977a). Importantly, for our co-creative perspective, these are skills that the client may bring to therapy and, in any case, can be encouraged to develop in therapy and, in this way, develop their own "articulation" of their experience.

Our understanding of the distinction between what is explicitly and what is implicitly known has, of course, been informed by neuroscience and neuropsychology and research into different memory systems: the conscious memory system, which involves the hippocampus and related cortical areas, and the implicit, emotional memory system, which involves the amygdala and related structures, which respond more quickly to stimulus (see, for instance, LeDoux, 1998). The point of this is that it means that, as I sometimes put it, we don't have to dig around in the unconscious trying to find repressed, introjected or archaic material; we simply have to work with what's present, and, through that, what becomes explicit.

I am encouraged that this is also being thought about and discussed in disciplines other than psychotherapy; Mattingly (1991), an occupational therapist, has described "clinical reasoning" as "a largely tacit, highly imagistic, and deeply phenomenological mode of thinking ... based on tacit understanding and habitual knowledge gained through experience" (p. 979).

This implicit or tacit knowing is something on which Clark Moustakas (1923–2012), the founder of heuristic research, commented: "Such knowledge is possible through a tacit capacity which allows one to sense the unity or wholeness of something from an understanding of the individual qualities or parts" (Moustakas, 1990, pp. 20–21), a sense and an outcome that, of course, fits with my interest in the organism, organismic psychology, and holism (see Chapter Three), and in phenomenological, and person-centred, research.

This tacit capacity is enhanced by what Moustakas refers to as "indwelling", which, as he described it, refers to:

> the heuristic process of turning inward to seek a deeper, more extended comprehension of the nature or meaning of a quality or theme of human experience ... [which] involves a willingness to

gaze with unwavering attention and concentration into some facet of human experience in order to understand its constituent qualities and its wholeness. (ibid., p. 24)

Preconscious

I notice in your chapter that you refer to the concept of the "preconscious", albeit only briefly, defining it as referring to "experiences, thoughts, or memories that while not in present consciousness are readily accessible through an introspective search and then available for conscious attention" (pp. 94–95). A common example of this would be those "thoughts" that we may say are "on the tip of my tongue". In classical Freudian psychoanalysis, the preconscious is applied to thoughts that are unconscious but that are not repressed and so, therefore, (more) available for recall—but, if those "preconscious" thoughts are unconscious, how do we know how repressed they are until we make them conscious in some way, at which point they are no longer preconscious/unconscious? Does something that was on the tip of my tongue but, in the end, I do not remember become preconscious or more unconscious because I can't recall it? As you gather I am sceptical about the value of the preconscious as a layer of the unconscious. I have to say that I've never been very drawn to or convinced by Freud's (1915e) topographical system of the mind (the conscious, the preconscious, and the unconscious)—or, for that matter, the archaeological view of the psyche implied by the term "depth psychology" (for a critique of which see Tudor & Worrall, 2006). If we take the definition of the preconscious as that which is *capable of becoming conscious*" (Freud, ibid., p. 173, original emphasis; an expression that Freud attributed to Bleuler (1914)) then surely this applies equally to the unconscious?

Non-conscious and unconscious

As you know, I also like and appreciate Daniel Stern's work and think—or, until recently, have thought—that his (2004) distinction between the repressed unconscious and the non-repressed non-conscious a useful one. The concept that we have within our psyche/body unintegrated or archaic fragments (from the Latin *fragmentum*, meaning a remnant, or a piece broken off) that are not necessarily defensive or organised defensively is consistent with a vision of human nature and experience that holds health alongside illness; and the idea that we may or may not integrate such fragments but are able to tolerate those vague feelings of discomfort, and known uncertainty, as well as the unknown, is consistent with a humanistic vision of the essence of things (ontology).

However, whilst Stern's non-conscious is a conceptual distinction rather than a topographical one (see Table 5.1), I have been (re)thinking that, in some ways, such a distinction is buying into psychoanalytic claims about the nature of the unconscious. Just because some people view "the unconscious" as comprising repressed material doesn't mean to say that it does. There are other ways of thinking about the unconscious and I prefer a more straightforward way of viewing it as that which is, well, "un" or not conscious, a conceptual state or potential process that encompasses:

• The lack of consciousness
• An altered state of consciousness in which we have no conscious awareness
• Processes in the mind/body that occur automatically (thought processes, memory, affect, motivation) but that are not available to introspection
• Phenomena such as repressed feelings, automatic skills, subliminal perceptions, habits, automatic reactions, dreams, forgotten memories, fleeting perceptions
• Hidden beliefs, fears and attitudes.

I don't think that you, I or anyone else need the concept or conceptual framework of the non-conscious in order, as you put it: "to locate the Child–Parent ego states and Adult ego states, each underpinned by 'Representations of Interactions that have been Generalized' (RIGs) (Stern, 1985, p. 97) within implicit memory in the unconscious and non-conscious, respectively" (p. 91). I think it's more straightforward to say that we have unconscious processes that are unknown until we know them.

I am interested that in the second edition of his book, Stern (1998) revised his reference to internal objects as RIGs, preferring the term "ways-of being-with", arguing that this de-emphasises "the process of formation in favour of describing the lived phenomenon in a more experience-near and clinically useful way" (p. xv). As someone who identifies with the person-centred approach to therapy (and life), this echoes with Rogers' (1980a) use of the phrase "a way of being". In practice, I embody a way of being that, I think, offers clients—and supervisees and trainees—ways-of-being-with or, as we put it, "new relational possibilities", the specific newness of which is often unknown until it's known and the fragment mended (as the above example, p. 103).

Recently, I've been reading more about Harry Stack Sullivan (1892–1949), who I think has been enjoying something of a renaissance as one of the fathers or, by now, grandfathers of the "relational turn" in psychotherapy. When referring to the unconscious, Sullivan (1937/1964) wrote about the "unattended". I like this as it promotes the concept of the unconscious as something to which we may—or may not—attend; and it supports the view that "unconscious" is perhaps better thought about as an adjective: a description of an aspect of the whole human organism, rather than a noun—that is, a substantive and reified "thing".

Just as I was finishing this, I was re-reading parts of Berne's (1972/1975b) book *What Do You Say After You Say Hello?* and was interested to come across his view that "The unconscious has become fashionable, and hence grossly overrated" (p. 404). He followed this by stating that "by far the larger percentage of what is called unconscious nowadays is not unconscious, but preconscious" (p. 404), what he referred to as "vaguely conscious"—which, although Berne categorised as preconscious, I would argue, lends more weight or width to the conscious.

Finally (on this), I rather like this quotation from Klein (1960), which links the unconscious and integration. She suggested that the need for integration is derived from "the unconscious feeling that parts of the self are unknown, and there is a sense of impoverishment due to the self being deprived of some of its parts … [and this feeling] increases the urge for integration" (p. 241). This supports my/our view that physis reflects a conscious and unconscious force, urge or motivation for life, health, and growth.

Integration

In your chapter you make some remarks about integrating and integration. I think we'd agree that it's useful to distinguish between *integration* as a noun that names a concept, and *integrating* as an adjective that describes something, such as the Adult ego state—and that as it's an adjective that derives from a verb form (the present participle) it both indicates the present and implies continuity. As some of what you say about integrating relies on the nature of integration, I address this first.

In a number of ways, my ideas about integration have developed since I wrote the neopsyche/integrating chapter. Stimulated by the work I'd done for that chapter and by my subsequent research into Berne's (1961/1975a) model of ego states (see Figure I.1, p. xxv, and my comments at the end of Chapter Three, pp. 85–88 above), I became more interested in the background to Berne's thinking about ego states, especially in the context of the development of ego psychology (Federn, 1928, 1932; Weiss, 1950). It became clear that the differences regarding child and human development, expressed in differing views in transactional analysis about ego state development (for a summary of which, see Tudor, 2010b), are based on differences regarding the nature of integration.

In the first set of models, "the three ego state model" ("set 1" in my analysis), integration takes place as human beings develop and distinguish between natural and adapted states, *in all three ego states*, through a process of decontamination, and as they move through various identified stages of development; for example, C_1, A_1, A_2, P_1, P_2, and recycling (Levin, 1974) or C_1 and A_1, then P_1 and A_2 then P_2 (Klein, 1980) are epigenetic sequences reminiscent of Erikson's (1968) "eight ages of man". Erikson's influence on Berne, who was in analysis with Erikson between 1947 and 1949, is clear and well documented and discussed by Cheney (1971), Jorgenson and Jorgenson (1984), Stewart (1992), and Barnes (2007). The proposition that development takes place through the resolution of a series of psychosocial crises, in effect means that such models are based on a conflict model of development and integration (see Clarkson & Gilbert, 1991).

The second view of integration, "the Integrated/integrating Adult model" (set 2 in my analysis) also derives from Berne (1961/1975a), who, as I have noted above (p. 43), suggested that: "it appears that in many cases certain child-like qualities become integrated into the Adult ego state *in a manner different from the contamination process*" (p. 194; my emphasis)—and went on to acknowledge that: "The mechanism of this 'integration' remains to be elucidated" (ibid., p. 194). In my original chapter on the neopsyche, I commented on the significance of this passage as it hints at an integrative mechanism or process whereby qualities, attitudes, feelings, behaviours and thoughts are integrated by the (integrating) Adult from the environment in an uncontaminated and unproblematic way and not via archaic Child or introjected Parent states. In his work on *Ego Psychology and the Problem of Adaptation*, Hartmann (1939/1958) argued that:

> Not all adaptation to the environment, or every learning and mat-
> uration process, is a conflict. I refer to the development *outside of
> conflict* of perception, intention, object comprehension, thinking,
> language, recall-phenomena, productivity, to the well-known
> phases of motor development, grasping, crawling, walking, and
> to the maturation and learning processes implicit in all these and
> many others. (p. 8)

For Hartmann, psychoanalytic ego psychology had, up to 1939, been predominantly a conflict psychology, with the conflict-free aspects of what he refers to (ibid., p. 13) as "reality-adapted development" periph-eral or underdeveloped, a phrase that predates Berne's (1961/1975a) definition of the Adult as "characterized by an autonomous set of feelings, attitudes, and behavior patterns which are *adapted to the current reality*" (p. 76; my emphasis) by some twenty years. Although, in his work, Berne did not refer to Hartmann directly, he did cite Federn (1928, 1932), with whom he was in analysis between 1940/1941 and 1943, and he also cited Weiss (1952), and Glover (1955).[1] In this sense, the inte-grating Adult model of ego states and, more broadly, our co-creative approach, with its acknowledgement of health, growth, and adaptation, may be viewed as a development from Hartmann's views of adaptation, and, thus, represent a growth model of development and integration. I think this fits well with your perspective on health (which I like so much that I quote it again!) that it: "provides opportunities for further growth and development" (p. 78). Moreover, this perspective on the nature of integration, which sets alongside the working through of past archaic or introjected experiences the view that we integrate directly from the environment, is entirely in keeping with our view of the origin of physis (see Tudor, 2003).

I also want to acknowledge the work in transactional analysis of James and Jongeward (1971) who, in a final, short chapter in their book *Born to Win*, wrote something about the Integrated Adult; they also used the term "Integrated Adult ego states" (p. 298), plural. They quoted Berne (1961/1975a) on the (different) manner of integration—that is, including integration from the environment; wrote about the

Integrated Adult before Erskine (1988) (who does not reference them in this article), and about the process of integration, which has informed my work (Tudor, 2003). They also made links between the Integrated Adult and the concepts of "the fully developed person" (Fromm, 1968), and "the self-actualizing person" (Maslow, 1954). They were then (in 1971) clearly still working on how they squared this integrated state or states with the "data-processing machine" view of the Adult they also held, concluding that: "We believe that unless integrated, the Adult functions only as a data-processing machine … [and] think it is the Integrated Adult that contains Adult feelings and ethics as well as technical skills and ability" (p. 299). Note also their use of the lowercase "i" in "integrated".

All of this is supported by research in developmental psychology (see, for example, Stern, 1985, 2004), and in neuroscience (see, for example, Cozolino, 2002), and by the relational, narrative and even social turns in psychotherapy across theoretical orientations. Cozolino (2002) discussed the importance of helping the client to shift her or his experience of anxiety from an unconscious trigger, which causes avoidance, to a conscious cue for curiosity and exploration. A psychotherapy that offers such exploration may be viewed as offering integration of cortical linguistic processing along with conditioned sub-cortical arousal in the service of inhibiting, regulating and modifying erstwhile maladaptive reactions. Psychotherapy, and other healing relationships, enable the client to regain a sense of psychological control and biological homeostasis, both of which help to resolve her or his reactions to trauma. Writing about what clients gain from psychotherapy, Cozolino (2002) argued that: "Narratives co-constructed with therapists provide a new template for thoughts, behaviors, and ongoing integration" (p. 28).

I hope that this part of my response clarifies my earlier words on integration, in terms of the capacity to reflect upon and make sense of our worlds, and extends my—and, perhaps, our—thinking about integration, as a conscious, non-conscious and unconscious process (see Klein, 1960).

Integrating

Viewing integration as a process rather than, for instance, a mechanism, brings me to the word and concept of "integrating". Despite your preference for the language of process over state, you appear to have three issues with the term integrating—or, more accurately, my use of the term:

1. That it "leans (too) heavily towards explicit consciousness" (p. 93); and
2. That it implies "a level of developmental achievement way beyond that of a foetus or neonate" (p. 93); and also
3. That you are less inclined to use the term as a prefix for the Adult as you want to acknowledge those "unintegrated fragments [that] are not defensively organised" (p. 94).

In response to the first two criticisms, I hope that what I have written in the previous section on integration addresses your critiques and concerns. Just in case it hasn't, I thought I might quote Damasio (1994/1996), who links integration with regulation:

> The human brain and the rest of the body constitute an indissociable organism, integrated by means of mutually interactive biochemical and neural regulatory circuits … (2) The organism interacts with the environment as an ensemble: the interaction is neither of the body alone nor of the brain alone; [and] (3) The physiological operations we call mind are derived from the structural and functional ensemble. (pp. xiii–xiv)

You'll appreciate that I particularly like this quotation as it brings together the organism with integration and the necessity of regulation—as Schore (1994) put it: "the core of the self lies in the patterns of affect regulation that integrate a sense of self … thereby allowing for a continuity of inner experience" (p. 33)—and the "integration" or inseparability of the body–brain.

As far as your third critique is concerned, I agree about the importance of accounting for different experiences and that we may also need to "dis-integrate". Although I don't think of "integrating" in terms of certainty, I take your point and, as you may know, have been somewhat critical of certainty, specifically in transactional analysis (see Tudor, 2007b), viewing it as one of four ways in which dogma and dogmatism are maintained (the other three being purity, conformity, and priesthood). I also like your acknowledgement of integrating, disintegrating, and non-integrating. I think of this as supporting entropy alongside syntropy (see Rogers, 1980a). As you and others have acknowledged, my original proposal to use "integrating" rather than "Integrated" for the Adult ego state was, has been, and, I think, probably still is useful; at the same time, in the spirit of the continual process of reflection, critique, deconstruction, and reconstruction, I am actually more inclined to use the term "neopsyche" rather than "integrating Adult" (see Figure 3.1, p. 87) as this makes it clearer that this "state" is different from Parent and Child ego states, and that it is more of, as you put it, an "open space" in which we need also "to dis-integrate our familiar ways of meaning-making", which, in turn, creates more and new open space—that is, a *neo*psyche. In my mind, this supports our view of flow, and connects to Rogers' (1958/1967a) concept of fluidity, and to his view of the integrative (integrating) nature of psychotherapy, which he (Rogers, 1942) defined thus:

> It aims directly towards the greatest independence and integration of the individual … The aim is not to solve one particular problem, but to assist the individual to grow, so that he can cope with the present problem and later problems in a better-integrated [integrating] fashion. (p. 28)

Rejoinder from Graeme

Thank you Keith for your responses and for expanding upon your latest thinking on the themes I have raised. I will respond here to each theme in turn.

The idea of conceptually differentiating unconscious and nonconscious processes was introduced to me by Daniel Stern (2004) a year after your publication on the neopsyche. His work helped me see a dimension of our original co-creative paper, which, in hindsight, was clearly implied through our emphasis on experience rather than insight, but not well or explicitly articulated. I continued to ponder Stern's distinction and first presented the dynamic ego state model (Figure 4.1) in my keynote speech at the 2008 Australasian Transactional Analysis Conference as a development of our co-creative perspective (Summers, 2008).

However it was not until 2010 that I began to formulate some critique of your paper through my participation in an online colloquium discussion (Summers, 2010). I was immersed in a stimulating trialogue with Ray Little and Jo Stuthridge on the theme of ego states that prompted me into re-reading our work. It was then that I noticed the increasing emphasis on conscious reflection in your chapter on the neopsyche. This emphasis is further reinforced in your empathy article, which we discuss later. So, like you, I am delighted to be taking time to gather our thoughts and engage in discussion throughout this book.

Dynamics

The Freudian echo is important to me because there are psychoanalytic influences within our work. We make specific uses of co-transference and intersubjectivity, and implied use of Fairbairn's object relations through adopting and adapting Erskine's ego state model. Transactional analysis literature has been and continues to be influenced by psychoanalytic ideas, which I personally appreciate even though, at heart, I locate myself within the humanistic tradition.

I clearly intend the term "dynamic" to represent two different meanings within my ego state model.

Since we consider Parent and Child as defensive patterns, the concept of "dynamic repression" makes sense here. Note that I incorporate Fairbairn's perspective to suggest that experiences are repressed from relationship rather than, as Freud suggested, consciousness. Parent and Child denote defensive patterns, which we substitute for Adult vitality in response to experiences that we cannot (or implicitly feel we cannot) tolerate in a given context. We hold back and protect ourselves from a perceived hostile or indifferent environment. The "holding back" is, therefore, a dynamic process.

When considering Adult process, dynamic has a different meaning much more in line with your suggestions. I think of Adult in terms of "dynamic expression" or "dynamic being" to represent the process of being more fully alive and natural within our varied life space.

So, in the context of my paper, I like the term "dynamic" because I think it does reflect my intentions and some of my influences. In practice, however, I usually present co-creative models without using any prefixes for ego states and simply refer to them as Parent, Adult, and Child. I do tell people who have previously encountered transactional analysis that this may be different from their current understanding and that I am open to discuss this in more depth if needed.

Different consciousness

Your table, "Senses of self and domains of relatedness and conscious-ness" (Table 5.1, p. 102), makes sense and accounts for both health and disturbance across different domains of self-development. The valid-ity of the "conscious" domain for the early infant also hinges on your definition of "conscious", since reflective consciousness will not have developed at that age although this will become available as the infant develops.

I appreciate your incorporation of the significance of non-conscious processes within your formulation of integrating Adult and self-development in general.

Implicit knowing

I think your suggestion that "we don't have to dig around in the uncon-scious, trying to find repressed, introjected or archaic material" (p. 104) is an objection to method rather than to theory. The point about implicit knowledge is that it may not become explicit or, for that matter, even conscious, yet it remains influential. With the relatively recent advent of neuroimaging techniques, Freud's basic claim that much of our behav-iour is influenced by processes outside of conscious awareness has been vindicated, even though more specific psychoanalytic propositions and methods may remain questionable (Mlodinow, 2013). The implication here is that there can be a significant gap between what we think we do and what we actually do that has a positive or negative impact on oth-ers. This is why 360 degree feedback sessions, carefully debriefed, are so helpful to organisational leaders.

Your proposition that "we simply have to work with what's present, and, through that, what becomes explicit" (p. 104) is a way of describing of phenomenological method. However, I think that implicit influences, which may not become explicit yet remain influential, are worthy of our speculative attention. This is why reflective practice is important, medi-ated by supervision, reading, training, and periods of contemplation. Even though we are condemned to not knowing (for certain) what may be happening in any given interaction, it is still important to ask ques-tions that help us consider how we may be influenced by or influencing of others for better or worse, in and out of awareness.

For example, in a group coaching session a client interrupts my exchange with another group member to ask "what's the point of trying to improve yourself?" Whilst I and others respond to him in various ways, I am asking myself: "What does this mean for him, me, the group and our work together?", "What is being demanded of me?", and "What response might be useful for him, me, the group and our work?" As the heat of the interaction passes I am still wondering about its significance. When I later met this person for an individual session he, once again, gave the impression that the coaching was somewhat unnecessary and that he was OK as he was. I reflected and respected his stance and stayed listening. Then, unprompted, he went on to discuss a rupture with his boss that was painful and still unresolved. He told me what was bothering him and invited me to talk about it with him. So was this issue "hidden" behind the provocative question in the group? I had done a little digging in response to his initial question (not into his personal history, though I did ask if there was anything behind his question) and got pushed back. I think, however, that his provocation demanded that I pay attention and that something significant (even though I didn't know what) might emerge if the conditions were right. He had stimulated in me a heightened state of alertness, receptivity, and respect for his boundaries. I think that much of this was co-navigated between us at an implicit level. This is, of course, a plausible interpretation of events informed only by my theoretical proclivities.

Preconscious

Your scepticism of this concept comes through very clearly. I find it a useful way to account for everyday experiences; for example, how a familiar song on the radio might stimulate a range of associated memories and feelings. Context-dependent learning operates in a similar associative way—that is, we are more likely to remember something we have learned previously when the conditions in which the original learning took place are re-created. This is perhaps why hierarchy in organisations often primes individuals at a psychological level to create Parent–Child dynamics. Under stress, people may be more susceptible to relate to their boss as Child to Parent and their direct reports (i.e., staff) as Parent to Child. I therefore prefer to use the iconic three stacked circles to represent ego states even though this could theoretically be reduced to two ego states as you suggest above. Coached clients often find the visual metaphor of the Parent–Child transaction helpful for illuminating and managing organisational politics and power plays.

The developmental challenge here is to create ways of crossing these transactions, from Adult, both up and down the hierarchy. In an attempt to balance idealism with realism I often suggest that clients think in terms of increasing their percentage of Adult–Adult transactions within their area of influence.

Unconscious and non-conscious

You don't seem keen on these ideas either, at least within the psycho-analytic frame. I share your caution but more in relation to how these ideas can be misused rather than the ideas themselves. The notion of the unconscious is vulnerable to being employed as a self-sealing doctrine (Riebel, 1996) by people who claim to know the unconscious motivations of others and who then claim that any resistance to their interpretation is evidence of being right. In skilful hands, however, these ideas can be used speculatively and respectfully to open up new lines of enquiry and perceptual vantage points. This was my personal experience of Jungian psychotherapy. I brought a range of experiences, dreams, and desires, which we explored from many different angles without fixing on any one in particular as being "true". What stays with me is a rich sense of freedom to accept and explore in partnership with an imaginative and curious other.

However, even if we don't specifically attempt to name or work with implicit processes they happen anyway and form the substrate of our dis-ease or well-being with others, conceptualised and differentiated here as unconscious and non-conscious processes, respectfully. I think this distinction provides a useful extension to our theoretical frame by counterbalancing your emphasis on reflective consciousness with an appreciation of adaptive non-conscious processes within Adult being and relating.

Integration and integrating

I hope it is clear from my description above that I utilise a one ego state model *of health* within a three ego state model *of personality*, which is consistent with our original formulation and our respective elaborations. The three ego state model of personality represents the contextual field of possibilities and probabilities from which we selec-tively draw to perpetuate regressive or progressive ways of being influenced by our previous experience, present environment, and personal resourcefulness/resilience. The idealised end of therapy that is the "one ego state model" is just that—"idealised". If we do not at least feel the edges of our defensive potential then we are probably coasting in our comfort zones, which paradoxically is a defensive orientation. I am, of course, in danger of articulating my own self-sealing doctrine here. The point I wish to make, however, is that even though I consider Parent and Child to be defensive they remain part of who we are as fallible, imperfect human beings. We may be able to reduce the frequency or intensity of our defensive responses and create more fulfilling alternatives but we will not eradicate them and nor should we expect to do so. People often express the apparently contradictory desires to be more deeply self-accepting on the one hand and to change, improve or develop on the other. I think this ongoing contradiction needs to be acknowledged and accommodated rather than resolved.

You refer to two modes for the integration of experience. The first is the unproblematic or, at least, the non-traumatic assimilation of experiences gained through normal experiences and developmental challenges. The second is "helping the client to shift her or his experience of anxiety from an unconscious trigger, which causes avoidance, to a conscious cue for curiosity and exploration" (p. 110). This echoes our original distinction between learning and healing, respectively, which still resonates as coherent.

You emphasise reflective consciousness in the healing process by helping the client a) move from an unconscious trigger to a conscious cue and b) co-construct new narratives with the therapist. This helps me understand your thinking and practice. I personally still believe it is the direct experience of being with the other that has primary significance. This is the emergent, implicit "lived story", which is experientially co-created in the dyad in contrast to the new "told story" co-created through conscious narrative. Of course, both processes can happen simultaneously and both are important. My aim here is to reinstate the significance of the implicit within our co-creative framework.

Emphasising reflective consciousness in the process of normal maturational development I find more problematic, especially in relation to early infancy. This just does not make sense to me. If you were to drop this emphasis in favour of a broader organismic definition of integrating, I would readily concur with you.

I enjoyed your reflections on integrating, dis-integrating, and non-integrating, together with your rationale and preference for the term "neopsyche". Like you, I think language matters, and consider the nuances of intentional, accidental and layered meanings worth considering, changing or refining as we continue exploring and learning.

Note

1. In terms of the development of ideas about the ego and respective influences, Federn (1928, 1932) did refer to Hartmann (1939/1958), and (Federn, 1929/1952b) to Glover's work but with only a passing reference. Hartmann (1939/1958) referred to Federn's work, and cited Weiss (1937). Weiss (1950) also referred to Glover's work but, similarly, with only a passing reference, and not to Hartmann's, although he did refer to Hartmann in his introduction to Federn's papers (Weiss, 1952).

CHAPTER SIX

Empathy: a co-creative perspective*

Keith Tudor

This chapter presents a co-creative transactional analysis of empathy as the principal method of co-creative transactional analysis. As such, it represents a further development of the author's work with Graeme Summers on co-creative transactional analysis (Summers & Tudor, 2000, 2005b) and on the neopsyche or integrating Adult (Tudor, 2003). The chapter locates co-creative transactional analysis as a relational transactional analysis and considers its similarities and differences with the integrative approach to transactional analysis of Erskine and others (Erskine, 1988, 1991; Erskine & Moursund, 1988; Erskine & Trautmann, 1996; Moursund & Erskine, 2004), and the relational transactional analysis of Hargaden and Sills (2002).

The original article outlining a co-creative transactional analysis (Summers & Tudor, 2000) offered a constructivist re-reading of transactional analysis and its four theoretical foundations: transactions (viewed as ways of co-creating reality), ego states (as co-creative

---

*Originally published in the *Transactional Analysis Journal*, 41(4), October 2011, pp. 322–335, © ITAA. Reprinted with permission.

personality), scripts (as co-creative identity), and games (as co-creative confirmations). Two major implications emerged from this original work:

1. The central and expansive role of the Adult ego state; and
2. The significance of present-centred transacting or relating.

As a result of reflecting further on what appeared to me as an underdeveloped view of the Adult ego state in transactional analysis, I went on to research the transactional analysis literature and to develop ideas about the integrating, neopsychic Adult ego state. This was published as a chapter (Tudor, 2003) in the book *Ego States* (Sills & Hargaden, 2003a). In a number of ways this chapter laid the theoretical foundations for a more expansive view of neopsychic functioning as represented by the (lowercase) *integrating Adult*. [James and Jongeward (1971) had written briefly about Integrated Adult ego states, and] Trautmann and Erskine (1999) had referred to an "'integrating' Adult [that is] fully in contact both internally and externally" (p. 16), though neither set of authors developed the concept further.

Almost immediately following the publication of this chapter, I had a number of conversations with colleagues who encouraged me to develop, demonstrate and describe the method of facilitating the client to expand her or his Adult as the goal of therapy (see Gobes in Novey, Porter-Steele, Gobes, & Massey, 1993), which I have now done in workshops in a number of countries.[1] This chapter outlines this co-creative method and, thereby, forms the third [now fourth, with Summers, 2011] in the series of papers on co-creative transactional analysis. In their book *Sociological Paradigms and Organisational Analysis*, Burrell and Morgan (1979) identified four sets of assumptions that elaborate the nature of social science: ontological assumptions—that is, assumptions about the essence of things; epistemological assumptions, or those about the nature of knowledge; assumptions about human nature; and assumptions about methodology (see Table 6.1, reading from the bottom up). Burrell and Morgan viewed these as lying on a continuum, the ends of which represent objectivist and subjectivist views of these four assumptions. This continuum, together with another related to assumptions about society, which represent views from social regulation to radical change, form axes that define four paradigms, an analysis I (Tudor, 1996a) have presented with regard to transactional analysis theory. I suggest that these three papers on co-creative transactional analysis represent an exploration of the four assumptions about the nature of social science (see Table 6.1), and, therefore, offer a significant development of transactional analysis from a co-creative relational perspective. This perspective offers a clear view about ontology, understood primarily in terms of the neopsyche or integrating Adult ego state (Tudor, 2003); human nature, based on the human organism and the fact that it tends to actualise (see Tudor, 2003; also Tudor & Worrall, 2006); the epistemological foundations of transactional analysis, analysed in terms of transactions, ego states, scripts, and games (Summers & Tudor, 2000); and methodology and method in terms of both principles and the practice of empathy and empathic transactions or, more accurately, empathic transactional relating. (As these assumptions build on the previous one, they are described and are to be read from the bottom up, indicated by the vertical arrow in Table 6.1.)

In the first article on co-creative transactional analysis, Graeme Summers and I (2000) acknowledged that two theoretical strands from field theory and social constructivism had influenced the emphasis in co-creative transactional analysis on interrelationship and the construction and narrative view of reality—or, rather, realities—respectively. By way of providing more background and context to co-creative method, in the first part of this current chapter I expand and elaborate these

Table 6.1. Assumptions about the nature of social science applied to the development of co-creative transactional analysis.

Empathy (Tudor, 2011d) and co-creative empathic transactional relating (present chapter; [see also discussions in this present work])
Method

Phenomenological (hermeneutic) and heuristic
Methodology

Implicit in "Cocreative transactional analysis" (Summers & Tudor, 2000) and explicit in "Understanding empathy" (Tudor, 2011d) [and this present work]
Epistemology

Based on the nature of the organism (Tudor, 2003)
Human nature

Understood in terms of the neopsyche or integrating Adult ego state (Tudor, 2003)
Ontology

theoretical influences. Again, in the original article, we identified three principles that guide a co-creative approach to transactional analysis:

1. The principle of "we"ness;
2. The principle of shared responsibility; and
3. The principle of present-centred development.

In the [then] ten years since the publication of the original article, I have found these principles to be useful in guiding my practice, and in the second part of this chapter I elaborate a method of practice that embodies them. Following this, in the third and final part of the chapter, I consider the similarities and differences between the co-creative approach and the work of Erskine and others (Erskine, 1988, 1991; Erskine & Moursund, 1988; Erskine & Trautmann, 1996; Moursund & Erskine, 2004) and locate co-creative transactional analysis as a form of, and an influence on, the development of relational transactional analysis, one that has both similarities and differences with the work of Hargaden and Sills (2002).

Theoretical influences

In developing co-creative transactional analysis, four strands of thinking have influenced my practice, philosophy, methodology, and method:

1. Rogers' client-centred perspective and, specifically, his sixth necessary and sufficient condition (Rogers, 1958/1967a);
2. Social, political, and cultural contexts of people's lives and of the field of psychotherapy;
3. Constructivism and, in particular, social constructivism; and
4. An interest in time, the present moment (Mead, 1932/1980; Stern, 2004), and working in, and with, the present as a way of working with the past (see Embleton Tudor & Tudor, 2009).

A client-centred perspective

In his seminal statements about therapeutic change and personality change, Rogers (1957, 1959) hypothesised six necessary and sufficient conditions involving both the therapist and the client. The sixth condition states that the therapist's unconditional positive regard and empathic understanding needs to be communicated to the client (Rogers, 1957) or, as he put it in a paper published two years later, perceived/experienced by the client (Rogers, 1959). In another paper summarising the therapeutic conditions, Rogers (1958/1967a) referred to being fully received as the "assumed" condition (p. 130; see also Tudor, 2011b). This is a phenomenological and constructivist perspective: acceptance and empathy only exist as such in the eye—or the experience and perception—of the beholder—that is, the client. I think of this condition as a touchstone for working with clients and for checking their experience and the meaning they are making of their experience, including their experience of me, my empathy and understanding, my misunderstanding or misattunement, and how we are relating. Thus, in terms of practice, I draw on ideas about empathic attunement and resonance, affective responsiveness, and visceral and relational empathy. In practice this means that I pay close attention to the client's response to me and what I say and do, especially when I observe or think that she or he is out of contact or has broken the contact between us. I focus on when I miss or do not "get" the client, when the client misunderstands what I am saying, and any interruptions and occasions when the client or I talk over each other, in which case I invariably pause and wait for the client to continue, finish—or, indeed, start—what she or he is saying.

Context counts

The second strand of thinking that influences my practice derives from a long interest and, at times, active involvement in politics, the social sphere, culture, and social psychology (see Tudor, 1997; Tudor & Hargaden, 2002); radical psychiatry (see Sanders & Tudor, 2001); and cultural perspectives on therapy (see Singh & Tudor, 1997). Many thinkers, from Aristotle onward, have considered people as social— and political—animals/beings. From this, it follows that clients' social context—how they are or are not in the world, and how alienated they are from themselves, others, and the world—is a matter that is relevant for psychotherapy and psychotherapists. This is supported by research into the significance of client factors on therapeutic outcome. This represents a sociocentric, as distinct from an egocentric, psychology and has led me to an interest in "relational empathy" (O'Hara, 1997). From this perspective I am interested in taking Kohut's methodology of introspection and empathy as the basis of interspection: a process of reflecting on what is in between and beyond therapist and client.

The phrase, "I count, you count, context counts" has been attributed to the family systems therapist Virginia Satir and has also been said to be the inspiration for Berne's (1972/1975b) three-handed life position: "I'm OK, You're OK, They're OK." In practice, this means that, as a therapist, I am interested in the client's context and what she or he brings or does not bring of that context to therapy, whether therapy is a part of her or his life or apart and separate from that life.

This is crucial when working with children and young people, in which case one corner of the "three-cornered contract" (English, 1975) or one party to the contract sits outside the therapy room and needs to support and not undermine the therapy (see Tudor, 2006, 2007c). While the importance of holding the client's context in mind may be obvious to some, even most, I think it is worth stating that this contextual attitude is important when working with anyone in relationship because that relationship is part of the client's phenomenological and social "field." I am interested in which aspects of the background field the client brings into the foreground and what she or he and I together make of them. For example, one group, which had met regularly in the same room for years, was disrupted by the advent of building works, which were due to continue for some time. Some of the group wanted to do something about the noise; for example, to negotiate with the builders to take a break for an hour during the meeting time of the group, or to relocate the group for the duration of the building works. Other members were drawn to understanding or exploring the meaning of the noise for them as individuals and as a group. Interestingly, the group remained where it was, which led me to reflect on whether psychotherapy, and perhaps certain approaches to therapy, privilege reflection over action.

Constructivism and narrative

Hoffman (1993) suggested that "constructivism holds that the structure of our nervous systems dictates that we can never know what is 'really' out there" (p. 34). All we can ever know about anything is our construction or construing of people, events, phenomena, and "reality," so, in this sense, the truth is not "out there" but "in here" and/or "here between us." As Schafer (1983) put it, "For the analyst the analysand is not someone who is somehow objectively knowable outside this model" (p. 39). Moreover, constructivist empathy (also sometimes referred to as empathic constructivism) refers to the perspective that when we empathise with another, we are, in effect, constructing a concept or model of that person. This narrative view of reality is familiar to transactional analysts in the form of script theory (see Allen & Allen, 1997). This view of the world may be traced back, philosophically, to the tradition of European rationalism, which held that the mind is active, not passive, and that it constructs reality rather than being informed by it. Social constructivism, which is closely aligned with the postmodern tradition, understands that everybody has equally valid perspectives and that, as Gergen (1991) put it, there is no "transcendent criteria of the correct" (p. 111). That "truth" is subjective and knowledge is local supports the importance of Rogers' sixth condition: that the client experiences/ perceives the therapist's positive regard and empathy. No matter how accepting or empathic a therapist is or thinks she or he is, it is the client's experience and perception of these qualities—or their absence—that is most important, at least from a classical client-centred perspective.

That there is no "truth" or that truth is constructed or, more accurately, co-constructed, means that both client and therapist are involved in reflecting on their impact and influence on each other, a process that Mearns and Schmid (2006) referred to as co-reflectiveness; moreover, both client and therapist are also involved in how each and both construe this impact and influence. From a constructivist perspective, as meaning evolves through dialogue, there is an emphasis in constructivist therapy on the dialogic relationship. As discourse creates systems, ego states and transactions are elicited from meaning, rather than the other way around (see Summers & Tudor, 2000), and since therapy is the co-creation of new narratives that name new possibilities, script becomes a changing story. For example, as a practitioner in Aotearoa New Zealand, when I greet a client or student by saying "Kia ora" I am conveying something of my relationships and politics and, specifically, referencing a bicultural relationship between Māori as tangata whenua (people of the land) and non-Māori New Zealanders or more recent immigrants. It represents a construction and a narrative—and a complex one at that. Of course, the terms "Aotearoa New Zealand," "New Zealand," "Aotearoa," "New Zealand/Aotearoa" and others all represent different constructions of, and narratives about, the same geographical land mass.

The present moment

The fourth strand of influence on co-creative methodology comes from an interest in the nature of time (see Tudor, 2002) and, specifically, in working in and with the present. As a result of this I increasingly view therapy as present-centred as much as person-centred. As human beings we grow, develop and age over time, and, when we talk about our development and our personal history, we tend to think of it as time passed and in the past. This is confirmed by child development theory and especially stage theories such as Erikson's (1950/1965, 1968) eight ages of man (sic), which propose or imply a fixed sense of developmental stages and of the past. At the same time, people across cultures and theoretical orientations acknowledge the significance of the past, the "there and then," on who and how we are in the present (i.e., the here and now). In general, we may consider that each biological, neurological, developmental and historical occurrence impresses itself on the personality and leaves some trace. In this sense, the whole personality is present, although influenced by the past. This led Angyal (1941, 1965/1973) to view personality not as a constellation of simultaneous factors but, at any given moment, as "a temporarily extended whole or as a 'time Gestalt'" (Angyal, 1941, p. 347). This prefigures Stern's (1985, 1998) layered view and model of development as ongoing over time. For Stern (1998), this development "assumes a progressive accumulation of senses of the self, socioaffective competencies, and ways-of-being-with-others … [that] *remain with us throughout the life span*" (p. xi, emphasis added). Even when a client is severely dissociated, or dissociating, she or he will have sufficient Adult available with which to work. She or he may not be whole, but she or he is present (see Embleton Tudor & Tudor, 2009). From this perspective, there is no need for the therapist to dig around in the client's problematic past—which, in integrative and co-creative transactional analysis terms, refers to the archaic Child and introjected Parent ego states—because the past emerges in the present. As Murakami (2006) put it:

> She waited for the train to pass. Then she said, "I sometimes think that people's hearts are like deep wells. Nobody knows what's at the bottom. All you can do is guess from what comes floating to the surface every once in a while." (p. 50)

As I work with clients, from the first moment we meet, greet, and seat [– or greet, seat, and meet, a reordering that is influenced by being more aware of different cultural protocols about such contact and engagement –] through the ways we continue to meet in the ways we relate to each other, I endeavor to pay attention to the surface and the detail of that surface as well as what floats to the surface. Often this is in simple ways: noticing what happens in the first moments of that contact—and noticing that I originally typed "fist" instead of "first"!—as well as what happens with regard to the first contact on the phone, the first thing someone says as she or he comes into the room, and so on. Berne (1966) devoted a whole chapter to the first three minutes of a group and the therapist's preparation for her or his work, including the importance of fine observing and listening with all five senses, a prerequisite for working with present moments.

Co-creative methodology and method

Having outlined some of the development and theoretical influences on co-creative transactional analysis, in this second part of the chapter I clarify what I consider to be the methodology (i.e., the philosophy and process of practice, which is certainly phenomenological and arguably hermeneutic) and the method (i.e., transacting empathically). Here, I summarise the methodology and method of co-creative relational transactional analysis: the first three statements describe the methodology and the following four describe the method.

Methodology

The therapist works in partnership with the client

As an approach, this reflects Berne's (1961/1975a) view of the importance of the "togetherness" (p. 146) of the therapist and client and of the therapist "working with" the client (p. 146). Berne, however, also extolled "dignified 'apartness'" (p. 146), which, as far as the therapist's role is concerned, represents more of a one-person or a one-and-a-half-person psychology (Stark, 1999) than a two-person or a two-person plus psychology (see Tudor, 2011d). While Stark has made the point that all modes of psychology may be relevant with each client at different points in treatment—and they are certainly relevant with different clients—she has also acknowledged the challenge for the contemporary therapist "to hold in mind, simultaneously, the three different perspectives without pulling or premature closure" (p. 148), a point that represents a pluralistic, if not an integrative, perspective.

At the same time, just as "dignified apartness," "working with," and "togetherness" represent different attitudes and modes, I think that the various modes carry different implications for the therapist in terms of her or his attitude to the formulation of interpretations (one-person psychology), the provision of corrective experiences (one-and-a-half-person psychology), active engagement in a reciprocal and mutual relationship (two-person psychology), as well as the acknowledgment of the place of the external world in therapy (two-person-plus psychology). Although Stark invites therapists to adopt a both/and or, in this case, an "all modes" approach, I think this can be confusing because there is a significant difference in the therapist's role, attitude and method between the modes of a one-and-a-half person psychology and a two-person psychology, which may compromise the repertoire or at least make the transition between these modes more difficult for both therapist and client. Working in partnership, and even viewing the client as a partner in the therapeutic action, reflects a particular paradigm and politics of therapy as well as a phenomenological and heuristic methodology.

The therapist works with what is present and what is past in the present

This reflects one of the influences on co-creative transactional analysis (i.e., present-centred development) and represents a philosophical perspective about the phenomenology of the present in which the past (and future) only exist in the present [see Embleton Tudor & Tudor, 2009]. In practice, this includes paying as much attention as possible to the present moment (Stern, 2004) as a lived story, and a "temporal contour along which the experience forms during its unfolding" (p. 219). The present moment comprises: (1) the "now moment," an emerging, interpersonal process, which is unpredictable and uncertain, which illustrates both the therapist–client dyad as well as the client's original family parent–child dyad; and (2) the moment of meeting or encounter, which alters the emerging relationship and leads to moments of movement (see Rogers, 1942; O'Hara, 1999; and the next statement).

The therapist works with the client's present-centred neopsychic functioning/integrating adult

The therapist transacts and interacts with the client in ways which co-create a climate and relationship of acceptance, empathy, and reflexivity. This in itself is often a helpful learning, and even transformative, experience/process. The emphasis is on working with the neopsyche because, from this perspective, it is the client who "works with" her or his archaeopsyche (archaic Child ego states) and exteropsyche (intro-jected Parent ego states) (see Figure 6.1). Again, this represents a meth-odology based on phenomenology as well as heurism. In her work developing Rogers' concept of moments of movement, O'Hara (1999) described a client who had a transformative experience in four sessions, and commented that:

> it was the quality of the change that marks it as significant. It would miss her achievement altogether to think of what occurred in terms of "numbers of sessions", "symptom reduction", [or] "problem-solving." … This change permeated her whole existence. She had not only changed what she thought about the situation she was facing, she had changed how she was thinking. She had made an epistemological leap. (p. 73)

This leap is what we may term "self-Adulting", [or, simply, "Adulting"], as distinct from self-reParenting or self-reChilding.
    This methodology underpins the following method.

Method

The therapist facilitates the client in expanding her or his neopsychic functioning

The therapist does this through a series of Adult–Adult transactions (see Figure 6.1 and notes). The therapist does not intend to offer or develop complementary ulterior transactions between the therapist's integrat-ing Adult and the client's archaic Child. This co-creative empathic transactional relating differs from Clark's (1991) and Hargaden and Sills' (2002) empathic transactions and from Shmukler's (1991) associa-tion of empathy with being parental (Parental) and transferential, by which "the therapist provides a quasi-parental model by being warm and empathic" (p. 132) and because of which, "the therapist's warmth and empathy as he or she meets the patient's expectation of a benign parent figure quickly establishes a positive transference" (p. 131). In Stark's taxonomy, this is a good example of a corrective provision and a one-and-a-half person psychology. Co-creative transactional relating as described in Summers and Tudor (2000) and co-creative empathic (transactional) relating as described here and as represented in

Figure 6.1, represent a different methodology and a shift in attitude and method with regard to empathic transactions. [Here, the emphasis is on what the client does, as distinct from what the therapist provides.]

The client abstracts empathic knowledge from the experience of her or his emotional resonance at both social (conscious) and ulterior (unconscious) levels

The client takes in her or his experience of being received (accepted and understood), as well as of not being received and being misunderstood, and takes out or abstracts this experience. As a process, it is parallel to breathing and, as such, is both simple and powerful. Through this process of abstraction, the client, in effect, integrates this experiential knowledge into responses that are increasingly acceptant and empathic of herself or himself and others, including the therapist. This is the intrapsychic aspect of the integrating and expanding Adult process (see Figure 6.1). This integration is the therapy. Writing about the nature of psychotherapy, Rogers (1942) defined it thus:

> It aims directly towards the greatest independence and integration of the individual … The aim is not to solve one particular problem, but to assist the individual to grow, so that he can cope with the present problem and later problems in a better-integrated fashion. (p. 28)

When this present-centred process is interrupted in whatever way, then the therapist and/or client re-experience some past relational pattern(s)

When an interruption or rupture occurs—and it always does—for example, through a game, then client and therapist have the opportunity, as Summers and I (2000) put it, to "explore the process through which Child or Parent ego states are co-created within the co-transference of the therapeutic relationship/relating" (p. 20). Game theory gives us a good framework for understanding and analysing ways and patterns of ways in which we play out or confirm, according to Berne (1964/1968a), "positive or negative feelings and beliefs about self or others" (p. 44). This approach develops Atwood and Stolorow's (1984) view of transference as a creation rather than a distortion. The process and experience of reflection on both the rupture and the repair of this relationship offers new "relational possibilities" (Summers & Tudor, 2000, p. 20). This is the extrapsychic or transactional aspect of the integrating and expanding Adult process.

Both intrapsychic and extrapsychic aspects of therapeutic relating are based on, and reflect, not only explicit interruptions or ruptures, but also implicit knowledge or "scenic understanding" (Lorenzer, 1970), which is also co-created. As Bohart and Tallman (1999) put it: "the therapist's empathic attempts may be particularly useful, as therapist and client together 'co-create' an articulation of implicit or unconscious experience" (p. 403).

When the client expands her or his Adult, she or he in effect decontaminates and/or deconfuses her/his Introjected Parent and Archaic Child ego states

This is represented in the visual image (in Figure 6.1) of the neopsyche/ integrating Adult not only expanding outwards into the relationship and the environment, but also into introjected, archaic and fixated Parent and Child ego states. As Summers and I (2000) put it: "This perspective shifts the therapeutic emphasis away from the treatment of ego state structures and toward an exploration of how relational possibilities are co-created on a moment-to-moment basis" (p. 20). As this method is relational and dialogic, so it is ethical, for discussion of which see Cornell et al. (2006). The emphasis in this co-creative approach on relational possibilities echoes von Foerster's (1981/1984) ethical imperative: "Act always so as to increase the number of choices" (p. 60).

The methodology of co-creative transactional analysis and, specifically, the method of empathic transactional relating is represented in Figure 6.1 and elaborated in notes to the Figure. Whilst this is written from a psychotherapeutic perspective, it should be noted that this approach is applicable in educational and organisational settings with individuals, groups, and systems.

Having set out the methodology and method of co-creative transactional analysis, I now consider the similarities and differences between this approach and the integrative transactional analysis of Erskine and others (Erskine, 1988, 1991; Erskine & Moursund, 1988; Erskine & Trautmann, 1996), and the relational transactional analysis of Hargaden and Sills (2002).

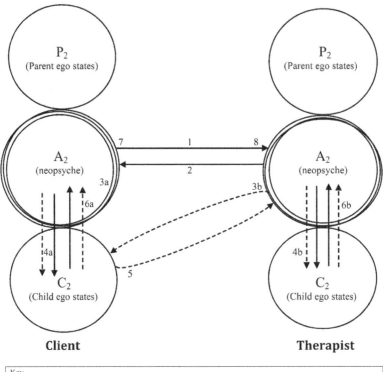

Client   **Therapist**

Key
1 The client offers an initial stimulus.   2 The therapist responds.
3a The client resonates with a feeling state in
   response to the therapist's response ...   3b ... and so may the therapist.
4a ... which, in this case, has an impact on
   the client's archaic Child ego state(s)#,
   consciously and unconsciously ...   4b ... as it may in the therapist.^
5 The client *may* experience the therapist's
   empathy also at an ulterior level, although
   it is not the intention of the therapist to
   "send" an ulterior Adult–Child transaction.*
6a The client abstracts empathic knowledge from
   the experience of her or his emotional resonance
   at both social (conscious) and ulterior
   (unconscious) levels ...   6b ... as may the therapist.
7 ... and integrates this abstracted empathic
   knowledge into responses that are increasingly
   acceptant and empathic of self and others ...   8 ... including the therapist who also is affected
                                                        and expanded by this process.

Notes
This transactional process is the same with regard to introjected Parent ego states (but for reasons of clarity
  and simplicity is only shown here with regard to the Child ego states; see Figure 7.2).
^ A point and a theme that acknowledges the intersubjective nature of this process [see Newton's contribution
  in Chapter Eight].
* If this is idealised then it would be represented as a Child–Parent and/or Parent–Child idealising ulterior
  transaction and, as such, offers a representation of how narcissism can be encouraged and perpetuated in
  therapeutic relating.

Figure 6.1. Co-creative empathic transacting.

Co-creative, integrative, and relational transactional analysis

Integrative transactional analysis

Citing Berne's (1961/1975a) definition of the Adult ego state as "auton-omous", Erskine (1988) suggested that this refers to "the neopsychic state of the ego functioning without intrapsychic control by an intro-jected or archaic ego" (p. 16). In this I agree with Erskine and, in terms of the structural analysis of ego states and the concept of the Adult, it is clear that co-creative transactional analysis shares much with Erskine's (1988, 1991) concept of the "Integrated Adult" (see Table 6.2). Erskine continued: "the healthy ego is one in which the Adult ego state, with full neopsychic functioning, is in charge and *has integrated* (assimilated) archeopsychic and exteropsychic content and experiences" (p. 19, emphasis added). In this regard I disagree with Erskine's view that inte-gration or assimilation is completed and with what follows from this— that is, the view, definition and implication of the Adult as an (upper case) "Integrated" *state*. I think about integration as a process rather than an outcome and, therefore, prefer the (lower case) term integrating (see also Tudor, 2008c, 2008d). Perls (1969/1971) argued that: "there is not such a thing as total integration. Integration is never completed. It's an ongoing process for ever and ever … There's always something to be integrated; always something to be learned" (p. 69). In the chapter on the neopsychic integrating Adult (Tudor, 2003) I wrote: "What distin-guishes the current, present-centred *neo*psyche from its *archaeo*psyche (archaic, experienced) and *extero*psyche (archaic, introjected) counter-parts is precisely its integrated and integrating process of changingness: experiencing, reflecting, mediating, and integrating" (p. 49).

There are certain other differences between integrative and co-creative transactional analysis with regard to their respective theoretical influences, and the relative acknowledgement of the importance of context, differences that are summarised in Table 6.3.

Table 6.2. Similarities between the theory of the Integrated Adult (Erskine, 1988, 1991) and of the integrating Adult (Tudor, 2003) and co-creative transactional analysis (Summers & Tudor, 2000).

Integrated Adult	*integrating Adult*
The distinction between Adult integration, and fixated archaic responses that is, Introjected Parent and Archaic Child ego states	

Table 6.3. Differences between the theory of the Integrated Adult (Erskine, 1988, 1991) and of the integrating Adult (Tudor, 2003) and co-creative transactional analysis (Summers & Tudor, 2000).

Integrated Adult	*integrating Adult*
Term	
Integrated Adult (a fixed state)	integra*ting* Adult (not fixed, fluid, moving) *neopsyche*
Metaphor	
"Integrated Adult" is (still) a mechanistic metaphor	integrating Adult is a metaphor of possibility and, specifically, relational possibilities
Theoretical base	
Work based on and in object relations theory	Work based on field theory, social constructivism and intersubjectivity; and in organismic psychology (see Hagehülsmann, 1984; Tudor & Worrall, 2006)
Represents a "one-and-a-half person" psychology (Stark, 1999)	Represents a "two-person" psychology (Stark, 1999) or a two-person plus psychology (Tudor, 2011d)
Context	
Not developed	Emphasises social/political context and culture
Theoretical implication: For the structure of personality	
Integrated Adult has an "either/or" quality: either health and functioning or fixation and pathology	integrating Adult accommodates some Child or Parent relational possibilities within the ongoing process of personal integration
Theoretical implication: For human development	
Not elaborated	Adult begins at conception (Tudor, 2003)
Practice	
Tends to focus on the capacity of the therapist for empathy, contact, enquiry	Focuses on the quality of therapeutic relating, co-created by therapist and client
Encourages and works with regression	Encourages present-centred relating as the medium for healing and learning; and acknowledges the co-creation of regressive experiences

Another difference is in the method. Whilst both approaches view empathy as the principle method, the integrative approach tends to rely on the potency of the therapist and the therapist's empathy, whereas in the co-creative model, the therapist's empathic resonance and responsiveness is a stimulus for both client and therapist to engage in a search for further understanding of the *client's* experiencing process and internal frame of reference. Whilst the power is still in the patient (see Goulding & Goulding, 1978), from a co-creative perspective, it is more accurate to say that the power or potency of the therapeutic encounter lies in the co-created relational field—which is why co-creative transactional analysis reflects and represents a two-person psychology if not or as well as a two-person plus psychology. Finally, this perspective also acknowledges the impact of these transactions and the relational encounter on the therapist, who may well also experience a sense of expansion (see Figure 6.1).

Relational transactional analysis

The term "relational transactional analysis" is perhaps most associated with the work of Hargaden and Sills—that is, Hargaden (2001) and Hargaden and Sills (2001, 2002), work for which in 2007 they were jointly awarded the Eric Berne Memorial Award (specifically for two of the chapters in their book on transference and countertransference). They and others have continued to develop their work—see Hargaden and Fenton (2005), and Fowlie and Sills (2011). Despite their own view, which as the subtitle of their book suggests theirs is *a* relational approach to transactional analysis, Hargaden and Sills' model has been taken by some as *the*—and, by implication, the only—relational approach in transactional analysis. It is clear, however, that with its way of understanding people, transactions and human development based on relationship, on relating, and on the relational field, co-creative transactional analysis is also relational, and, indeed, Cornell and Hargaden (2005) have included co-creative transactional analysis as part of what they have identified as the emergence of a relational tradition in transactional analysis [see also my Introduction].

The difference between these two relational approaches is based on their different theoretical influences: Hargaden and Sills' work is influenced predominantly by psychodynamic thinking, object relations, and self psychology, whereas co-creative transactional analysis is influenced by field theory and social constructivism, and specifically by person-centred and gestalt psychologies.

In their work, and particularly their book *Transactional Analysis: A Relational Perspective*, Hargaden and Sills (2002) outlined a model that they referred to as relational for two reasons:

a. Because of the research evidence that the therapeutic relationship is a key factor in therapeutic outcome; and
b. Because, they argued, deconfusion (of the Child) can only occur in the transferential therapeutic relationship by which they meant: "that unconscious developmental issues—those early Child ego states—can emerge to be seen and addressed within the safe bond of the relationship" (p. 1).

Their work provides a theory and methodology that allows for an exploration of the unconscious, specifically:

i. They have developed a theory of the self in terms of the Child ego state;
ii. Drawing on previous work by Menaker (1995), they have developed three categories of transference phenomena: projective, introjective, and transformational; and
iii. They have represented Berne's therapeutic operations as empathic transactions, and have added "holding" to this sequence (between illustration and crystallisation).

Their theory is influenced by humanists such as Rogers and Perls; by psychoanalytic thinkers such as Bollas and Pine; by developmental psychologists, notably, Stern; and neuropsychologists such as Shore, Panksepp, Damasio, and Watt.

The differences between the relational approaches of Hargaden and Sills (2002) and Summers and myself (2000) lie:

1. In a different analysis of the self—Hargaden and Sills conceptual-ise the self in the Child ego state and thus take a "three ego state" model of the healthy person, whereas [we] (Summers & Tudor) view the Adult ego state as healthy, and the Archaic Child and Introjected Parent as metaphors for different aspects or configurations of psy-chopathology (see Tudor, 2010b).

2. In a different view of the empathic transaction—for Hargaden and Sills these are conceptualised and diagrammed as a social level Adult–Adult transaction with an ulterior level transaction from the therapist's Adult to the client's Child, whereas for me this is referred to as "empathic transactional relating" or "empathic relating" (with and diagrammed as a series of integrating Adult–integrating Adult transactions with the purpose of helping the client to expand their neopsyche or Adult (see Figure 6.1, and Tudor, 2003 [present Chapter Two]).

3. In a different emphasis on ways of relating and working—in their practice, Hargaden and Sills emphasise and focus on working with and through different forms of transference phenomena, whereas Summers and I tend to work more in the present with an emphasis on co-creating different relational possibilities. This does not mean that we do not work with unconscious processes; it does mean that we place a different emphasis on working with and confronting such processes through engaging with present, conscious processes (see Summers & Tudor, 2000). In one of his discussions of empathy, Rogers (1975/1980b) described this as having several facets:

> It involves being sensitive, moment by moment, to the changing felt meanings which flow in the other person … It means temporarily living in the other's life, moving about it delicately without making judgements; it means sensing meanings of which he or she is scarcely aware, *but not trying to uncover totally unconscious feelings, since this would be too threatening*. It includes communicating your sensings of the person's world as you look with fresh and unfrightened eyes at elements of which he or she is fearful. (p. 142, emphasis added)

I think this is an interesting passage with a significant perspective on the unconscious, and one that supports the method outlined (above) in the second part of this chapter: as a therapist *I* am not trying to uncover my client's unconscious feelings by facilitating more expansiveness, extensionality (Rogers, 1959), and integrating, I am helping *her/him* to uncover, discover or rediscover her/his unconscious and non-conscious feelings and processes (see Figure 6.1 and, specifically, notes 4a and 6a). This perspective is supported by Klein's (1960) view of our motivation for integration, which follows from having parts in and of a whole or, as she described it: "the welding together of the different parts of the self" (p. 241). She suggested (ibid.) [as I noted in Chapter Five] that the need for integration is derived from "the unconscious feeling that parts of the self are unknown, and there is a sense of impoverishment due to the self being deprived of some of its parts … [and this feeling] increases the urge for integration" (p. 241).

Notwithstanding the differences between these relational models, Hargaden and Sills, and Summers and I are united in promoting relationality in transactional analysis in all its applications. However, whilst this interest and "relational turn" is reflected in a number of approaches across the theoretical spectrum of psychotherapy, and in a number of disciplines and fields, relational ways of being and working are under attack from ideologies and governments, which promote happiness as an easy and accessible alternative to the existential realities and anxieties of life, and which fund short-term, solution-focused forms of therapy and so-called evidence-based practice, which, in turn, is based on certain methodologies, such as randomised controlled trials, which are privileged over other methodologies (for a critique of which see Freire, 2006).

In this social and political context, a number of relational transactional analysis practitioners and theorists [including myself and Graeme] came together in 2009 to form, and later launch, the International Association for Relational Transactional Analysis (IARTA) to promote the development of relational transactional analysis—or, perhaps more accurately, transactional *analyses*. In coming together as a group of practitioners and theorists we identified eight relational principles that we hold in common:

1. The centrality of relationship
2. The importance of experience
3. The significance of subjectivity—and of self-subjectivity
4. The importance of engagement
5. The significance of conscious patterns as well as of non-conscious and unconscious patterns
6. The importance of uncertainty
7. The reality of the functioning and changing adult/Adult
8. The importance of curiosity, criticism, and creativity. (IARTA, 2010)

Clearly, co-creative transactional analysis has influenced these principles, and reflects them in practice.

Since then, these principles have been explored in a book on relational transactional analysis, edited by Fowlie and Sills (2011), in which over thirty different authors take and apply these principles to practice.

Conclusion

It is clear that co-creative transactional analysis is a relational approach to transactional analysis, and contributes to both the understanding and application of relational principles. Whilst originally developed in the field of psychotherapy, it is applicable to the other transactional analysis fields of application, in which further work may be done to elaborate its method.

Note

1. In England, Wales, Lithuania, Italy, Australia, and Aotearoa New Zealand.

CHAPTER SEVEN

Response to "Empathy: a co-creative perspective", and rejoinder

Graeme Summers and Keith Tudor

This chapter comprises Graeme's responses to Keith's article "Empathy: A cocreative perspective" (Tudor, 2011a, and the previous chapter in this volume). It is followed by a brief rejoinder from Keith.

Response from Graeme

I have shared some general responses to this paper in my Introduction (pp. xxxvi–xxxvii). Here I reflect more specifically on aspects of your latest co-creative transactional paper. I am particularly interested to explore where we agree and where we have differences of opinion.

Theoretical influences

I appreciate you mapping significant influences behind your thinking. The client-centred influence comes across strongly, given your choice of empathy as the principle method, and I enjoyed your creative juxtaposition of this with constructivism.

Your touchstone interest in the quality of contact or interruptions to contact resonates with me. However, I would not necessarily be primarily concerned with the presence or absence of empathic experience. I am interested in the range of ways we might experience each other and subsequently seek to navigate the limitations and potential of our relationship moment by moment.

With respect to your discussion of context, the term "sociocentric" (from O'Hara, 1997) offers a useful contrast to an "egocentric" standpoint. I would, however, add that it is equally important for the practitioner to account for their own context and not just that of the client. Echoing Winnicott (1952), I would challenge the one-person psychology assumption to suggest that in the therapeutic setting "There's no such thing as a client; only a therapist–client dyad." Both parties are, in part, a function of their past and present environments and will bring these influences to the interaction, in and out of awareness.

The constructivist influence is clear in your work and has political as well as clinical significance. Whoever gets to define the predominant reality or truth often gets to dominate social and political interactions, and it is important to be aware of how this can manifest in a clinical or consulting context. However, my stance here does not mean that I will automatically accept the client's reported experiences or perceptions as the only significant "truths". I may instead see them as contributions, perhaps a stimulus, to further explorations in our work together. I think that ideally, consensual, working definitions of truth or reality necessary for mutual understanding and social functioning get negotiated and updated through verbal and non-verbal communication. This is another way of saying that "meaning evolves through dialogue", a principle that helps us to allow "truth" or, more accurately, "truths" to emerge and evolve from relational process rather than being unilaterally defined by practitioner or client.

You state that "therapy is the co-creation of new narratives that name new possibilities" (p. 125). Are implicit stories and "unnamed possibilities" as important as "named possibilities"?

I agree with all you say about using a present-centred focus and differentiating from archaeological approaches. I think you communicate here an implicit trust in organismic process—that is, readiness for material to "float to the surface", alongside respect for whatever may remain below. I also think there may be times when digging, provoking and disturbing interventions (from practitioner or client) are useful, albeit uncomfortable. A key therapeutic attitude that is important here is one of openness to experiences and meanings that emerge in response to such relational risks.

Co-creative methodology and method

I clearly recognise the following points in this section as co-creative transactional analysis and appreciate your categorisation of methodology and method. I include responses to each in turn.

Methodology

The therapist works in partnership with the client

You usefully acknowledge Stark's (1999) framework and the difficulty for therapists to switch flexibly between modes, at least in part, because of the differing paradigms implied within each mode. In emphasising the mutual and reciprocal nature of relating I believe that we offer an interpretation of transactional analysis that predominantly sits within a contemporary two-person psychology or therapeutic mode. It is perhaps important here to emphasise the distinction that you already make between methodology and epistemology. From an epistemological perspective we might consider that all three therapeutic modes are "co-created" relational patterns, even though, from a methodological perspective, we seek to work in partnership with clients within a two-person or two-person-plus paradigm, or at least be prepared to work that way.

The therapist works with what is present and what is past in the present

I agree with you. This is a cornerstone of phenomenological method employed for many years within gestalt and existential psychotherapies, a fact acknowledged by Stern (2004) prior to his sophisticated elaboration on the significance of the "here-and-now" in everyday life as well as psychotherapy.

The therapist works with the client's present-centred neopsychic functioning/integrating Adult

In principle I agree with you here, too, with the following qualifications. The therapist cannot "co-create" an optimal therapeutic climate for the client. The therapist's contributions are important but, by definition, this is co-created together. At times the "optimal" climate for growth may also require adversarial elements; for example, challenge or conflict. When you say "it is the client who 'works with' her or his archaeopsyche (archaic Child ego states) and exteropsyche (introjected Parent ego states)" (p. 129) you also emphasise—and, I think, overemphasise—client responsibility. For me this contradicts the co-creative assumption of shared responsibility. My epistemological assumption is that, through my presence or actions, I am a contributory influence in my client's experience and that at least some aspects of this co-created experience can be explicitly explored. As we put it: "It is this juxtaposition of co-transferential and present-centred relating, developing in parallel, that facilitates the therapeutic emergence of transference. This duality of relating enables transferential phenomena to be experienced, compassionately identified and contained in the relationship" (Summers & Tudor, 2000, p. 14 above). If we implicate our involvement in our client's experience through our epistemological assumptions then I don't think we can deny this in our methodology. I think, however, the main thrust of this third methodological point we might agree upon is that therapeutic "work" happens through present-centred Adult development, and that both (work and development) will include recovery from and/or reflection upon inevitable transferential enactments.

Method

The therapist facilitates the client in expanding her or his neopsychic functioning

I agree with your statement that the "therapist does not intend to offer or develop complementary ulterior transactions between the therapist's integrating Adult and the client's archaic Child" (p. 129) and that facilitation occurs through a series of Adult–Adult transactions. What is missing for me is any reference here, or in your diagram, to Adult–Adult ulterior transactions, which I would regard as the main channel through which therapeutic empathy (rather than transferential empathy) is communicated and received. Your diagram suggests that you restrict Adult–Adult transactions to conscious communication, leaving unconscious/non-conscious processes to occur only at an intrapsychic level.

The client abstracts empathic knowledge from the experience
of her or his emotional resonance at both social (conscious)
and ulterior (unconscious) levels

I think this is an interesting way of accounting for ongoing intrapsychic processing and the way a set of transactions may reverberate at
different levels and stimulate internal re-writing of relational expectations, both during and after therapeutic work. In line with my work
on dynamic ego states I would use the term non-conscious (Adult) to
reference implicit knowledge (abstracted from the Adult–Adult ulteriors) at the implicit level, and unconscious (Child or Parent) to reference
implicit defensive reactions against it. Whilst I agree with you about
the inevitability of ruptures and that "process and experience of reflection on both the rupture and the repair" (p. 131) offer new possibilities, I would also suggest that the therapeutic benefits of such reflection
as well as the process of repair will be significantly mediated through
Adult–Adult ulterior transactions. I would, therefore, add complementary Adult–Adult ulterior vectors to this model to conceptualise mutual
influence between therapist and client at an implicit level of relating.

You state: *"When the client expands her or his Adult, she or he in effect
decontaminates and/or deconfuses her/his Introjected Parent and Archaic
Child ego states"* (p. 131). I think this statement holds true if we mix ego
state models. As such it provides a useful translation between the one
ego state model of health adopted in co-creative transactional analysis and the three ego state model of health in traditional transactional
analysis. However, I don't think it holds true "within" our one ego
state model of health where Child and Parent ego states are considered
defensive relational possibilities and probabilities rather than structures
to be modified. I don't therefore think in terms of Adult expanding into
the Child but would consider that as Adult relational capacities expand
and become increasingly probable, Child possibilities and probabilities
diminish. I think this further reinforces the relevance of your reference
to von Foerster's (1981/1984) ethical imperative.

Co-creative, integrative, and relational transactional analysis

Comparison with integrative transactional analysis

I agree with most of your comments here, particularly your descriptions of our differentiated emphasis on ongoing processes and relational

possibilities rather than finite processes and fixed entities. I also agree with your re-statement of our emphasis on the potency of the relational field rather than the therapist's empathic capacity.

I do, however, want to acknowledge more overlap with Erskine regarding our theoretical base, as indicated in my Introduction, particularly in relation to Fairbairn (1952). I also resonate with much of Ray Little's (2001, 2006, 2011) work, which also draws strongly on Fairbairn's ideas to conceptualise personality in terms of ego states. My theoretical departure from Erskine is marked by his incorporation of Kohut's (1971, 1977) emphasis on the empathic stance of the therapist—and the therapist alone. Whilst the intersubjective approach of Atwood and Stolorow (1984, 1996), who we reference, stems from the Kohutian tradition, it marks, at least in theory if not always in practice (see Ringstrom, 2010), a significant shift into a two-person paradigm.

Comparison with relational transactional analysis

I agree that the relational transactional analysis approach might be considered by some to mean one specific version of relational transactional analysis. However, I personally feel that co-creative transactional analysis has been recognised through its inclusion in two edited books on the subject (Cornell & Hargaden, 2005; Fowlie & Sills, 2011), both of which show diversity of independent thought whilst maintaining collective coherence. Also, in the last three years, I have been actively involved in IARTA, through which I have also developed a sense of belonging and acceptance within the "Relational TA" world, whilst also feeling free to explore and express my own ways of seeing and understanding.

You make specific comparison of co-creative transactional analysis with the work of our colleagues Hargaden and Sills. I agree with your comparative analysis apart from two instances: first, regarding theoretical influences, my comments about overlapping influences in relation to integrative transactional analysis also apply here; and second, regarding our different emphasis on ways of working you state that: "This does not mean that we do not work with unconscious processes; it does mean that we place a different emphasis on working with and confronting such processes through engaging with present, conscious processes" (p. 137). Here I don't agree with your emphasis on "conscious" processes, as I have already discussed in Chapter Three.

Conclusion

I think this is a characteristically thorough reflection on methodology and method within co-creative transactional analysis alongside an updated account of theoretical influences and current context. Your clear structure and coherent arguments have helped me both to understand your perspective and to clarify my own. Thank you for another stimulating and engaging contribution.

Rejoinder from Keith

Thank you again, Graeme, for your close reading of this article (present Chapter Six). As before, I rejoinder your response.

Implicit and explicit narratives

I think that stories, narratives, myths and legends are enormously important—and powerful. As a boy I was interested in both Greek myths and Norse legends; now living in Aotearoa New Zealand, I am aware of a rich tapestry of Māori legends, some of which I am beginning to get to know. People often think about such stories as "working" on a different, or some, "level" which, I think, is interesting on two counts: first, that stories, narratives, etc., "work" on us or for us in some way, as a connection and perhaps as a guide; and second, that they work on some "level" other than the conscious or explicit suggests that they impact, I think we would say, non-consciously and/or unconsciously. I remember some years ago coming across the following example, which, I think, illustrates this well. It's from a book called *The Way of Council* by Zimmerman with Coyle (1996) in which they tell a story about a young part Hispanic, part Native American boy who was invited by his grandfather to a tribal Council of Elders that had been called to decide its response to a Federal government proposal concerning land trade and mineral rights. The council began in silence, following which the leader unwrapped a bundle, took out a pipe stem, and began to tell a story; when he'd finished he passed the pipe on to an elder on his left who, in turn, told a story; one by one all the elders told one story after another; after some four hours, the pipe returned to the leader and the meeting ended with a silence. The boy, Joe, couldn't make out what had happened; after everyone had left, he caught up with his grandfather.

"What's going on?" he blurted out, a little out of breath. The old man stifled a smile and kept on walking. "I thought the council was going to take up the proposal," Joe continued in confusion.

"We did," his grandfather said in a quiet voice.

"I didn't hear any debate—and I certainly didn't hear any decision," Joe responded, still mystified.

"Then you weren't listening," his grandfather answered, and lost his battle with the smile. "In council one listens in the silences between the words with the ears of a rabbit."

"You mean the council actually took up the proposal and reached a decision?"

"Yes."

"In the silence?"

"And in the stories," his grandfather added, laughing. (pp. 3–4)

Thus, I would say that "implicit stories" and "unnamed possibilities" are important. Whether they are *as important* as "named possibilities", I am less certain—and hence my "maybe". I think that the impact of such stories, resonances, and so on, are in the eye of the beholder or perhaps more in the breath (as in "That took my breath away") or the gut (as in having a "gut feeling" or "gut response") of the person experiencing and thus evaluating their impact.

Now we come to therapy, which, as it creates—or co-creates—new relational possibilities, creates new narratives; and, as a narrative is fundamentally about telling a story, I do think that therapy is about *naming* these new possibilities. So, whilst the implicit and the unnamed may be as important or significant as the explicit and the named, I think it is the purpose and point of therapy to name things. This is, of course, not about the therapist naming things as *the* reality or *the* truth. It is about the client being facilitated by the therapist to name their own reality or realities, their new relational experiencing in therapy, and the possibility of taking that out of therapy into the rest of their lives. A good example of this is Rogers' (1951) point about therapy and diagnosis:

Therapy is basically the experiencing of the inadequacies in old ways of perceiving, the experiencing of new and more accurate perceptions, and the recognition of significant relationships between perceptions.

In a very meaningful and accurate sense, therapy *is* diagnosis, and the diagnosis is a process which goes on in the experience of the client, rather than the intellect of the clinician. (pp. 223–224)

Digging, disturbing, and disconcerting

As you—and others—know, I am generally not shy about impacting on my environment! In this context I particularly like Berne's (1966) definition of confrontation, which involves the use of information previously elicited "in order to disconcert the patient's Parent, Child or contaminated Adult by pointing out an inconsistency" (p. 235). I also agree that when considering, making and processing such interventions, (the therapist's) attitude is crucial. One aspect of Rogers' (1959) description of congruence is a person's openness to experience, and I think that openness, and non-defensiveness, is a core quality of therapists, trainers, and supervisors—or, at least, those trainers who operate from Adult–Adult. Only in this way can the therapist (and trainer and supervisor) process any rupture(s) caused by such interventions or interpositions. My caution about digging (and delving) is specific to therapists who rush in to the unconscious, trying to find repressed, introjected or archaic material or "the problematic past", where, rather, like angels, they might better fear to tread. I agree with you about the necessity and the desirablity of disturbance and, therefore, of the therapist's role as a disturber of what is often an uneasy peace. I think that to disturb (from the Latin *disturbare*)—to stir, discompose, agitate, move from a state of rest, interrupt, and throw into disorder—is good psychosocial praxis. The difference for me is in the fact that, as Berne defined it, such material has been previously offered or elicited.

With regard to your comment about optimal growth also requiring challenge or conflict, I agree, and I certainly did not intend to imply that the therapist creates the climate or anything else, or, for that matter, "provides" anything on his or her own (see Tudor, 2011b).

Congruence between methodology and method

I appreciate you promoting the importance of the theoretical and practical alignment between epistemology and methodology. When I originally made the point that it is the client who works with her or his own material, I was wanting to emphasise that it is not the therapist who is "sending" an ulterior, empathic angular transaction from her or his Adult to the client's Child (see Figure 6.1, p. 132 above) or to the client's Parent (see Figure 7.2, p. 152 below); rather, it is the client who is reflecting and processing, both during the therapy session and outside the therapeutic hour—in the other 167 hours in the week. Again, I was not intending to imply that it is only the client who does this work, or that the therapist is not contributing to or sharing the responsibility of this work.

Expanding neopsychic functioning

I agree with the point you make about Adult–Adult ulterior transactions. At the time I wrote the original chapter, I know I was concerned about the diagram (Figure 2.4, p. 51) becoming too complicated and layered. Notwithstanding that, however, I think that in our conversations and in your writing (Summers, 2011; present Chapter Four) you are generally inviting me to make the implicit explicit. So, to clarify, I think there are two levels to Adult–Adult transacting (see Figure 7.1):

1. The social or explicit level—which I think is fundamentally about awareness expanding awareness; as Yontef (1976) put it: "Awareness is integration. When one is aware, one does not alienate aspects of one's existence. One is whole" (p. 67).
2. The ulterior or implicit level—which, I think, is both inevitable and desirable, and, I agree, is a channel for therapeutic empathy, though I'm not sure that I agree that it is the "main channel" for this, as I would argue (as I have done) that the impact of empathy is in the eye of the beholder—that is, the experience of the client (see Tudor, 2011b), whether that is explicit or implicit.

I like the contrast you draw between therapeutic and transferential empathy: I think it adds something to the distinction we have drawn between

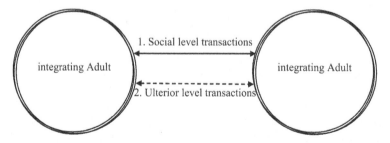

Figure 7.1. Social and ulterior level transactions between integrating Adults.

co-creative empathic relating and other perspectives in transactional analysis on empathy such as Clark's (1991) empathic transaction and Hargaden and Sills' (2002) empathic transactions, and also Shmuckler's

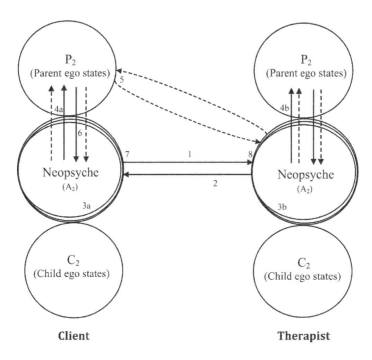

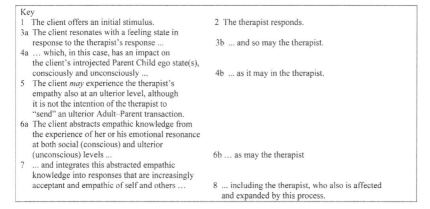

Figure 7.2. Co-creative empathic transacting (showing the client's work with the Parent).

(1991) association of empathy with being parental (Parental) and transferential. As described (and represented in Figures 6.1 and 7.1), co-creative transactional relating represents a different approach and a shift in attitude and technique with regard to empathic transactions (see also Tudor, 2011a).

My concern about over-complicating matters—I don't mind complexity but I would prefer not to overcomplicate things!—was also why I did not reproduce the same set of transactions as diagrammed in relation to the Child also in relation to the Parent. However, I think this is a sufficiently important point that I want to take the opportunity to present this here (Figure 7.2).

Decontamination and deconfusion

Regarding the point you make about expansion and decontamination and deconfusion, I both agree and disagree!

If we take this back to considering contamination and the traditional notion and representation of this in transactional analysis as an intrusion by (and overlapping of) the Parent and/or the Child into/of the Adult (see Figure 7.3), then I agree that in the integrating Adult model

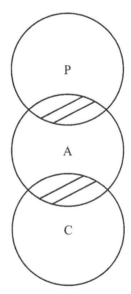

Figure 7.3. Double contamination (three ego state model).

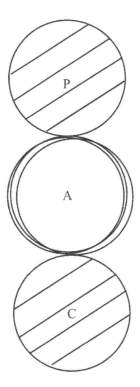

Figure 7.4. Contaminations (integrating Adult model).

this makes no sense, as "contaminations" would, by definition, be an aspect of an Introjected Parent and/or Archaic Child (see Figure 7.4).

If we now consider *de*contamination—and *de*confusion (usually represented on another level within the Child), then I don't agree with you or, at least, I think I am using the words "decontaminate(s)" and "deconfuse(s)" differently. Basically, I am saying that the more we integrate and expand, or are integrating and expanding (Adult), the more we diminish the power of, or cathexis in, introjected (Parent) or archaic (Child) ego states and, in this sense, decontaminate or deconfuse those rigid and fixed states or relational schema. The important aspect of this (at least, for me) is that the focus is on the Adult and the co-construction of new relational possibilities and, therefore, the deconstruction of defences, and not so much on the Parent or Child. I think this is consistent with our original critique of deconfusion and redecision "work" on and in the Child when they are based on regression to childhood scenes.

I agree that in the three ego state model, Parent and Child (and, for that matter, Adult) are "structures" and that in transactional analysis the concepts of contamination and confusion (as nouns) are used to refer to modifications of these structures. I think this highlights a problem when we use words and, specifically, nouns (substantives) in this way as it tends to substantiate and reify the "object". In such circumstances I am interested to use verbs or verb forms (see Tudor, 2008c, 2008d) as they suggest not only action but process. Maybe the problem is the image—and metaphor—of the Adult expanding *into* the Child and/or Parent, whereas, in my mind, it's more as you say, that with such expansion (or, better, expanding), Child—and Parent—relational patterns become redundant or less useful.

This said, I am interested in your first point about translation or, as it were, bridging between the two different sets of models of ego states (see Tudor, 2010b), as when I present this material I am often asked how I integrate the two sets of models—which I don't! However, if you're right, maybe this statement about method is helpful for those wanting to square things (as it were) between the two models or sets of models of ego states.

Co-creative transactional analysis and relational transactional analysis

I agree about the acknowledgement of our work (as I acknowledge in my Introduction) and, in this regard, I particularly appreciate Helena (Hargaden), Charlotte (Sills), Bill (Cornell) and, of course, others who have contributed to this book, as well as others who have not but who have acknowledged our work in their writing and/or teaching and training. I also recognise that, as I have not been actively involved in IARTA, I have not had the benefit of that sense of belonging and acceptance. However, I'm less sure that this acceptance from our colleagues and friends translates into training rooms where I still think that Hargaden and Sills' work = psychodynamic = relational transactional analysis. I think a case in point is Fowlie and Sills' (2011) book, which I like, but in which, although you cite it as demonstrating the influence of our ideas, the majority of the contributors draw on, assume and present Hargaden and Sills' work as *the* relational perspective. I am also concerned that "relational" has become the new norm: now everyone's "relational"! I hear this, for example, with regard to how some trainers and supervisors are preparing candidates for qualifying exams, advising them to say that they're "relational"— even if they're not! I think this is a concern that echoes your comment (in Chapter Three) about the idealism—and, I would say, the danger—of the universal or universalism; and also of dogma and the dogmatic; of certainty and attempts to make certain (see Tudor, 2007b); and of advocating and preparing exam candidates for conformity (see Cornell, 2000). This is, of course, particularly ironic and frustrating in that, as you know, neither Helena or Charlotte claim such privileging of their work and model, and are open and supportive of pluralism (see Samuels, 1997).

Conscious, non conscious, and unconscious

I'm not sure that I agree with your reading of my emphasis. I think that I was—and also, originally, we were—talking more about conscious processes and processing in order to redress what I certainly have experienced as an overemphasis on the unconscious and, in some quarters, an obsession with defining and structuring it, a project that I think is a somewhat fruitless attempt to define the unknown (see my comments in my rejoinder in Chapter Five). I do acknowledge that in my attempt to redress what I see as an overemphasis, ironically, I, in turn, may have overly overemphasised the conscious! I guess that's partly the stuff and process of developing ideas—from a Hegelian perspective, through thesis, and antithesis, to a synthesis, which then becomes the new thesis for which there is an antithesis, and so on. In terms of your disagreement, I hope that the material in Chapter Five addresses this or, at least, clarifies any differences of emphasis.

Final comment

As ever, it's great to have the dialogue, which, I think, opens up more space both for ourselves and for others. For my part, I love your attention to the nuances of language and your alertness to consistency, to the non-conscious and unconscious, to flexibility, and to possibilities. I have always appreciated that, despite our differences—and we have had and continue to have them—we are generally able to work through them, with the result, I think, that our theory and practice is clearer and better.

CHAPTER EIGHT

Co-creative contributions

Helena Hargaden, Laurie Hawkes, Marco Mazzetti,
Trudi Newton, and Gregor Žvelc

This chapter comprises contributions from five respected international colleagues who have been informed by, and some of whom have informed, the development of co-creative transactional analysis. In the following chapter we both respond to each of the contributions.

The tango of therapy: an improvisational dance?

Laurie Hawkes

Psychotherapists and their patients are in the same boat. To play mentalising duets effectively they must rely on whatever developmental competence they have achieved. At any given moment their performance will depend on the same factors: the extent of secure attachment (i.e., mutual trust in the relationship), and an optimal level of arousal (Allen & Fonagy, 2006).

What is "co-creative" to me?

I am dancing the tango with a partner I know well. At times I close my eyes and just melt into the experience of sensing the music and sensing what he wants to do with it; what he wants me to do with it. Then the music speeds up, and I open my eyes as our embrace opens and he suggests faster, more vigorous moves. We concentrate and smile, and often laugh to one another. Then comes a time when he changes the embrace, letting go of my right hand, letting me take hold of his right hand, as now I encircle his body. For a few moments, as we glide into the switch, we are co-dancing, no one in particular leading; but very quickly one of us must lead again: someone must be in charge so we don't crash into the other couples. Perhaps it was I who initiated the change, when a possibility came up. I might have released my hold on his hand, slightly, and if he agreed, he'll have let go lightly and we'll have taken a step or two that way, in an intermediate state, until I took the lead and tried to communicate to him what I wanted to do with the music and what I wanted him to do with it. It is particularly thrilling, this (uncommon) form of dancing: the uncertainty of who will lead when, taking the lead and playing with the music, then relinquishing that choice to the partner; and, as suggested by Allen and Fonagy (2006), it requires a mutual trust in the relationship, and wide-awake energy.

Thus with the tango of psychotherapy: there are moments when we lead, moments when the client leads, moments when we are co-leading, moments when we are mostly leading but are exquisitely aware of the client's reactions. This, to me, differs quite a bit from the traditional "therapeutic leverage", which, according to Boyd (1976), the therapist should strive not to give away to the patient.

To me, "co-creative" means, first, that we are creating together, not one person creating and the other adapting to them, not one person responsible and the other passive; and, second, that we are not following a plan, a treatment protocol, but improvising our shared creation in the present moment.

Am I a co-creative transactional analyst?

I have never managed to situate myself in only one of the transactional analysis currents—co-creative, relational, integrative, redecisional, body-oriented, cognitive-behavioural, etc. All of those seem to suit me and the work with my clients at different times. Each of these terms come to my mind at some time or another, to describe the kind of work I am doing or have just been doing. I tend to think "co-creative" during moments when my client and I are understanding, seeking, searching, experiencing, feeling together, moments that are also relational, I would say. In the training group I run, I also think "co-creative", especially when we think together and each person's view makes up a piece of the mosaic: a much richer picture than I alone could have painted.

In tango, as in psychotherapy, I am often struggling with this: striving to be fully in the present, yet calling on what I have learned, on techniques. In therapy, my effort needs mostly to go in the other direction: my natural tendency goes to just being with people, and I must discipline myself to think "diagnosis", "treatment plan", etc., except in those anxious moments when I lean on such modes, hoping to reassure myself that I know what I am doing. When I teach things such as diagnosis and treatment planning, I try to convey the constant weaving of those threads: the thread of categorisation and the thread of present contact, in order that trainees may learn to balance planning, even directing the therapy, and improvising. Probably this best happens when the learning has become a sort of second nature, and the person has become "unconsciously competent" (Robinson, 1974; Barrow, 2011), leaving them freer to go with the "music" of the present moment. Since this is long in coming, I wonder to what extent one can be co-creative without a fair amount of experience.

Sometimes or partly co-creative?

To me, co-creation is a state to which I often aim, but which is not easily attained, and usually not held, maintained, or static. It is more a state of trust that the right thing will emerge, that you and your dance partner, or you and your client, will know how to move next.

In tango, when you're the one leading, it is much simpler just to remain in charge. Sure, you take your partner and the other couples into account, adjust to their level or speed, and dance according to the music, but you're the boss, you hold the reins. Likewise, in therapy, it is simpler to be the therapist, easier to do one-person psychology therapy with a classical medical stance than look together at what ails the client and how that came about.

Co-creating, and improvising, requires much more refined attention, because one is always dancing at the edge of a mess; nobody is leading the dancing couple, or, in therapy, becoming too symmetrical, self-revealing, disorganised, or familiar.

It is often said that tango is an improvisational dance, meaning that you don't usually choreograph it or put together pre-established figures but, rather, you listen to the music and (co-)create a shape to fit it and to fit a particular dancing couple, a sequence of shapes of varying amplitude and speed. However, to me, there is no such thing as total improvisation in tango. The myth that "a good dancer can lead any woman into a good dance" is just that—a myth. I have never seen anyone dance a decent tango without a pretty good technique. So there must be learning, practicing, and training one's body to hold a good posture, to recognise subtle cues, and to perform unusual movements.

Likewise in psychotherapy, even though any good empathiser can participate in a conversation with therapeutic effects, you can't improvise the art of psychotherapy. You need the learning (of diagnoses, treatment plans, techniques, etc.) in order to get more and more skilled at improvising: learning to be anew with each person, on any given day.

As for the theory developed by Summers and Tudor over the years, one aspect that has particularly stuck with me is their script helix (Summers & Tudor, 2000), which, as distinct from the traditional script matrix, shows the many categories of people who influence a person's script development—more than simply two parents—and, following Cornell (1988), shows how mutual the influence can be. I come and go with the "one healthy ego state model" they describe so convincingly. From a gestalt perspective, and having learned much from Richard Erskine (see Erskine, 1988), I find this view very attractive, and yet I often use the "three healthy ego state model", too, because sometimes that is most evocative for me. Therefore, even in terms of theory, I stand at the edge of the co-creative movement, not quite in, not quite out.

As a conclusion

In my understanding of co-creative transactional analysis, it is a way of working and conceptualising that I use and am "in" fairly often. I find it a good term, especially in transactional analysis, with our "I'm OK, You're OK" foundation, and a term that, ideally, for me, would not set apart another group of transactional analysts, but, rather, would enrich the way all of us think about our work and ways of relating with our clients. My aim is to be a relational, integrative, co-creative, cognitive-behavioural, body-oriented transactional analyst who may also incorporate a few other adjectives that I may have forgotten!

Co-creative transactional analysis in a cross-cultural setting

Marco Mazzetti

In and on the terrain of cross-cultural encounters, the co-creative approach appears to be really promising. The main challenge when a patient and a practitioner from different cultural environments meet each other is to define a common, co-constructed and co-constructive territory by negotiating some kind of frame of reference that, at the beginning, is acceptable to both, and later, hopefully comfortable for both. In this sense this territory and relationship may be experienced as the best of "mixed race" or "dual heritage".

This negotiation can be fruitful as far as the first two main principles of co-creative transactional analysis are concerned and implemented: of "we"ness and of shared responsibility (Summers & Tudor, 2000), which, later (Tudor, 2011a), are included in the methodological principle, *"The therapist works in partnership with the client"* (p. 127), while the third (that of present-centred development) plays a significant role for treatment strategies.

To co-create a common relational field, it is necessary to honour the cultural worldview of clients, their understanding of their problems, their causes, and their explanation for their situation (Mazzetti, 2010, 2011). It can be surprisingly useful to enquire into, and respect, the patients' opinions about their suffering, and to support their strategies of self-care. In order to promote this process, the first step is to become aware of our expectation of the meeting with the patient, which is very often influenced by what we may call a cultural countertransference; in other words, the expectations we have for a person coming from, or belonging to, a specific environment.

To offer an example of a co-creative approach to this issue of cross-cultural work, I wish to draw briefly the story of a brief therapy with a Bangladeshi patient, who immigrated to my country of Italy. Even though, at the beginning of my practice, I spent some years working as physician in different continents, most of my experience in the cross-cultural setting comes from working with immigrants, and there are good reasons to take an example from this field. Working with immigrants is different from working in a specific environment; thus, a doctor practising among the Dogon in the heart of Mali, or the Yanomami in the Amazon forest, first of all has to adapt to these environments. Therapeutic practice with immigrants is more a matter of dual, reciprocal adaptation, and in a setting that naturally facilitates co-creativity.

At this particular time I was working once a week as the responsible doctor of the psychiatric department at a surgery in the centre of Rome, run by a Catholic non-governmental organisation, where free general and specialist medical assistance was offered on a voluntary basis to (mostly illegal) immigrants. One Thursday afternoon, having just arrived, I had a glance at my schedule: the first appointment was with a man from Bangladesh. Before meeting him I sat down in my office and unchained my fantasies about the meeting. I revived images of the summer weather in the Gulf of Bengal—the sudden violent showers followed immediately by a beating sun over hot wet air; the presumed Islamic faith of my patient; the centuries of fighting against Hinduism, which permeates so much of the culture of his country, as I myself witnessed with the several cases of Dhat, a culture-bound syndrome well rooted in the Hindu tradition, and which I have treated among Bangladeshi patients. I wondered also about the effect on him of being treated in a Catholic service, especially coming from such as religiously troubled area. I recalled the independence war against Pakistan and the most recent political disorders; the floods and the extreme poorness of Bangladesh; and the gender inequality, etc. My cultural countertransference was ready for meeting him! At least, I was aware of it.

Alì entered my office. He showed a sad face and a depressed mood, and was complaining of serious insomnia: he wanted something to be able to sleep at night. I reassured him: I would prescribe him a drug for the purpose. Meanwhile, I showed my interest in knowing something more about his life; he described his painful homesickness: he missed his young wife and two small children, a boy and a girl. He wasn't at all worried, as his father, who was running a successful carpentry business, which had several employees, was taking care of them, but Alì felt ashamed and guilty: he didn't send money home, and he didn't play the role of a responsible breadwinner for his family. He spoke about his migration: after leaving Bangladesh, he had headed to Germany where he spent some months. He had then moved to Holland and, later, after a short period in Belgium, to France; from France, Alì had tried to go to Switzerland, unsuccessfully, and then came to Italy. From Italy he had tried again to move to Switzerland, successfully this time, and he had stayed there some weeks. Finally, a few months before I met him, he had come to Rome where he was now living as an illegal immigrant and a flower seller. At the end of the session I prescribed him something to help him sleep, and made a date for a session the following week.

I had to admit that nothing of my anthropological, historical and social knowledge seemed to be useful: all my expectations were unmet, and my cultural countertransference frustrated! I'd just had a meeting with a sad man, with a very strange migratory story: he left his country to be successful abroad, but had had a job and a good financial situation at home, and a beloved family. He had moved between several countries in Europe. I had never met a single emigrant/immigrant doing this unless forced to, as, in each new country, they need to start from scratch, to learn a new language, etc. I felt a strong impact of this man, but didn't understanding why; I felt frustrated in my knowledge about his country and supposed culture, and, at the same time, very much involved with his story and life experience.

During the next sessions, while he was exploring why he had left his country and had had such an unusual migratory journey, I was also exploring how he was impacting on me. We took some time to explore reciprocally a way to stay together, to reflect on his story and his present, and to share the responsibility of the therapeutic journey.

Very soon we discovered he had two different migratory plans. The migratory plan is a powerful resilience factor for immigrants (Mazzetti, 2008); it not only contains motivations that have led the immigrant to undertake the difficult adventure of migration, but also, on a deeper and probably more relevant level:

> the migratory plan can provide the individual with a sense of history and help to maintain and connect, through narrative, two images of self: one pre-migration and the other post-migration. This helps the person to avoid the fracture that often results from migration, and provides meaning that mends the existential plot. (Mazzetti, 2008, p. 289)

His original environment heavily influenced Alì's first migratory plan, as the social pressure to migrate was very strong in his small town: the brave, brilliant young men had to migrate. For Alì, migration was a way to demonstrate his courage, to be proud of himself, and in order to achieve this goal he adopted, on a conscious level, the most common project: to go abroad to make money. Then, in our work together, we discovered a second, hidden and unconscious plan. It happened that he talked to me about his collection of world maps he had when he was a child, and how much he dreamed about travelling and seeing the world, with a special preference for the most exotic continent, Europe. At that moment I was enlightened: I saw the bedroom I had when I was a child, with the walls covered by maps of the continents, with a special preference for Africa, and I realised how probably this had influenced my decision years later as a young doctor to migrate to Africa! I decided to disclose this to Alì: I told him about my dreams as a child to travel and see the world, and he did the same with me. He listened to me very carefully, with an empathic participation in my story, and suddenly he also had an insight: the reason for the several changes (of country) were inconsistent with the formal aim of his migration (having a financial success), but very consistent with the real, unconscious one: to see as much of the world as he could!

At that point the short therapy had almost ended, after a handful of sessions. "We" worked together and shared the responsibility of the therapeutic journey (Summers & Tudor, 2000; Tudor, 2011a) by co-creating our micro-cultural environment, which, interestingly, was significantly influenced not by "high" culture (anthropological, social and historical elements such as religion, traditions, etc.), but by the common experience of growing up in an environment that we had each perceived as confined and scanty, and by our wishes to discover the vast world. Finally, we accepted that, through our relationship, we were transformed by each other: hearing his story, I gained insight into my life story, as he gained insight when I disclosed mine.

We were ready for the final step: present-centred development. Alì planned to work a few more months, until the end of the year, in order to earn some money to show his success at home, and to buy presents for all his nearest and dearest, and planned that he would travel home the following January. He felt relieved and started to sleep well again, without medication. He realised that his migratory plan had been successful, and that it was time to go home. He said goodbye, and I wished him good luck.

Alì's therapeutic experience focuses on another element: the positive approach frequently underlined in co-creative transactional analysis. We didn't attack any pathological, scripty issues, but followed his physis in searching for the healthy answers to his present life.

This is a rather paradoxical story, and not the rule. In working with immigrants I often have to take into account what, to my Western mind, are magical, religious and exotic beliefs, to co-create a common environment in the cross-cultural setting. I particularly love this story, as it reminds me of the need to be and remain open and free-minded when we meet new patients to begin the fascinating process of co-creating a therapeutic journey with them.

Two aware minds are more powerful than only one: mindfulness, relational schemas, and integrating Adult

Gregor Žvelc

In this contribution I expand on the idea of integrating Adult and connect it with relational schemas and mindfulness. Erskine (1991) described the integrating Adult ego state as consisting of age-related motor behaviour; emotional, cognitive, and moral development; the ability to be creative; and the capacity for full, contactful engagement in meaningful relationships. Tudor (2003) further developed and expanded this concept and described the integrating Adult ego state as present-centred and as a continual process of integration. The Adult ego state is thus a process, not a static entity. It is characterised by a "pulsating personality, processing and integrating feelings, attitudes, thoughts and behaviours appropriate to the here-and-now—at all ages from conception to death" (Tudor, 2003, present p. 31). I proposed that the integrating Adult is influenced by relational schemas, which are defined as schemas of an individual's subjective experience of a relationship (Žvelc, 2009b, 2010). Relational schemas implicitly organise our experience and are often non-consciously guiding our behaviour. This is similar to Summers' (2011) view regarding non-conscious implicit processes, which form the ongoing experiential basis of Adult ego states. In his view, Adult–Adult relating does not necessarily imply consciousness.

Relational schemas can be adaptive or defensive (Žvelc, 2010). In my view, adaptive relational schemas are connected with Adult ego state and defensive relational schemas with Child and Parent ego states. Adaptive relational schemas are open to change with each new experience and are thus constantly in flux. Such schemas serve an adaptive function by enabling individuals to gain a quick orientation in interpersonal relationships and to have healthy relationships with themselves. In my view, the Adult ego state cannot be "objective." We experience the world through structures that give meaning (schemas), and we process our experiences based on our schemas. So our experiencing is always subjective, with different people reacting to experiences in different ways. I agree, therefore, with Summers and Tudor (2000), who questioned the notion that the Adult ego state is the basis for objective processing and suggested that the ego state model describes different kinds of subjective experience.

The integrating Adult involves a constant process of integration and restructuring of relational schemas (Žvelc, 2010). Healthy, integrated schemas are adaptive because they spare us from having to learn everything from scratch, and they are appropriate to the current situation. The adaptive relational schemas, which are influencing our integrating Adult ego state, are quite different from defensive relational schemas, which are fixed structures that inhibit our spontaneity, creativity, and intimacy. These schemas are expressed in Child and Parent ego states.

Tudor (2003) described seven key features of the integrating Adult, having: autonomy, relational needs, consciousness, reflective consciousness, critical consciousness, maturity, motivation, and imagination. He wrote: "Whilst I believe that these are key features of the neopsyche (and in this context it behoves me to advance them), of course there are others" (p. 54). I proposed that mindfulness is another key feature of the integrating Adult and one that may be at the heart of the integrating process of the Adult ego state (Žvelc, 2010; Žvelc, Černetič, & Košak, 2011). In the last decade, there has been a growing interest in mindfulness in research as well as in psychotherapy. Kabat-Zinn (1994) defined mindfulness as: "paying attention in a particular way: on purpose, in the present moment and non-judgmentally" (p. 4). Mindfulness can also be defined as the non-judgmental, accepting awareness of one's own experience in the current moment (Černetič, 2011). Such awareness can include internal experience and/or external stimuli of which an individual becomes aware in an allowing manner, without trying to avoid or suppress such stimuli (Žvelc, Černetič, & Košak, 2011). Mindfulness is characterised by stable, non-reactive awareness of the present moment.

In previous writings I have introduced the concept of mindful Adult ego state (Žvelc, 2009a, 2010). Being in the mindful Adult means that we are present in the moment, receptive to whatever experience arises and accepting it without judgment or evaluation (Žvelc, 2010). The metaphor of a mindful Adult, then, refers to a capacity of the integrating Adult that is central for the integrating process, a process that involves:

- Integration and processing of undigested and fixated experience of Child and Parent ego states.
- Integration of Adult thoughts, feelings and physiological reactions, which arise from moment to moment and are reactions to present external or internal stimuli.

Getting in contact with the mindful capacity of the Adult ego state can be healing on its own. In the article "Mindfulness-based Transactional Analysis" (Žvelc, Černetič, & Košak, 2011), we wrote:

> Being centred in our mindful Adult gives us inner peace because we no longer identify with our Parent and Child ego states. We do not even identify with the contents of our Adult ego state. This means that we can observe our current thoughts, feelings, and sensations. The mindful Adult reveals another dimension of the human being: a dimension of pure awareness of the mind and the external environment. (p. 245)

Mindfulness can be a powerful ally in the process of change in psychotherapy (Žvelc, 2010). It promotes awareness of the contents of relational schemas—that is, structures that organise our subjective world. Such de-centring from schemas can provide psychotherapeutic change. When our relational schemas are activated, we can start using our mindful Adult ego state. The aim is to observe what is happening in our moment-to-moment awareness from a third-person perspective. Such activation of the mindful Adult ego state can change and restructure defensive relational schemas when they are activated.

Being in the Adult ego state does not automatically lead to a state of mindfulness. Adult ego state can function in two basic modes: of doing and of being (Žvelc, 2010). The doing mode describes problem-solving, a faculty that was traditionally attributed to the Adult ego state (Berne, 1961, 1964). We are not truly at peace in this mode because we are constantly evaluating where we are now and where we want to be in the future. This involves escaping the present moment for something that has yet to happen. The other mode of Adult functioning, the being mode, is concerned with immediate experience in the present moment, which is a characteristic of the mindful Adult. The focus here is on accepting what is, without pressure to change it.

One of the key ideas of co-creative transactional analysis is the principle of present-centred development (Summers & Tudor, 2000; Tudor,

2011a) and working in and with the present. Tudor (2011a) wrote that "the whole personality is present, although influenced by the past" (p. 126). Summers' and Tudor's ideas are similar to my own interest in developing mindfulness in psychotherapy. I use mindfulness within overall relational framework, though there are quite different formulations of what relational really means. I use the word "relational" for describing the co-creation of the relationship between the client and the therapist. This means that client and therapist are influencing each other on both conscious and unconscious levels and are creating an intersubjective field of reciprocal influence (Stolorow, Atwood & Brandschaft, 1994). I think that therapists who are aware and use this dynamics of reciprocal influence are "relational therapists". However, there can be different modes of working with the client that exist within the overall intersubjective field of client and therapist:

1. The intrapsychic mode (the relationship of the client with himself); and
2. The relationship mode (the relationship between client and therapist).

Both of these modes are important in psychotherapy, and the focus of therapy is sometimes more on the intrapsychic and sometimes more on the relationship. In the intrapsychic mode the client is attentive to his/her inner processes (thoughts, feelings, memories, body sensation), and the focus of psychotherapy is on relationship between client and his/her internal world. The relationship between client and therapist is in the background; however, the therapist provides the atmosphere of presence, attunement and acceptance of the client. In the relationship mode the focus is on relationship between client and the therapist. As Stark (1999) noted, this relationship can be based more on provision of corrective experience or active engagement in a reciprocal and mutual relationship. In my view the word "relational" has to do more with basic philosophical assumption of the therapist and not necessarily with the mode of relating.

Mindfulness in psychotherapy can be used in both intrapsychic relationship modes within an overall relational philosophical framework. Summers (2011) wrote of the importance of cultivating mindfulness and curiosity in relation to emergent relational dynamics. Activation of defensive relational schemas in the therapist and client can lead to enactments in games (Žvelc, 2010). Recognising and becoming aware of such enactments is crucial to preventing repetition and reinforcement of script. The therapist's goal is to become mindful of what is going on in the relationship with the client and to promote mindfulness in the client through the use of phenomenological enquiry (Erskine, Moursund, & Trautmann, 1999) and metacommunicative transactions (Widdowson, 2008).

I think that some "relational-based" therapists, by being focused on the relationship itself, sometimes forget about the importance of intrapsychic mode of relating with the clients. In my own psychotherapy practice I have become increasingly interested in how to promote mindfulness within the intrapsychic mode. I think that mindfulness promotes the natural healing of the organism, where the change comes spontaneously by acceptance and awareness of internal experience (Žvelc, 2012). Such a process has been described as "mindful processing" because, with mindful awareness, disturbing experiences can be processed and integrated (Žvelc & Žvelc, 2008, 2009). When clients learn to accept and tolerate their internal experience, experience starts to transform, and change can take place.

The mindful processing method invites clients to become aware of their moment-to-moment subjective experience with acceptance (Žvelc, 2012). The role of the therapist is to facilitate a mindful stance in the client. He or she invites the client into a state of awareness and acceptance. The therapist is also supposed to be in a mindful state of mind, aware of what is happening within him or her and what is happening with the client. The therapist's role is to offer an accepting space to all of the client's experiences that are emerging from moment to moment. The therapist is not trying to change anything, he or she has to be curious and open to whatever experience is arising. In this approach the therapist cultivates the attitudes of quietness, presence, curiosity, warmth, and acceptance.

In mindful processing the therapist helps clients establish a mindful stance, which involves the capacity to observe inner experience. We can say that: "Two aware minds are more powerful than only one aware mind" (Žvelc, 2012, p. 47). The therapist's presence can actually promote a mindful stance in the client, which would be difficult to achieve alone. Moreover, such a stance actually promotes processing and integration of disturbing experience.

Mindful processing starts with focusing on body sensations connected to the issue the client is bringing to the therapy. Mindful processing involves attention to body-felt experience from which other elements of subjective experience arise. In mindful processing the client alternates between awareness of internal experience and description of his or her experience to the therapist. The client is invited to pay attention to any experience that emerges from moment to moment. This process involves lots of silence in psychotherapy and gives clients space for just being with him or herself. In this way the client can develop a new relationship with themselves that is based on acceptance, compassion, and awareness. I think that mindful capacity of integrating Adult is especially important for the integration of implicit and non-verbal experience, and, thus, I agree with Summers (2011) that critical and reflective consciousness is not the only way (and often not enough) for integrating process.

In this contribution I have written some of my thoughts regarding relational schemas and mindfulness in connection to the concept of integrating Adult. I hope that the concept of integrating Adult will grow and develop further and that the process of theoretical integration will continue.

Learning to be transactional designers

Trudi Newton

In this contribution I aim to explore the links between co-creative transactional analysis and the educational field by considering what is happening when learning is effective. Three key ideas common to both are identified and used to highlight four points for co-creating better systems for learning.

When a new idea appears it challenges accustomed attitudes and practice. The "new idea" will be emerging from a context in which its originators are passionately engaged and they will be attempting to integrate their own experience and observation with what they have learned and inherited. So it was with Berne. Emerging out of the increasingly esoteric complexity of psychoanalysis came the accessibility and insight of transactional, game and script analysis. So it is with co-creative transactional analysis. The original spark and energy of transactional analysis concepts are being reignited by the experience of using and thinking transactional analysis in practice, with clients, observing one's own and one's clients' responses and enlivening and re-evaluating theory.

I believe the co-creative approach expresses something universal found in other fields too: medicine (radical psychiatry), religion (liberation theology, non-realist philosophy), formal education (humanistic *vs.* traditional schooling), sociology, politics, and economics. All at some point confront the question: "Do we solve this together, cooperatively, as a community, or do we ascribe power to some and compliance to others?" In these various arenas we witness the emergence of similar contextual solutions: experience-focused ways of being with others that challenge received traditional knowledge-based systems and uphold appropriate responsibility for all.

When I first encountered transactional analysis I was able to make sense of, and articulate, ideas I had been using for years in pastoral counselling, community development, and adult education. I didn't have the words to convey meanings, which were important to me, and which I very much wanted to share. I had met and studied with Paulo Freire in Switzerland and felt at home with his radical ideas and philosophy about learning (Freire, 1973/1996). I wanted to bring these insights into my work and, to the best of my ability, I did so. Ten years later I came across transactional analysis. Suddenly I found a language with which I could name, describe and explain what I saw happening around me (and in me), and share it with others too. Experiential learning, radical education and student-centred teaching all made more sense with the accessible psychological perspective promoted by transactional analysis.

When the original article on co-creative transactional analysis was published (Summers & Tudor, 2000) it had a great impact on me—with its exhilarating ideas of "we"ness, present-centredness, future possibilities, and the script helix—but, most of all, a little phrase that moves transactional analysis into a new paradigm: "Perhaps we need to see ourselves as transactional *designers* as well as transactional analysts" (present p. 21). The authors saw that (designing) as intuiting possibilities, for and with clients, and exploring and developing these possibilities for their future: the clients' future and maybe the therapists' too.

In this contribution I want to move on further and consider what transactional design can mean for learning and education, not only for individuals but for whole communities. In the critical pedagogy of Freire, the situated, problem-posing approach, first to literacy and then to all areas of learning, confronts the elitist, traditional, "banking" model of education.

This is a familiar experience, probably because education is where a society most clearly shows its beliefs about itself and how it values—or doesn't value—its members. Everything we believe is revealed by the way we perceive learners and teachers, what we elect to teach, and who and what is rewarded and with what—who decides and by what right? When we think about co-creative transactional analysis and learning together we soon find ourselves in the political arena—and why not?

I want to pick up three words that seem significant to me, are expressive of the essence of the co-creative approach, and are resonant with education: empathy, mutuality, and context.

Empathy: a source of play, co-operation, and narrative

Tudor (2011b) has described empathy as the principle method of co-creative transactional analysis. Robert Bellah (2011) has suggested that empathy is the key capacity that emerges during human development. This is not surprising. The ability to understand, accept and share feelings with others gives rise to bonding (attention, cooperation), play (intention), and meaning. Describing factors in the emergence of religion in human evolution, Bellah related the process of creating ritual and narrative to stages both in infant development (Piaget, 1973) and in human culture (Donald, 1991). I think his ideas can be applied to any cultural system, not only religion; from our personal and joint narratives we derive concepts and ideas. We may then stay with the systems we create and the concepts they embody—features of our everyday lives that Bellah has called "online"—or we may challenge them by staying aware of the "offline" consequences of empathy, bonding, playfulness, art and story, and so continually co-create new meanings in the present.

Mutuality: a two-person enterprise

I chose the word mutuality to convey the two-person shared experience of learning. This is the key to radical education: we teach each other, though sometimes in an equal but asymmetric relationship (Freire, 1973/1996). Learning is a "two-person" endeavour: the learner is not an object to be "taught" or instructed but an equal partner (Rogers, 1978).

Teacher and learner are both actively involved in the process; and the teacher is engaged, not neutral.

This characteristic of both co-creative transactional analysis and authentic learning has been diagrammed recently in two ways: by Sills and Mazzetti (2009), based on script, and very differently by Tudor (2011a), based on transactions. Both these visualisations show the engagement and openness to change of the therapist—or, equally, of the teacher. For Sills and Mazzetti this is the "relational field", which, as Chinnock (2011) has described it: "represents the mutuality and bidirectional nature of the relationship between supervisor and supervisee" (p. 343). This inter-subjective relational field also exists between teacher and learner; if learning is a change in, or expansion, of Adult we can also think of it as each "re-doing" our meaning-making and some aspect of our identity. In Tudor's (2011a) diagram (present p. 132), the reciprocal, repeated description in transactions "and so may the therapist" could equally apply to a teacher, trainer, facilitator, or animator. Both diagrams aim to make visible an unconscious and conscious process: mutual availability to change in the two-person endeavour.

Context: the social perspective

When lived experience is at the centre of learning it opens up the political dimension and the possibility of freedom. Freire (1973/1996) was clear that he was not seeking the overcoming of a powerful hierarchy through his critical pedagogy but the liberation of all.

With regard to a shift from two-person psychology to two-person plus psychology, Tudor (2011b) has stressed the importance of taking account of the social, political and cultural context when working with therapy clients. In education the social and political context is always present, impacting on the teaching/learning; and education influences its context by reinforcing or challenging it. The contract is always multi-party and, hopefully, "socially intentioned" (Tudor, 1997), a perspective that helps us to understand ourselves and our clients in the social context, to reflect critically on it, and to take account of the impact of the changes we choose to make. Problems and pathology are located in the external as much, or more than, in the internal world—as are solutions and health.

How can the education field and co-creative transactional analysis inform and enrich each other?

I see this in a number of ways:

1. First, through a shared understanding of the process of learning as rooted in experience and relationship—learning is the major process of human adaptation (Kolb, 1984), a holistic, continuous, lifelong process which extends to all parts and situations of our lives. Learning in school (or in any other formal setting) is much more than a curriculum—as learning is the means by which growth and development (and problem solving) happen in therapy.

2. Second, through the concept of the integrating Adult (Tudor, 2003)—the consequent idea of "expanding the Adult" captures the aim and purpose of learning: to enable autonomy, wider frames of reference, and interdependence (homonomy). Again, the diagram of co-creative empathic transactional relating (Tudor, 2011a, p. 132) shows what occurs in the moment-by-moment (and day by day) relationship as this expansion and learning happens.

3. Third, through education as one container for the learning process—which is accustomed to the public space and to taking account of—by adapting to or confronting—the social and political factors of everyday life. There is a storehouse of experience among educators that can benefit other transactional analysis fields by sharing and debating effective methods, and by describing the philosophical ground (see, for instance, Barrow, 2011).

4. Fourth, all of this comes back to the idea of transactional design—not only for individuals but also for communities. We can focus on the future as well as the present moment, or focus on the present moment and learn from it to create new possibilities for the future.

Designing learning and learning to design

By maintaining our awareness of the "offline"—play, friendship, bonding, shared narratives, art, music—everything that gives meaning and carries meaning, we become involved in a continual evaluation, reflection and exploration of possibilities. This is what leads us to tell better stories and so create better societies.

Lily, Anna Karenina, and the co-created unconscious relational third

Helena Hargaden

"[C]o-creative transactional analysis is best considered as a generative approach" (Summers, 2014, p. xxxvii). In this contribution I introduce the idea of the "third", a concept that, I propose, has the potential to expand and enrich the theoretical range of co-creative transactional analysis. In the following case study I demonstrate how the "third" is generated by the co-created relational unconscious and facilitates "the emergence of new contextually viable possibilities grounded in relational experience" (ibid., p. xxxvii).

When invited to write this contribution I thought of "Lily" because of what happened between us, about which I say more later. The "third" refers to the creation of a triangular space, alongside the therapist and client, which enables the therapy to move beyond an impasse in the dyadic relationship, and "allows for more nuanced and 'mature' forms of relating to both self and others" (Gerson, 2006). The original idea of the "third" derives from an understanding of how the "father"—a metaphor that stands for any other person or object such as the mother's work, for instance—interrupts the Oedipal process so that mother and child are separated by a "third" other, enabling the child to move out of the symbiotic relationship with mother. In the therapeutic relationship, the "third" is characterised by many things, one of which could be the therapist's thoughts, which may be experienced as an intrusion into the empathic flow of the therapeutic relationship. Gerson (2004) suggested three categories of potential thirds: developmental, cultural, and relational. Developmental thirdness acknowledges the third position as an Oedipal constellation and is represented in the work of Britton (1998); the cultural third is one that envelops and shapes the interactions of the dyad and is represented by the work of Chasseguet-Smirgel (1974) and Lacan (1977); the relational third is most frequently associated with an intersubjective perspective, as developed in the work of Bollas (1992), Ogden (1994), Benjamin (1995, 2004), and Orange (1995). My focus here is on the relational "third", the emergence of which changed the course of the therapy in the following account.

When Lily first walked into my consulting room I did not see a thirty-year-old woman. From the way she moved, her childish dress, her hair in bobbins, I saw, instead, a child: demure, pretty, and dainty. Her name is of course not Lily—that is my name for her, and there must be some meaning in that. Lily is the name of a flower that is pretty, fragrant, elegant, and a mark of culture. There is "something else", though, about the name, for I found myself humming a folk song called "Lily of the West", which is the name given to a woman who betrays her lover by falling in love with another man. Lily's rejection turns him into a killer and yet despite being sentenced he still loves his "faithless" Lily of the West. My association with this folk song reveals the shadow side of "Lily", which makes her more interesting, opening up a secret domain of a woman who has sexual power and independence of mind.

The thoughts of Lily as a powerful, sexual, independent, although "faithless" young woman, if they existed at all, were remote from my conscious mind as I embarked on my work with Lily. I experienced her as childlike, unnecessarily adapted to others' needs and emotionally hidden. It turned out that Lily was no stranger to therapy, having been in classical transactional analysis, which seemed to reinforce her belief that there was something pathological about her feelings, which she defined as rackets. This made it impossible to get close to her as she described herself and her feelings in such concrete and derogatory terms. When telling her story she showed little affect: her father had left her mother when Lily was twelve; her mother was devastated and had gone into a depressed fugue. The family's circumstances deteriorated and Lily lost the security of home and parents. Lily seemed to have no feelings about any of this. Both parents sounded self-absorbed as, too, was her new stepmother, who had no daughters of her own, and for whom Lily felt obliged to be the "cute" and loving object.

The atmosphere that emerged between us in the relationship was one of me feeling irritable, sometimes angry, even enraged as Lily smiled and twinkled her way through the sessions. In her current life she was in an unsatisfactory relationship with a man whom she felt she must placate, and around whom she had to be cute and "supportive" of his needs, dreams and requests of her, with little thought of her own ambitions and needs. It was confusing to me that she was clearly well educated and articulate, and even held down an important job for a prestigious organisation, yet Lily felt to me like a girl who experienced herself as quite powerless, and whose main function was to play supportive roles to others in her life, and to be whatever they needed her to be. Stuck in a crippling paralysis of internalised symbiotic relationships,

Lily felt required to be compliant, adapted, and to repress her true experiences.

The co-created dynamic that ensued involved me in "chasing" Lily with my thoughts, and although I introduced my countertransference reflectively, and Lily did make some changes, there was a deep reluctance on her part to let me really know her. She resisted my curiosity, for instance, about her work, and any of my attempts to relate to her as a powerful adult woman. The therapy felt polarised into a Parent–Child configuration.

The incident that altered this dynamic was the emergence of the co-created "third" between us in the form of the book *Anna Karenina* by Leo Tolstoy (1877/2000).

A few weeks before my summer break, Lily arrived for her session looking even more childlike than usual in a floral pinafore dress and white socks. As she sat down she smilingly told me that as she had walked up the hill to my house, she had been reading her book and a man had behaved inappropriately towards her. I was infuriated, as though with a daughter who had put herself in danger. I shared my thoughts rather more forcefully than usual and, for her part, Lily felt hurt and angry with me, feeling criticised and blamed for attracting unwelcome male attention. Unusually, over the following weeks, she expressed her anger with me, saying that she thought I had been too harsh with her, and that she felt hurt by me. We talked about the situation at length in a way that felt as though the roles had been reversed: I was the Child and she was the Parent, telling me off for being impatient with her and saying "horrible" things. We were stuck in an impasse when, on the last day before my holiday, I found myself, slightly impatiently, cutting across the repetitive dialogue with a question: "What were you reading anyway?" "Anna Karenina", she replied. In that moment I saw Lily afresh: who was she? I was curious.

So, on holiday, I read the book. In it, Tolstoy describes a society that is obsessed with status, image, material gain, easy pleasures gained through gambling, sex, intrigues, mindless projects, and a narcissistic community full of its own self-importance. Anna, although fascinating and wonderfully seductive, is essentially self-absorbed, amoral, and self-pitying. Levin, an anti-hero, on the periphery of the "in" crowd to which Anna belongs, turns out to be the unlikely but real hero of the story. At the beginning of the book he seems boorish, moralistic, too serious, and unpopular, but, unlike Anna, he is willing to struggle with himself, to engage honestly with his frustration. By the end of the book he finds how to live a satisfying life whilst Anna is destroyed by her narcissism.

I found the book deeply satisfying and was grateful to Lily for reintroducing me to Tolstoy. Lily was very surprised when I told her that I had read the book, and shocked to hear that I was interested in her views about the characters and what she thought about the moral tone of the book. Her reflections on the themes, including the fantasy of narcissistic love and the reality of love, led to her musing on what really mattered to her; on what she wanted from life. The emergence of this "third" into our work provided Lily with a language to discover domains of herself that had hitherto been hidden. This "third" enabled us to move beyond our individual psyches, and a stale impasse, into here and now Adult–Adult relatedness.

Thirdness, as Gerson (2006) has described it, is: "that quality of human existence that transcends individuality, permits and constricts that which can be known, and wraps all of our sensibilities in ways that we experience as simultaneously alien as well as part of ourselves." The "third" allowed the therapy to become more vital, when it had previously suffered from elements of deadness, to evolve, take on a more improvised feel; it became more possible to play around with ideas. As Summers puts it his Introduction: "The principle method of co-creative transactional analysis is play" (p. xxxvi).

Our reflections helped Lily to disentangle from the crucifying symbiotic relations. She became more conscious of her stuckness and the rage she felt with her parents. This acknowledgment enabled her to become more autonomous. There is of course so much more to say about Lily. The major focus of this case, however, is to illustrate an understanding of how the "third" can bring about a more co-created dynamic within transactional analysis.

References

Allen, J. G., & Fonagy, P. (Eds.), (2006). *Handbook of Mentalization-Based Treatment*. Chichester, UK: Wiley-Blackwell.

Barrow, G. (2011). Educator as cultivator. *Transactional Analysis Journal*, 41(4): 308–317.

Bellah, R. N. (2011). *Religion in Human Evolution: From The Paleolithic to The Axial Age*. Cambridge, MA: Harvard University Press.

Benjamin, J. (1995). *Like Subjects, Love Objects*. New Haven, CT: Yale University Press.

Benjamin, J. (2004). Beyond doer and done to: An intersubjective view of thirdness. *Psychoanalytic Quarterly*, *73*: 5–46.

Berne, E. (1961). *Transactional Analysis in Psychotherapy: A Systematic Individual and Social Psychiatry*. New York: Grove Press.

Berne, E. (1964). *Games People Play: The Psychology of Human Relationship*. New York: Grove Press.

Bollas, C. (1992). *Being a Character*. New York: Hill & Wang.

Boyd, H. (1976). Therapeutic leverage. *Transactional Analysis Journal*, *6*: 401–404.

Britton, R. (1998). *Belief and Imagination*. London: Routledge.

Černetič, M. (2011). Odnos med anksioznostjo in uje nostjo [The relationship between anxiety and mindfulness]. Unpublished doctoral dissertation, University of Ljubljana, Ljubljana, Slovenia.

Chasseguet-Smirgel, J. (1974). Perversion, idealisation and sublimation. *International Journal of Psycho-Analysis*, *55*: 349–357.

Chinnock, K. (2011). Relational supervision. In: H. Fowlie & C. Sills (Eds.), *Relational Transactional Analysis: Principles in Practice* (pp. 295–303). London: Karnac .

Cornell, W. F. (1988). Life script theory: A critical review from a developmental perspective. *Transactional Analysis Journal*, *18*: 270–282.

Donald, M. (1991). *Origins of the Modern Mind: Three Stages in the Evolution of Culture and Cognition*. Cambridge, MA: Harvard University Press.

Erskine, R. G. (1988). Ego structure, intrapsychic function, and defense mechanisms: A commentary on Eric Berne's original theoretical concepts. *Transactional Analysis Journal*, *18*: 15–19.

Erksine, R. G. (1991). Transference and transactions: Critique from an intrapsychic and integrative perspective. *Transactional Analysis Journal*, *21*: 63–76.

Erskine, R. G., Moursund, J. P., & Trautmann, R. L. (1999). *Beyond Empathy: A Therapy of Contact-in-Relationship*. Philadelphia, PA: Brunner/Mazel.

Freire, P. (1996). *Pedagogy of the Oppressed* (2nd Revised edition; M. Ramos, Trans.). Harmondsworth, UK: Penguin Education [original work published 1973].

Gerson, S. (2004). The relational unconscious: A core element of intersubjectivity, thirdness, and clinical process. *The Psychoanalytic Quarterly*, *73*: 63–98.

Gerson, S. (2006). On analytic impasse and the third: Clinical implications of intersubjectivity theory [posting]. In: L. Aron (Ed.), & B. Reis & D. Shaw (Moderators), *Analytic Impasses and the Analytic Third*. International Association for Relational Psychoanalysis and Psychotherapy.

Online Colloquium No. 9. www.iarpp.net/resources/colloquia/ colloquium_9.html [last accessed 30/11/ 2006].

Kabat-Zinn, J. (1994). *Wherever You Go, There You Are: Mindfulness Meditation in Everyday Life*. New York: Hyperion.

Kolb, D. (1984). *Experiential Learning*. Englewood Cliffs, NJ: Prentice Hall.

Lacan, J. (1977). *Ecrits: A Selection* (A. Sheridan, Trans.). New York: W. W. Norton.

Mazzetti, M. (2008). Trauma and migration: A transactional analytic approach toward refugees and torture victims. *Transactional Analysis Journal, 38*(4): 285–302.

Mazzetti, M. (2010). Cross-cultural transactional analysis. *The Psychotherapist, 46*: 23–25.

Mazzetti, M. (2011). Cross-cultural transactional analysis. In: H. Fowlie & C. Sills (Eds.), *Relational Transactional Analysis: Principles in Practice* (pp. 189–198). London: Karnac .

Ogden, T. (1994). The analytic third: Working with intersubjective clinical facts. *International Journal of Psycho-Analysis, 75*(1): 3–20.

Orange, D. (1995). *Emotional Understanding*. New York: Guilford.

Piaget, J. (1973). *The Child's Conception of the World*. St. Albans, UK: Paladin.

Robinson, W. L. (1974). Conscious competency—The mark of a competent instructor. *Personnel Journal, 53*: 538–539.

Rogers, C. (1978). *Carl Rogers on Personal Power*. London: Constable.

Sills, C., & Mazzetti, M. (2009). The comparative script system: A tool for developing supervisors. *Transactional Analysis Journal, 39*(4): 305–314.

Stark, M. (1999). *Modes of Therapeutic Action*. Northvale, NJ: Jason Aronson.

Stolorow, R. D., Atwood, G. E., & Brandschaft, B. (1994). *The Intersubjective Perspective*. Northvale, NJ: Jason Aronson.

Summers, G. (2011). Dynamic ego states: The significance of nonconscious and unconscious patterns, as well as conscious patterns. In: H. Fowlie, & C. Sills (Eds.), *Relational Transactional Analysis: Principles in Practice* (pp. 59–69). London: Karnac .

Summers, G. (2014). Introduction. In: K. Tudor & G. Summers (Eds.), *Papers, Responses, Dialogues, and Developments* (pp. xxi–xxviii). London: Karnac.

Summers, G., & Tudor, K. (2000). Co-creative transactional analysis. *Transactional Analysis Journal, 30*(1): 23–40.

Tolstoy, J. (2000). *Anna Karenina* (R. Pevear & L. Volokhonsky, Trans.). London: Allen Lane [original work published 1877].

Tudor, K. (1997). Social contracts: Contracting for social change. In: C. Sills (Ed.), *Contracts in Counselling* (pp. 207–215). London: Sage.

Tudor, K. (2003). The neopsyche: The integrating Adult ego state. In: C. Sills & H. Hargaden (Eds.), *Ego States* (pp. 201–231). London: Worth.

Tudor, K. (2011a). Empathy: A cocreative perspective. *Transactional Analysis Journal, 41*: 322–335.

Tudor, K. (2011b). Understanding empathy. *Transactional Analysis Journal, 41*(1): 39–57.

Widdowson, M. (2008). Metacommunicative transactions. *Transactional Analysis Journal, 38*: 58–72.

Žvelc, G. (2009a). Between self and others: Relational schemas as an integrating construct in psychotherapy. *Transactional Analysis Journal, 39*: 22–38.

Žvelc, G. (2009b). The present moment in integrative psychotherapy. Keynote speech delivered at the 4th International Integrative Psychotherapy Conference, Bled, Slovenia.

Žvelc, G. (2010). Relational schemas theory and transactional analysis. *Transactional Analysis Journal, 40*: 8–22.

Žvelc, G. (2012). Mindful processing in psychotherapy: Facilitating natural healing process within an attuned therapeutic relationship. *International Journal of Integrative Psychotherapy, 3*: 42–58.

Žvelc, G., & Žvelc, M. (2008). The power of present moment. Mindful processing in psychotherapy and counseling. Workshop presented at 4th European Conference on Positive Psychology, Book of abstracts. Opatija, Croatia.

Žvelc, G., & Žvelc, M. (2009). Loss and regain of "now": Transforming trauma through mindful processing. Workshop delivered at the 4th International Integrative Psychotherapy Conference, Bled, Slovenia.

Žvelc, G., Černetič, M., & Košak, M. (2011). Mindfulness-based transactional analysis. *Transactional Analysis Journal, 41*: 241–254.

CHAPTER NINE

Response to "Co-creative contributions"

Graeme Summers and Keith Tudor

Response to Laurie Hawkes' contribution—from Graeme

I enjoyed Laurie's different meanings for the term "co-creative". For her this can variously imply: a developmental competence, an improvised shared creation, a state of trust in emergent process, a professional identity, and a way of thinking.

The overarching theme, though, is one of associating co-creativity with improvisational (rather than formulaic) contact between two or more people. Drawing parallels between tango and psychotherapy she stresses the paradox that it is a deliberate, disciplined skill-based practice that enables improvisational "co-dancing". Here our hard-earned competence can both consciously and non-consciously inform and extend the range of co-creative possibilities.

Laurie's is a convincing and beautifully illustrated account of "co-creativity" applied to sophisticated novelty in a developmental context. Given Laurie's associations to co-creativity, her statement that "co-creation is a state to which [she] often aim[s], but which is not easily attained" (p. 159) makes sense. From this perspective "co-creation" could be considered as a state of "flow" that occurs within and between people most evident during peak experiences.

In contrast, however, Laurie's description highlights how I think differently about co-creativity. For me, the purpose of any theory is to guide attention to aspects of experience that might otherwise be overlooked. So when I think "co-creatively", I ask how the event or experience under consideration might be "co-created" and see what gets illuminated in the process. I therefore apply co-creative thinking to apparently formulaic patterns and not just to improvised novelty. For example, if we consider the situation of "one person creating and the other adapting to them" (p. 158) as a co-created event we might ask the following questions:

"How does each person maintain their role?"
"How does each person encourage the other to stay in role?"
"How do they each benefit from this pattern?"
"How might they help each other risk something different?"

Co-creative questions become more complex and more interesting once we implicate ourselves in the process—that is, when we consider ourselves not as impartial observers, but participant observers in similar patterns with our clients or others in our life space.

Laurie's informed focus on developmentally earned improvisational contact is refreshing and enriching and helps counterbalance the traditional overemphasis on pathology in transactional analysis literature. I also appreciate Laurie's reflections on her professional identity. Her preference to remain informed and inclusive about different approaches without fixing her identity to one in particular sounds healthy to me, as does her caution to use differential terms in the spirit of mutual enrichment rather than entrenching divisiveness.

Response to Laurie Hawkes' contribution—from Keith

I appreciate Laurie's response and the way she structures her creative contribution in terms of the three questions she poses. It reminded me that there is often, if not always, a structure to creativity and to creative expression, not least in dance—and in the dance of ideas.

When discussing how she situates herself in transactional analysis, Laurie uses the word "currents" as distinct from the usual word "tradition" or "approach"—the latter of which is now used in the context of the CTA oral exam (see, for example, Training and Certification Council of Transactional Analysis, 2004; European Association of Transactional Analysis, 2013). Her use of this word appears congruent with her own interest in movement and flow, and I also find it interesting in terms of how co-creative transactional analysis is viewed within transactional analysis. I know that Graeme and I have both resisted the idea that "co-creative" is, or should be, a "school" or even a "tradition", and we certainly would not seek to copyright the term or to restrict its use. Clearly, it is associated with and, in a number of ways, elaborates the constructivist tradition (see Tudor & Hobbes, 2007), and, in this sense I see it as reading or re-reading of transactional analysis. This was very much the spirit of our original analysis (Summers & Tudor, 2000), which was a deconstruction and reconstruction of the four building blocks of transactional analysis—that is, ego states, transaction, scripts, and games. In this sense I rather like Grégoire's (2007) identification of it as an "orientation". Whilst, at times, I have experienced this co-creative reading and, perhaps, project, as more of a tussle than a tango with transactional analysis, there is something that resonates for me in Laurie's image of dancing with a partner, in this case, a theoretical orientation I know well. Given my criticism of the infantilisation of trainees (Tudor, 2003, Chapter Two), and concerns about examining for conformity (see Cornell, 2000), I like the idea that transactional trainers and supervisors would encourage trainees and supervisors to "dance" with transactional analysis, and that examiners would enquire how candidates are "dancing" with transactional theory in their practice. Writing about "the dance of psychotherapy" and, specifically, person-centred therapy, Mearns (1994) suggested that this involves the therapist in a "following role" (p. 12). I recently edited for a professional journal an article written by a dance therapist. In working through the various drafts of the article (and there were many), we tussled; in the published version, the therapist/author was kind enough to acknowledge the work I had put into helping her to express herself in this written form. Following the publication she wrote to me: "This writing— I could not have done it without you. Now you need to learn how to dance" (J. de Leon, personal communication, 17 October, 2012). She had—and has—a point. Such reflections, associations, and challenges raise, at least, for me, the question of whether therapy is a science, as Freud intended psychoanalysis to become, and as Rogers in his early writings framed client-centred therapy, or an art, or, if we embrace this dialectic, both (see Hofmann & Weinberger, 2006; Schore, 2012).

The second point I want to respond to from Laurie's contribution is her wondering whether "one can be co-creative without a fair amount of experience" (p. 159). I think this is a particularly interesting point and one I hear a lot, especially when I teach the co-creative approach/perspective/current and do a demonstration. It seems that deconstruction, working relationally and (for myself) being at times quite minimalist in my interactions are all associated with a certain quantity of training and (postgraduate) level of learning; a certain length of experience, and a certain depth or intensity of self-knowledge. Whilst I appreciate these elements of training as a clinician (i.e., acquired knowledge, supervised practice, and personal psychotherapy), I do wonder if we can do more to acknowledge, support and draw out or educate (from the Latin, *educare*) the adult trainee/student's experience, "first nature" learning, and intuition, and, in these postmodern times, to teach the latest theory first rather than to teach theory—some of which is over fifty years old and outdated—simply because "it's there". I have, for instance, taught introductory TA 101s from a co-creative perspective, including introducing the two sets of structural ego state model (see Tudor, 2011b)—which the participants "got" immediately! In this sense I think we can dance, and encourage others at all levels of experience and knowledge to dance and to play with ideas.

Response to Marco Mazzetti's contribution—from Graeme

Reflecting on his cross-cultural work with a Bangladeshi man, Marco describes his differential application of the three principles of co-creative transactional analysis. He found that the first two principles, "we"ness and "shared responsibility", are helpful in negotiating a shared frame of reference between himself and clients from different cultures, whilst the last principle, "present-centred development" informs his development of treatment strategies.

Marco vividly describes his "cultural countertransference"—his rich set of expectations prior to meeting "Alì", which were thwarted in their first meeting. Marco's elaborate (and knowledgeable) cultural expectations were soon replaced with his dominant impression of "a sad man, with a very strange migratory story" (p. 163).

Marco frames the ensuing short therapeutic journey as the shared co-creation of their "micro-cultural environment", strongly influenced by their "common experience of growing up in an environment that we perceived as confined and scanty, and by our wishes to discover the vast world" (pp. 163–164).

Whilst Marco is describing building a sense of "we"ness based on common experience, I want to stress that "we"ness does not equate to sameness. For me, "we"ness is the complex constellation of sameness and difference that is co-created through interpersonal relationships. Whilst sameness can offer therapeutic "mirroring", difference can offer stimulation, challenge and learning through interaction with other-ness. Mutual confirmation can occur across difference as well as within sameness.

I used to run an exercise in training groups inviting people, in pairs, to identity similarities and differences with respect to age, gender, race, class etc. I would then ask "So what then is the potential in this particu-lar relationship to reinforce self-limiting beliefs or to create/reinforce self-enriching beliefs and how might you do this?"

Marco defines the outcome of his contact with Alì in terms of mutual transformation: "I gained insight into my life story, as he gained insight when I disclosed mine" (p. 164). This is a story of an intimate and unex-pected exchange that Marco admits later is not typical but nonetheless reminds him to be "open and free-minded" (p. 165).

On present-centred development Marco states "We didn't attack any pathological, scripty issues, but followed his physis in searching the healthy answers for his present life" (p. 164). This latter point is gratify-ing, and one which, here, builds on Laurie's focus that positive develop-ment is a significant area of investigation in its own right, implying that therapy is more than just the identification and fixing of pathology. This echoes Marco's earlier comment that "we discovered a second, hidden and unconscious plan: it happened that he talked to me about his col-lection of world maps he had when he was a child, and how much he dreamed about travelling and seeing the world" (pp. 163–164). It appears that here Marco is pointing to a physis-driven unconscious—perhaps, in our current terms, "non-conscious" life plan. In terms of co-creative transactional analysis this would constitute a positive variation of "script" and a manifestation of preconscious/non-conscious Adult.

Response to Marco Mazzetti's contribution—from Keith

I really appreciate Marco's application of the three principles we origi-nally identified as underpinning the co-creative approach. Whilst it's good and even flattering to know that people read what one writes, it's something else entirely—perhaps a bullseye transaction—when they find it useful to apply it to practice, and, moreover, that they write or are responsive to writing about it.[1] Marco's brief therapy with Alì is a poignant story of a therapeutic encounter that is clearly informed not only by the principles of co-creative transactional analysis but also by Marco's support for Alì's health (and in the sense of health as more than illness), including his reframing of some aspects of Alì's migratory story. This is consistent with that aspect or tradition of script theory, which suggests that a life script is always self-defining but not always self-limiting (see Cornell, 1988).

I think that one of the reasons that the co-creative approach is, as Marco acknowledges, "promising" with regard to the terrain of the cross-cultural encounter, is that it represents attitudes of mutuality, as distinct from equality or symmetry (see Aron, 1996); of openness (of being "free-minded", as Marco puts it) or non-defensiveness in response to the experience of other; as well as a certain humility about one's own frame of reference, especially when it is the dominant and/ or assumed one (see, for example, Naughton & Tudor, 2006). Mutuality is a word that Trudi picks up in her contribution to describe "the two-person shared experience of learning" (p. 172), which, I suggest, equally describes Marco's experience of his relationship with Alì. Such attitudes or qualities on the part of the therapist/facilitator—which we could and I would frame in terms of Rogers' (1957, 1959) therapeutic conditions (for the therapist) of contact, authenticity (congruence), respect (positive regard), and empathy (originally, empathic understanding)— facilitates the co-construction of the, or a, "common relational field" in cross-cultural encounters. I note that Marco does not say "equal" relational field (and I agree with him) as the structural position of local therapist–immigrant client is not an equal or symmetrical one—which is why I would take issue with Marco's ascribing of the therapist's expectations as "cultural countertransference", preferring to view this generally, and certainly before she or he meet the client, as the therapist's cultural transference.

I have two personal associations with Marco's contribution, as well as the image he offers us of his bedroom as a child; with walls covered in maps, as I, too, love maps and travelling.

My first association is that, between 1985 and 1987, when I was in my early thirties, I lived in Italy and, especially in the second year of my time there, learned not only Italian but also about being "lo straniero" (the foreigner), the other (Other). Whilst aspects of my experience and learning were painful, it gave me what Rogers (1951) referred to as "a broad experiential knowledge of the human being in [and out of] his cultural setting" (p. 437), knowledge and learning that has since stood me in good stead. Whilst living in Italy I also learned more about my own English culture—and, as I was teaching English as a foreign language, about English language and grammar. Since that experience I think and hope that I have been more "intentional" about culture—see Shweder (1990), and Ivey, Ivey and Simek-Morgan (1993)—and understanding that culture is a crucial aspect/whole of how we experience, construct and negotiate our worlds.

My second association is that, having immigrated to Aotearoa New Zealand, I, too, am an emigrant/immigrant, have my own migration (emigration/immigration) story, as do my family, and to some extent, am "other" in my adopted homeland. I say "to some extent", as being a white middle-class man with secure employment, I enjoy a certain ease in a country that, historically, was colonised by the British. This twists the concept and experience of "otherness" so that, for the most part, it is indigenous Māori, who have become "the other" in their own country. The founding document of this country is Te Tiriti o Waitangi | The Treaty of Waitangi (Te Tiriti) (see Waitangi Tribunal, 2013), which was signed by representatives of the British Crown and by a number of Māori chiefs. To a greater or lesser extent, Te Tiriti informs the relationship between Māori and tau iwi, literally, "the other tribe" and Pākehā, a term used predominantly to refer to New Zealanders of European descent, through legislation and public policy, as well as social and personal encounters. Interestingly—and significantly for our present discussion—one of the principles of Te Tiriti is that of partnership (Royal Commission on Social Policy, 1988), which, I suggest, provides a political background and framework for negotiating and co-constructing a common relational field in therapy, education, and organisations, and, at best, a society that honours the cultural worldview(s) of the other.

Response to Gregor Žvelc's contribution—from Graeme

Gregor offers an articulate reflection of what he means by relational and describes some of principles he applies through his mindfulness work. He links his thinking to some of our co-creative perspectives, with particular reference to ego states.

It is clear that we have much in common. Gregor's conceptual base is rooted in an understanding of the significant implicit influence of relational schemas on both healthy and problematic subjective experience and in this sense is highly consistent with our emphasis on co-creative personality and co-creative reality. Our work was strongly influenced by Daniel Stern, whose original notion of "Representations of Interactions that are Generalised" (RIGs) (Stern, 1985) appears to correlate with relational schemas. In addition, Gregor's distinction between adaptive and defensive schemas resonates with our emphasis on differentiating between Adult as healthy (adaptive) and Parent and Child as pathology (defensive) relational patterns.

This conceptualisation concurs with Little's (2006) idea, who, drawing on Erskine (1988) and Rubens (1994), suggested that Child–Parent ego state relational units represent archaic, fixated introjections that defensively split and therefore structure the personality in contrast to good enough experiences that become assimilated into Adult.

Gregor appears to bridge an appreciation of the implicit organisation of relational schemas with a mindfulness approach that emphasises healing through non-judgemental awareness. His proposition of the mindful Adult as a capacity of integrating Adult aligns well with Keith's focus on both the importance of consciousness and the importance of empathy.

I was particularly interested that Gregor stresses the value of intrapsychic as well as interpersonal relating. I agree. In fact I often represent this when coaching clients, in the following way:

Superimposing Figure 9.2 over Figure 9.1 provides a visual metaphor of the consequences of activating internal defences—that is, we bypass our inner resourcefulness and interrupt our creative and open contact with others as we get caught up in our intrapsychic aggressive/defensive loops. These diagrams are based on differentiating between healthy and defensive RIGs or, in Gregor's terms, relational schemas.

The challenge, of course, is how do we recover and/or develop our healthy self and other relating? Stern (2004) suggested that: "to narrativize can be seen as an almost non specific, convenient vehicle by which the patient and therapist 'do something together.' It is the doing-together that enriches experience and brings about change in ways-of-being-with-others" (p. 215). For me, this speaks to Gregor's interest in both being and doing, and perhaps the importance of "being with-whilst-doing" therapy or coaching in some plausible form.

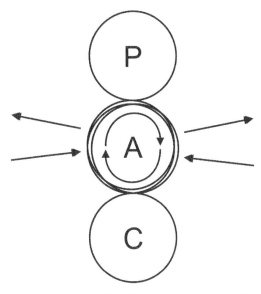

Figure 9.1. Healthy contact with self and openness to others via Adult.

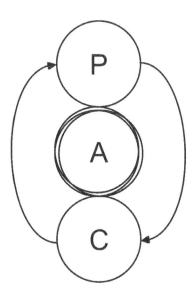

Figure 9.2. Defensive Parent–Child intrapsychic loop.

I concur with Gregor's assertion that learning to accept and tolerate internal experience is fundamental to growth, and that silence and space are important. Again, I am less sure about defining such growth as integration. I prefer to think of growth in terms of the co-existence of diverse and increasingly tolerable (positive and negative) human experience within ourselves and our relationships with others.

There is a clear coherence to Gregor's contribution, an internal consistency between his thinking, values and practice that stands out as a distinct and effective approach to expanding Adult capacity. In this sense he models the integration he seeks to promote, and I appreciate his interleaving of contemporary transactional analysis with his mindfulness approach to alleviating distress and promoting well-being.

Response to Gregor Žvelc's contribution—from Keith

I appreciate Gregor's work and, specifically, his contribution to the evolution of the concept of the integrating Adult, and so am particularly pleased that he has made a contribution to this book.

I like his use of the concept of "relational schemas" to acknowledge the implicit and the non-conscious aspect of the integrating Adult or neopsyche, and I particularly like the distinction he draws between adaptive and defensive schemas (Žvelc, 2010). Whilst I understand that the term "schema" is useful to describe a structure that gives meaning, similar to Stern's (1985) Representations of Interactions that are—or were—Generalised (RIGs), I prefer Stern's renaming of RIGs as "ways-of-being-with" (which he did in the second, revised edition of *The Interpersonal World of the Human Infant*, published in 1998), a preference born partly out of my association (though not Stern's) with Rogers' emphasis on a way of being (and the title of one of his last books—Rogers, 1980a), and partly out of my preference for the language of process as distinct from the language of structure.

I agree with Gregor's proposal that mindfulness is a key feature of the integrating Adult ego state (Žvelc, 2010; Žvelc, Černetič, & Košak, 2011), and of a mindful Adult (Žvelc, 2002, 2010) and its capacity for integration. Indeed, I would say that the way in which many authors and practitioners (such as Kabat-Zinn, 1994) describe mindfulness offers a language for describing the practitioner's attitude and process in helping the client to expand their integrating Adult, and to integrate implicit, non-verbal, non-conscious and unconscious material. I also agree that mindfulness "promotes natural healing of the organism," (p. 169)—and, given that I draw a lot on person-centred psychology, it's great to read someone else in transactional analysis refer to the organism! From what I have read of and about mindfulness, not least by Gregor, I think there is a real meeting between mindfulness and the person-centred approach—see Tophoff (2006), and Bazzano (2011).

I am less sure about the necessity of what Gregor refers to as a "third person" perspective. Whilst I have experience of being "in" (the) relationship with the client, supervisee, trainee, etc. and, at the same time, able to notice and reflect on what's happening in and to me, and between us (at least from my point of view)—that is, a mindful stance, I am less sure that I would or would want to describe this as a third person perspective, as I think this suggests that I—and, perhaps, I alone—have a perspective or (ad)vantage point that is somehow outside me (see also Helena's contribution to Chapter Eight and my response to this in this present chapter, pp. 198–200).

I perhaps resonate most with Gregor's point that "The therapist is not trying to change anything". This accords with my view of the role of the transactional analyst/therapist/facilitator being empathic—and mindful—with the client in the service of the client expanding their neopsychic/integrating Adult functioning, and working with their introjected (Parent) or fixated (Child) ego states (see Figure 6.1, p. 132 above). In my view of co-creative empathic transactional relating, it is important the therapist is working in the present (integrating Adult–integrating Adult relating), with no intention of offering an ulterior transaction, as described by Hargaden and Sills (2002).

Response to Trudi Newton's contribution—from Graeme

From an educational perspective, Trudi brings together the key ideas of empathy, mutuality and context to emphasise four guiding pointers to the co-creation of better learning systems and better societies. These are:

- That learning is rooted in experience and relationship;
- That the aim of learning is to enable autonomy, a wider frame of reference and interdependence through expansion of the Adult and empathic relating;

- That social and political context can be taken into account through adaptation or confrontation; and
- That individuals and communities can embrace transactional design.

It is this final point that echoes the title of Trudi's paper, highlighting the co-creative transactional analysis proposition that we might see ourselves as transactional designers as well as transactional analysts. I am grateful to Trudi for amplifying this idea because I think it is critical to the development of new possibilities; as de Bono (1992) put it: "With analysis we are interested in what is. With design we become interested in what could be" (p. 63).

Trudi mitigates the possibility of design being used as a form of oppression (i.e., in which I impose my design upon you) by setting this idea alongside mutuality and the radical educational philosophy of Paulo Friere. In hindsight, I remember that, prior to writing with Keith, Friere's work had been a significant influence in my thinking about psychotherapy. Friere's suggestion that "investigators and the people (who would normally be under investigation) should act as co-investigators" (Friere, 1970/1993, p. 87) resonated deeply—and still does. This appears to me to be the educational precursor to psychotherapeutic two-person psychology.

Friere is also distinctly humanistic, viewing oppressive patterns as dehumanising to both oppressor and oppressed, and sought to understand how such patterns can be reinforced or challenged through educational methodology. This perspective therefore equates genuine education (rather than indoctrination) with liberation, and balances critical consciousness with empathy—even for oppressors! I am delighted, therefore, to see Trudi represent this paradigm here with such clarity and make links between it and our co-creative project.

Trudi utilises a contemporary metaphor to signify either staying with the online "systems we create and the concepts they embody" or challenging them by "staying aware of the offline consequences" of meaningful human interaction.

I remember expressing some anxiety to a colleague as I was about to start training others in transactional analysis: "What if I have to teach material that I don't believe in?" He suggested that I might say: "You need to know this because it is on your syllabus. I don't agree with it and this is why. What do you think?" His words helped me remember that education is about facilitating interdependent thought and participation, not conformity, and continually to invite "offline" concerns and interests of trainees into play to shape our "online" content.

In my current coaching group work I make a point of proposing, rather than providing, learning structures, thus indicating my openness to counterproposals and co-created alternatives that work best for each group. I have also got into the habit of keeping my transactional analysis teaching slots very brief whilst emphasising the generative rather than prescriptive nature of the ideas. This way the transactional analysis theory remains in the background as a helpful framework that we can draw upon whilst the group members and our interactions together remain the central focus for our work.

I am grateful for Trudi's deeply considered thoughts and contribution to this "evaluation, reflection and exploration of possibilities" (p. 174) from an educational frame.

Response to Trudi Newton's contribution—from Keith

I, too, am grateful to Trudi for her contribution and, especially, for opening up the contextual, social and political dimension of co-creativity. Following the publication of our original article in 2000, I was curious that the re-reading of transactional analysis we offered and the principles and ideas we were—and are still—advancing seemed to "spark" more interest, at least, initially, amongst colleagues in the educational and organisational fields of application of transactional analysis than in the psychotherapy and counselling fields. Like Graeme, I, too, am delighted to see Paulo Freire (1921–1997), certainly one of my heroes, appear in these pages. I realise that, although I reference him quite a lot in my own work, it is mostly when I am writing about and within the person-centred approach, as distinct from transactional analysis.

In transactional analysis, at least in its psychotherapeutic application, there has, in my view, been too much emphasis on detection, as in "detecting driver behaviour" (see Stewart & Joines, 1987), which places the psychotherapist as expert on and over the client, and not enough emphasis on design—or co-design—which places the transactional therapist/educator/consultant as a partner (even with expertise) alongside the client. I think it is no accident that it is a colleague from the educational field, and one, moreover, who is influenced by progressive, humanistic and radical models or traditions of education (see Newton, 2003), who writes about design. I am reminded of another therapist and therapist educator, Carl Rogers (1902–1987), who, in an address to the American Psychological Association, offered some new challenges to the helping professions in the form of a series of questions that included the question: "Do we dare to be designers?" (Rogers, 1973, p. 381). As he articulated it then:

> Another great challenge of our times to the psychologist is to develop an approach which is focused on constructing the new, not repairing the old; which is designing a society in which problems will be less frequent, rather than putting poultices on those who have been crippled by social factors. The question is whether our group can develop a future-oriented, preventive approach, or whether it will forever be identified with a past-oriented remedial function. (p. 381)

Sadly, this and the other questions Rogers posed in this address/paper are still relevant today, although the good news is that they are still being read and reviewed (see House, Kalich, & Maidman, 2013; Tudor, 2013).

When teaching becomes facilitation; when learning involves students taking (more) responsibility and being involved in the design, process(es) and structure of their learning, including self- and peer assessment; when "teachers" and administrators share power, and we practice partnership and co-operation (for an account of which, see Embleton Tudor, Keemar, Tudor, Valentine, & Worrall, 2004), teachers, too, learn, and are affected by such praxis. In this context, I appreciate Trudi acknowledging the points we make about intersubjectivity ("and so may the therapist"—see Figure 6.1, p. 132 and 7.2, p. 151 above), and her drawing out the point about the impact of change or learning on the therapist and/or teacher/trainer.

Lastly, but not least, I very much appreciate how Trudi ends her contribution with her reflections on how the educational field and co-creative transactional analysis, in effect, *co-influence* each other. This is not only a specific example of mutuality with regard to this specific theory and practice, it is also a reminder that in all our fields of applications, and despite professional, political and personal differences, what transactional analysts have in common is transactional analysis.

Response to Helena Hargaden's contribution—from Graeme

Helena proposes that the psychoanalytic idea of the "third" has the potential to expand the theoretical range of co-creative transactional analysis and illustrates this with an intriguing case example. Among other descriptions she considers the "relational third" as a therapeutic interruption generated by the co-created relational unconscious enabling movement beyond "a stale impasse, into here and now Adult–Adult relatedness" (p. 178).

I am in agreement with Helena's proposition and the bridge it provides to this area of psychoanalytic thought, since she offers many parallels to co-creative transactional analysis.

First, she describes the therapeutic impasse as a "co-created dynamic" reflecting our proposition that: "the impasse that was originally co-created within a relationship is now co-maintained through transferential relating or co-resolved through Adult–Adult contact" (Summers & Tudor, 2000, present p. 12 see also Chapter Ten).

Second, the co-created relational unconscious tallies with our reference to the co-unconscious (Moreno, 1977), which fills a conceptual gap between the personal unconscious of Freud and the collective unconscious of Jung. Following my more recent work (Summers, 2011) I would now distinguish between the co-unconscious and the co-non-conscious and would consider the therapeutic co-created interruption (essentially the crossed transaction) to be a manifestation of the latter. What I find fascinating is that the therapeutic interruption could be considered here to be a constellation of events as distinct from a crisp intervention: the inappropriate behaviour of the man, Lily bringing her book into the discussion, and Helena's impatient question.

Third, the therapeutic thrust of the case example is represented by the movement away from a deadening transferential pattern to a more vitalising, improvisational aliveness that we would also promote and characterise as Adult.

When introducing the case, Helena expresses frustration that Lily was using the transactional analytic idea of rackets to pathologise her feelings and keep her distance, and felt irritable and angry in response to Lily's little girl persona. As the therapy unfolds therapist and client express frustration and anger with each other in different ways. Then, through the Anna Karenina story, Helena finds respect for the anti-hero/hero who "engage[s] honestly with his frustration" (p. 178).

Might this be part of unconscious (non-conscious) message from Lily to Helena that in some way predicts and affirms their journey together and awakens vitality in their contact? I don't think we can know the answer to this, but it is a plausible story that at least acknowledges the presence of curative dynamics beyond our conscious control. For me the retrospective speculation of how intrusions occur is less significant than the openness to the process as it unfolded, as ably demonstrated by Helena and her client, who made therapeutic use of the intrusions from outside and within the psychotherapy sessions.

The concept of the "third" may well prove a fruitful expansion of our theoretical range within co-creative transactional analysis, Helena's stimulating contribution being the first step.

Response to Helena Hargaden's contribution—from Keith

I have had the good fortune to have known Helena for over twenty-five years and I appreciate not only her friendship, but also her creative thinking and writing—which, of course, together constitute a "third" between us! Here, I take up Helen's invitation to reflect on the meaning of the "third" and how that links with co-creative transactional analysis.

In his original article on the subject, Ogden (1994) described the analytic third as "the intersubjectively-generated experience of the analytic pair" (p. 3). He described two clinical sequences in which the intersubjective experience created—or, more accurately, co-created—by the analytic pair became accessible through, in one instance, the analyst's experience of his own reveries and, in the other, by means of a somatic delusion. The (analytic) third, then, is a third subject, unconsciously co-created by the analyst and the analysand, which can take on a life of its own. In Ogden's original article, this is a purloined letter; in Helena's case vignette it is Tolstoy's *Anna Karenina*.

When I first read Helena's account of her work with "Lily", I immediately had another association with another Lily and another "third". The other Lily is a character in one of Bob Dylan's songs: "Lily, Rosemary and the Jack of Hearts" (Dylan, 1975); and the other third is Bob Dylan himself, whose music and poetry both Helena and I enjoy. The song has a complex plot involving the Jack of Hearts, the leader of a gang of bank robbers; Rosemary, the wife of "Big Jim"; Lily, Big Jim's mistress ("It was known all around that Lily had Big Jim's ring"); and Big Jim himself, the wealthiest person in the town ("he owned the town's only diamond mine"). The plot concerns a bank robbery, a murder (of Big Jim by Rosemary), and ends with a hanging (of Rosemary). The song, which has numerous references to card games, has been the subject of much interpretation, such as that it's an allegory about romantic facades that hide criminal motives—or, indeed, about criminal facades that hide romantic motives.

The point is that, just as there are many interpretations of a song or a story, there are many associations that can be made by both therapist and client—and, of course, by supervisor (another third), and, of course, a reader. Thus, I would suggest that in and outside this vignette there are a number of "thirds": Anna Karenina, Lily (the flower), Lily (of the West), Lily (of the Dylan song), and, perhaps, Bob Dylan himself.

As far as how the concept of the "third" links with co-creative trans-actional analysis, I have, perhaps unsurprisingly, three thoughts!

First, whilst acknowledging the importance of dis-integration (see discussion in Chapter Five), the concept of integration and integrating is still fairly central to a co-creative perspective on the Adult ego state. When I think about integration in the wider field of psychotherapy (as in psychotherapy integration or integrative psycho-therapy), I think of this as a meta activity, which requires knowledge of different (first-level) approaches *and* of a metatheoretical frame-work (see Tudor, 1996b). Such a framework both is, and represents, a third—that is, a third view by which at least two first-level views may be processed, assessed, and integrated. Similarly, as personal integra-tion or integrating requires a person to reflect on him or herself and on another or the other (person, people, or "the world"), this requires him or her to adopt or move to a third position, a process that is akin to the Hegelian dialectic method involving thesis–antithesis–synthesis, the last of which is a third thesis. One benefit of such a process is, as Klein (1960) observed: "Integration also has the effect of tolerance towards one's own impulses and therefore also towards other people's defects" (p. 241).

Second, and following on from this, as an approach to, or a read-ing of, transactional analysis in the constructivist tradition, co-creative transactional analysis offers a critique of the philosophy, theory and practice of tranactional analysis, especially in its more traditional forms and approaches. In our original critique (Summers & Tudor, 2000; Chapter One, as well as the work we have done since then), we have often taken an aspect of transactional analysis theory, compared or contrasted it with some other theory or tradition, and then developed something that we have named "co-creative". This, again, represents a "third" position.

Third, as co-creative transactional analysis is something that I and Graeme have developed, it is itself a third entity: of us but outside of or beyond us. It represents, of course, our individual and separate experiences, backgrounds, influences, views and emphases, but it is more than one plus one (equals two). As we have discussed, debated, and disagreed, as well as agreed about this material, one plus one has become three: we have co-created something that is genuinely a third entity, which is more and bigger than each and both of us.

Note

1. Lest the reader think that, with my reference to a bullseye transaction, I am mixing my ego state and transactional models (see Tudor, 2010b), I want to clarify that as there is only one centre on the dartboard and that only one dart can land in only one place at one time, we can reclaim the—or *a*—"bullseye transaction" as one that expands the integrating Adult (see Glossary).

CHAPTER TEN

Implications, developments, and possibilities

Graeme Summers and Keith Tudor

B y way of ending, though, of course, not concluding, this final chapter first discusses a number of implications and developments of our view(s) of co-creative transactional analysis with respect to language, impasses and impasse theory, power, games, and intuition. Some of these implications we thought about as we discussed and drafted our original article but, for various reasons, did not include; some implications we hinted at in our original and/or subsequent work; others we did not think about originally but have subsequently developed our ideas and perspectives through discussion and dialogue with colleagues over the years and, more recently and actively, with each other. Following discussion of these implications, we discuss "applications", both in terms of the four fields of transactional analysis, and of co-creative transactional analysis to group work. Finally, echoing the ending of our original article in which we posed a number of questions, we end this final chapter by posing some questions for future possibilities of co-creative transactional analysis.

Language

From our early discussions with each other about whether what we were proposing should be referred to as "co-created" or "co-creative" transactional analysis, we have paid close attention to language. Informed by constructivism and ideas about narrative and, of course, script theory, we hold the importance and significance of both what is said and how it is said, as well as what is not "said" but is communicated. Transactional analysis has always been interested in the "messages" people get, principally from parents and parent figures, and from these, what we internalise. The importance of language has been a strong aspect of co-creative transactional analysis from the outset of our original work (Summers & Tudor, 2000; Chapter One) in which we renamed the four fundamental elements of transactional analysis theory, and talked in terms of "relating" rather than "relationship"; through Keith's writing about metaphor (Tudor, 2013; Chapter Two); through Graeme's choice of the word "dynamic" in his work on ego states (Summers, 2011; Chapter Four); to our present dialogue, much of which begins with some attention to each other's use of language and the implications thereof; for example, using "expanding" instead of "decontamination", "unitary" to mean "not defensively split", and so on.

One of the things we have noticed in putting this book together is where we have retained words that have common currency and resonance in transactional analysis, such as ego states; where we have suggested the use of other words, such as (from Berne, 1961/1975a) the categories of psychic organs (neopsyche, archaeopsyche, and exteropsyche); where we have proposed new words or concepts, which are nonetheless familiar, such as the neo–archaeopsyche, two ego state model (Figures 3.1 and 3.2) or new, co-creative readings of old concepts; for example, the "bullseye transaction" (see Chapter Nine); and where we simply use a different language, specifically and consistently the language of health, possibilities, and design. Our choice of these options is quite strategic: sometimes, we use words and retain concepts to maintain a connection both with our audience and with the approach, to take people with us as we unfold and emerge our own thinking. This is based on a need or hunger to maintain contact with our reader/audience and, more widely, our community (theoretical, professional, and organisational), and for structure, through form and familiarity—perhaps as much for ourselves as the reader/audience. One example of this is our (general) retention of Parent and Child ego states when, arguably, the logic of our approach is to move to a two ego state model (see Chapter Three); another is our use of decontamination and deconfusion (which focuses on the Parent and Child) and, later, expansion and expanding (which focuses on the Adult). Our interest in the changing use of language led us, quite late on in our preparation of the manuscript of this book, to develop a Glossary.

We anticipate further developments in, and of, language that take the logic of what we have proposed from state(s) to process(es), from ego to psyche, from, as Cornell and Hargaden (2005) conceptualised it, transactions to relations, and from transactions and relations to transacting and relating; and further, perhaps, from ego to no ego, from self to no self, from script to no script (which is different from being script free).

Impasses and impasse theory across three domains of enquiry

In our original article (Summers & Tudor, 2000) we stated that we viewed impasse and impasse resolution primarily as relational phenomena. The theoretical development and distinction between intrapsychic and interpersonal impasses within transactional analysis literature has been clearly articulated by Cornell and Landaiche III (2006). In addition we propose here a further domain of enquiry within which impasses can be considered: the intersubjective impasse. Each domain refers to conflicts, which can become deadlocked. The intrapsychic, interpersonal and intersubjective domains each refer to conflicts within the person, conflicts between people, and conflicts between co-created fields of relating, respectively.

Using these distinctions it is clear that we highlight the interpersonal and intersubjective impasses, since our perspective emphasised—and still does—"that the impasse that was originally co-created within a relationship is now co-maintained through transferential relating or co-resolved through Adult–Adult contact" (p. 12). Here we describe the theoretical implications, which stem from our co-creative perspective to consider impasses within these three domains of enquiry.

Intrapsychic impasse

Our co-creative perspective on ego states has implications for our conceptualisation of intrapsychic impasses, which is represented in Figure 10.1.

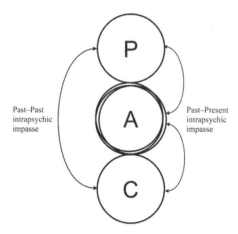

Figure 10.1. Intrapsychic impasses in co-creative transactional analysis.

Note that the Parent–Child Past–Past impasse (shown on the left hand side of Figure 10.1) represents intrapsychic conflict between introjected–archaic fixations. Little (2006) has incorporated Fairbairn's (1952) ideas to consider paired Child–Parent ego states as "relational units", which are created as defences against intolerable frustration and, yet, are also characterised by loyalty. From Fairbairn's (1952) perspective "the child internalized bad objects partly with a view to controlling them (an aggressive motive), but chiefly because he experienced a libidinal need of them" (p. 156). Building on Fairbairn's formulations, Little has stressed the importance of accounting for archaic Child loyalty to the introjected Parent, which can manifest as resistance to change. The Past–Past internal conflict between split parts of the ego is created and maintained to defend against "an intolerable situation of relational failure" (Little, 2006, p. 8).

By contrast, the intrapsychic conflict evoked by new relational possibilities is represented by the Parent–Adult/Child–Adult Past–Present impasse (shown on the right hand side of Figure 10.1). The conflicts represented by the Past–Present impasse is, therefore, between an archaic/introjected defensive probability and a present-centred possibility. The Past–Present intrapsychic impasse could be said to lie between the impulse to withdraw and the impulse to reach out. Following the logic of Little's proposition, however, that Child–Parent ego states are linked relational units, we would suggest that the presence of a Child–Adult impasse also implies the presence of a Parent–Adult impasse and vice versa. This is why we represent the complete Past–Present impasse (on the right hand side in Figure 10.1), which comprises both processes although at any given point in time one may appear more evident than the other.

In her contribution (in Chapter Eight), Helena Hargaden is focusing on the intrapsychic impasse when she evocatively describes her client: "Stuck in a crippling paralysis of internalised symbiotic relationships, Lily felt required to be compliant, adapted, and to repress her true experiences" (p. 177). Note that this first part of Helena's description emphasises a Past–Past impasse involving symbiotic internalised relationships, whilst the second part hints at a Past–Present impasse between feeling an archaic requirement to repress, and a present-centred desire to express, her true experiences.

Interpersonal impasse

As suggested in our original co-creative paper, the intrapsychic impasse described above may be viewed concurrently, if not primarily, as an interpersonal impasse that manifests between client and therapist. The interpersonal impasse can, therefore, be considered as the externalisation of the intrapsychic impasse as split off parts of the self are projected onto the other. In this way the internal conflict gets enacted in an external relationship. The dyadic interpersonal impasse is therefore characterised by two opposing positions, each represented by one person in the dyad.

The interpersonal Past–Past impasse is expressed and maintained *between* two people as each are relating from and projecting archaic/introjected ego states to influence (i.e., reinforce defences in) the other within the co-transferential psychological field. Figure 10.2 shows a Past–Past interpersonal impasse manifested between the Parent of one person and the Child of the other.

In Figure 10.2 we use curved arrows to represent the interpersonal impasse in order to differentiate from the parallel vectors of a parallel transaction. The shared co-transferential psychological field is represented by the dashed rectangle, which encompasses the archaic ego states and the relational "inbetween". (The diagrammatic overlap with

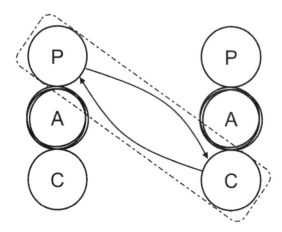

Figure 10.2. A Past–Past interpersonal impasse within the co-transferential psychological field.

Adult ego states is a non-intentional and non-significant consequence of this representation.)

For clarity we have chosen to represent the co-transferential psychological field as a Parent–Child dynamic. This is, however, a simplification used to illustrate the concept of a psychological field. The presence of Child dynamics usually implies the presence of an *internally* "influencing" Parent (see Berne, 1975a/1961) and, we think, that the presence of Parent dynamics will similarly imply *internally* "influencing" Child ego state processes. We consider that both overtly active and internally influencing introjected/archaic ego states will be shaping and, therefore, constituting the broader co-transferential psychological field. Once again, Helena's clinical case provides a good example. The interpersonal impasse is brought into focus when she describes the therapy as having become "polarised into a Parent–Child configuration" (p. 177).

An interpersonal Past–Present impasse could theoretically be located *between individuals* and represented by a series of crossed transactions whereby one person, most typically the therapist, aims to cross and interrupt the transferential stimulus of the other, most typically the client. The complication here is that a well-intentioned series of responses, designed to interrupt the transference, can reinforce the transference as the therapist unwittingly enters into the co-transference whilst believing they are grounded in Adult. This is why we originally suggested that "crossed transactions alone cannot support a sustainable form of relating. If the client is consistently relating transferentially, then it is often useful to assume that the therapist is in some way contributing to the transferential process" (p. 8). It is from this perspective that we propose, as before, that an apparent Past–Present interpersonal impasse between therapist and client will most probably be a disguised Past–Past interpersonal impasse.

The intersubjective impasse

The implication of acknowledging the existence and significance of these relational fields leads to a consideration of the impasse in a third domain. Here our enquiry moves beyond the individual and interpersonal into reflection upon the intersubjective, which we take to mean: "any psychological field formed by interacting worlds of experience, at whatever developmental level these worlds may be organized" (Stolorow & Atwood, 1992, p. 3).

An impasse created within the intersubjective domain represents the conflict created between two different psychological fields as distinct from a conflict manifest through polarised interpersonal stances. Little (2011) has proposed a variation on this perspective through his description of the impasse between the needed (or longed for) relationship and the repeated (or feared) relationship. Little has referred to this as the "relational impasse" (p. 30) and suggested that the therapeutically required relationship provides the context in which this impasse can be resolved.

In our formulation (Figure 10.3), however, we propose that relating can be distilled to two types, namely Adult–Adult relating and co-transferential relating, and that each are jointly created by client and therapist. Our interest here, therefore, is to represent these two psychological fields and the impasse between them. Using this level of enquiry we recognise that therapist and client can be mutually progressive as they build and deepen Adult–Adult contact. They will also at other times, and even to some extent simultaneously, be mutually regressive as therapist and client both engage defensive Parent or Child ego states. In our terms, we would consider regressive relating as co-transference.

We think that intersubjective enquiry complements rather than competes with enquiry at individual and interpersonal levels, and that

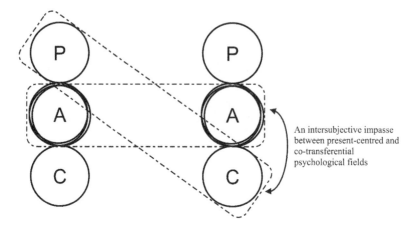

Figure 10.3. An intersubjective impasse.

all domains of enquiry might therefore be used to explore the same experience from different perspectives.

Somewhat synchronistically, we think that, once again, this concept is illustrated by Helena's reflections on her case: "The 'third' allowed the therapy to become more vital, when it had previously suffered from elements of deadness, to evolve, take on a more improvised feel; it became more possible to play around with ideas" (p. 178). Here Helena is describing "the therapy" in terms of changes in the quality of therapist–client interaction via the "third" and, in doing so, describes the movement from archaic deadness to improvisational play that we would conceptualise as a shift from the co-transferential to the present-centred psychological fields, respectively.

Eusden (2011) has used the metaphor of "one foot in, one foot out" (p. 106) to refer to the "capacity to reflect on the intrapsychic and inter-personal dance of therapy" (p. 106), which we understand as develop-ing reflective awareness and curiosity about our engagement in both here-and-now and co-transferential psychological fields. This is consist-ent with our original suggestion that:

> This duality of relating enables transferential phenomena to be experienced, compassionately identified and contained in the rela-tionship. Integration then occurs as the client gradually embodies and re-owns previously fixated aspects of his or her experience in

the context of freshly co-created support that was originally absent in childhood. (p. 14)

An impasse within the intersubjective domain may reflect *shared* ambivalence about relating, albeit expressed from different perspectives. As a client, do I stay loyal to my predictably unsatisfying introjects or do I risk reaching for increased need fulfilment along with the inevitable disappointments and frustrations that more open relating might offer? Will I risk feeling hurt (again) in order to know others and be known more deeply? As a therapist, will I relinquish the comfort of, as Hirsch (2008) has put it: "coasting in the countertransference?" in order to make more risky and potentially more fruitful interventions? In considering the ethical challenges of this two-person approach, Eusden (2011) asked: "How do we engage in risks with our clients, minding the gap between danger and inertia?" (p. 111), and suggested that: "Whatever we do, however we find ourselves relating with our clients, requires rigorous consideration and minding" (p. 111).

Even though we may expect ruptures to occur they can still take us by surprise. As we notice that the flow of interaction between us develops an aggressive or defensive tone, we might ask, "It was going so well; what happened?" Rigorous consideration challenges us to generate and explore a range of hypotheses, which provides a variety of lenses through which we can reflect. Was our experience of "going so well" a defensive collusion, a flight into health, repressing unwanted anger, vulnerability, difference, or disturbance—that is, were we engaging in Parent–Child dynamics under the guise of Adult–Adult contact? Did the positive flow stimulate fear of loss, engulfment, abandonment, or grief? Is the rupture a call to deeper engagement or a defensive deflection from novel and intolerable satisfaction or intimacy?

These and other questions we ask will be shaped by our theoretical orientation, current interests, and probably a whole range of unconscious and non-conscious influences. Of course, we can't know the answers for certain, or even if we are asking the right questions, but that is not the point. The point is to stay curious and engaged, utilising our self-support and professional networks for help and guidance to make use of the experience, to minimise harm, and to make a positive difference to our clients. This, in turn, involves developing our understanding and ability to explore and help, where possible, to resolve the impasses that we may variously conceptualise as residing within ourselves, within our interpersonal relationships, and/or between the relational fields we inhabit.

We end our theoretical reflections on impasses with a an acknowledgement and a reminder that we are interested in transactional design and not just analysis; as Petriglieri (2007) put it: "I shall look at impasses from a progressive, rather than from a regressive standpoint, asking the question 'Where is this leading?' rather than 'Where is this coming from?'" (p. 187).

Power

Since, in our frame, Parent and Child are defensive ego states, power dynamics between two people can be most simply expressed as a Parent–Child parallel transaction. This would represent a power over–power under dynamic in which the person in the oppressed, powerless Child position is, at worst, so oppressed, mystified and isolated that they have little or no power to resist or break free of the specific situation and/or dynamic; in other situations and dynamics they may *in some way* be colluding with it or them. In contrast, the Adult–Adult parallel transaction represents a "power with" interaction or psychological field. The horizontal vectors within the Adult–Adult parallel transaction then also resemble the mathematical equals sign, in this case symbolising equality of respect within the interaction even if there is a status differential between the dyad.

In our original article we proposed a co-creative script matrix, which amongst other changes proposed a horizontal diagram (see Figure 1.3, p. 23). At the time we acknowledged that: "Our horizontal diagram does not represent equality of power in parent–child relationships. It is intended to emphasise our ongoing capacity to influence and be influenced" (p. 23). Interestingly, this was one of Claude Steiner's criticisms in his discussions with Keith in 2008 (see Chapter Five): that, unlike his original script matrix (Steiner, 1966), which in its placement of the child below the parents offered a powerful visual representation of the power differential in such relationships, our co-creative script matrix did not show the power relationship. We think he has a point and our response is reflected in Figure 10.4.

It is important to note that the subject is not neutral. The example above might best represent power dynamics when the subject is female.

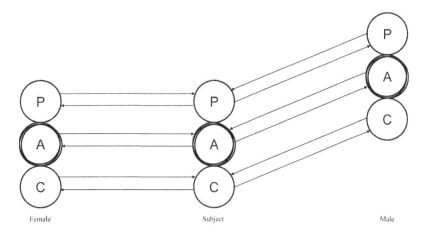

Figure 10.4. A co-creative script matrix (representing a power dynamic with regard to one polarity of influence).

Taking the identity of the subject into account with reference to a variety of polarities on continua under consideration is obviously significant. This visual metaphor could be developed to represent a matrix of constructs linked to our social and political identities, rather like the script helix, which also indicate power imbalance.

The prefix "co" (originally from the Latin) encompasses a number of meanings:

1. Together, mutually, and jointly, as in co-operant, co-operative, co-ordinate
2. Partner, as in co-habitee, co-operator, *or* subordinate, as in co-dependent
3. To the same degree, as in co-habit
4. (Mathematics) Of the opposite, as in cosine.

Thus, whilst the first meaning carries the sense of mutuality, this does not imply equality, let alone equity. When we discussed the principles of co-creative transactional analysis in our original publication (Summers & Tudor, 2000), we made the point that "shared responsibility" did not necessarily mean equal responsibility. In relation to this present discussion about power, we want to emphasise this point as we would not want "co-creativity" to be used as way to blame or allocate equal responsibility to those who are genuine victims of oppression, violence, and abuse. This is why when we talk about a "power over–power under" dynamic (as above) we talk first about oppression and in doing so refer to the radical psychiatry tradition of transactional analysis, which has contributed to our understanding of alienation, oppression, power, mystification, competition and co-operation by means of the stroke economy, the Pig Parent, powerless scripts, and an analysis of power—see Agel (1971), Steiner et al. (1975), Wyckoff (1976), Steiner (1981, 2000), and Roy and Steiner (1988). Thus, we would not see child abuse as co-created; however provocative the child and however damaged or disturbed the parent or adult, we would see it as a form of oppression whereby the adult is using their physical and/or psychological power over the child. The devastating impact of child abuse is well known; in working with victims or survivors of such abuse, from a co-creative perspective we would, first, be concerned about their current support systems and networks, including that these systems and networks supported their therapy; and second, be picking up and considering how the survivor presently co-creates with others—including the therapist—healthy or unhealthy patterns of relating. It is the therapist's professional responsibility to attend to the nature and significance of emergent patterns between her or himself and her or his client, including subtle symbolic re-enactments of abusive experience. The therapist's challenge is, therefore, to mind the therapeutic process: navigating the potential to be intrusive, neglectful, or disempowering. How we frame the emergent abusive patterns is critical. An oppressive frame would suggest the client is *inviting* abuse (and therefore deserves it). An anti-oppressive and therapeutic frame would regard the client as *communicating* disturbance, which requires a respectful and skilful response. Thus, a child does not share responsibility for being abused. The psychological fields within which the survivor can recover, survive and grow are co-created within the therapeutic relationship and the broader support networks of both client and therapist. In this regard, we find Aron's (1996) work on mutuality and asymmetry as useful in acknowledging that relationships that are mutual or mutually influencing are not necessarily symmetrical.

We also recognise that oppression takes many forms in adulthood. Accounting for the impact of oppression on our social identities along with the relatively high or low cultural value that is implicitly assigned is an important Adult capacity. A critical question here is: "How can the concepts of mutuality, co-creativity and shared responsibility address and change oppressive dynamics rather than perpetuate, rationalise or reinforce them?" In posing this question we recognise that these concepts, like any other, can be used badly or used well. In relation to class, for example, Freire (1970/1972) described how the concept of responsibility can be utilised from an oppressive perspective:

> For them, having more is an inalienable right, a right they acquired through their own "effort", with their "courage to take risks". If others do not have more, it is because they are incompetent and lazy, and worst of all is their unjustifiable ingratitude towards the "generous gestures" of the dominant class. (p. 41)

Here the "generous gestures" represent tokenistic displays of help, which do not address the fundamental inequality, which, when spurned, justifies continued deprivation of the other and over-entitlement of the self. We call this a negative game of "You get what you deserve"— a combined variation of "After all I've done for you" and "Now I've got you" (Berne, 1964/1968a).

In contrast, Friere made many references to shared responsibility as an essential principle of authentic education in which "The teacher is no longer merely the-one-who-teaches, but one who is himself taught in dialogue with the students, who in turn while being taught also teach. They become jointly responsible for a process in which all grow" (Freire, 1970/1972, p. 61). He further stated that, in order for this to work, "authority must be on the side of freedom, not against it" (p. 61). Again, we thank Trudi Newton (see Chapter Eight) for bringing Friere's work, which has relevance across many spheres of human interaction, into our present awareness and consideration of power dynamics.

Psychological games/Co-creative confirmations/Medium of co-regulation

In our original article we acknowledged and elaborated Berne's concept of a positive game. We proposed that James' (1973) game plan could be applied to positive or negative patterns of interaction, leading to "confirmations" of identity. "Games", however, are significant not simply in their outcomes and degree, but also in their process. Indeed, Berne (1964/1968a) chose the metaphor of children's games to describe these psychological patterns precisely because he recognised that: "The essential characteristic of human play is not that the emotions are spurious, but that they are regulated" (p. 18). Games are not only a means by which we confirm positive or negative beliefs about ourselves, they are also the medium through which we co-regulate emotions, and, thus, may be thought of, beyond confirmation(s), as a psychological medium of co-regulation. Within our framework, therefore, we consider negative games to be defensive attempts to regulate emotions, whilst positive games are the medium through which we effectively express and co-regulate our emotional experience with other people. For an historical summary of game theory with regard to positive, negative and what we refer to as "neutral" theory, see Table 10.1.

Table 10.1. Game theory analysed.

Negative game theories	Neutral game theory	Positive game theories
	A game as "an ongoing series of complementary ulterior transactions progressing to a well-defined, predictable outcome." (Berne, 1964/1968a, p. 44)	"The essential characteristic of human play is not that the emotions are spurious, but that they are regulated." (Berne, 1964/1968a, p. 18)
Psychological games (Berne, 1964/1968a)		A good game: "one whose social contribution outweighs the complexity of its motivations … one which contributes to the well-being of the other players and to the unfolding of the one who is 'it'." (Berne, 1964/1968a, p. 186)
Degrees of games (Berne, 1968)		

(*Continued*)

Table 10.1. Continued.

Negative game theories	Neutral game theory	Positive game theories
Drama triangle (Karpman, 1968)		
Formula G (Berne, 1972/1975b)		
		Game plan (James, 1973)
Goulding-Kupfer game diagram (Goulding & Gouding, 1979)		
Bystander role (Clarkson, 1987)		
		The winner's triangle (Choy, 1990)
	Games as co-creative confirmations (Summers & Tudor, 2000)	
	"Games are repetitive patterns of interaction that lead to negative or positive outcomes depending on the implicit and explicit exchanges between people." (Jackson & Summers, 2010, p. 2)	
	Game(s) as a medium of co-regulation (this present work)	

Intuition

With the benefit of having developed, played and, at times, tussled with co-creativity—and with each other—over fifteen years, one aspect of putting together this book we have most enjoyed is the time and space we have taken to draw out and develop some of the more subtle aspects of the co-creative approach, particularly with regard to implicit and tacit knowing, and to the unconscious, non-conscious—and even the preconscious, notwithstanding Keith's reservations about this as a concept (see Chapter Five). In our original article (Summers & Tudor, 2000), we, and in his work on the neopsyche (Tudor, 2003, Chapter Two), Keith, referred briefly to Berne's (1977a) and Schmid's (1991) work on intuition. Here, as we near the end of this work, we return to the subject of intuition, which was the focus of Berne's early research, and which was central to the development of transactional analysis itself (Berne, 1949/1977c).

Philosophers down the ages have addressed the subject and question of intuition. In the Western tradition Pythagoras (c. 570–c. 495 Before Common Era (BCE)) suggested that numbers existed in intuitive realms, Plato (c. 428–c.348 BCE) founded a school of idealism, which rested on intuitive knowledge; and others, including Aristotle (384–322 BCE), Plotinus (204–270 CE), Augustine (354–430) and Thomas Aquinas (1225–1274) all (variously) talked about forms of knowledge obtained without or beyond rational processes. More recently, Immanuel Kant (1724–1804) proposed that intuition was the non-rational recognition of an object, and Henri Bergson (1859–1941), on the basis that, whilst the intellect can analyse a person, situation, or event, it can never completely know it, argued that complete knowledge can only be obtained by intuition. Carl Jung (1875–1961) identified intuition or intuiting as one of four cognitive or mental functions (the others being thinking, feeling, and sensing).

This was the intellectual background against which Berne, as a young medical doctor and psychiatrist in the US Army (1943–1946), had the job of assessing young men for military service and on discharge. He realised that he was able to guess with some accuracy the men's occupations; he became curious about this, and began studying intuition. In his first paper on intuition, Berne (1949/1977c) talked in terms of "reflex imitation" and thinking "with our muscles" as a method of judgement that he called "thinking through subjective experience" (Berne, 1949/1977c), judgements that Cornell and Landaiche III (2008) liken to somatic resonance and countertransference. We would add that thinking through subjective experience sounds like the basis of intersubjectivity. In a later paper Berne (1955/1977b) defined intuition as: "the automatic processing of sensory perceptions" (p. 95).

Intuition may be thought of, in Bollas' (1987) phrase, as "the unthought known" (p. 277)—in their article on "Non conscious processes and self-development" Cornell and Landaiche III (2008) make this point and make useful connections between the work of Berne and of Bollas. Developing the implied taxonomy in Bollas' phrase, we suggest that intuition may also usefully be thought of as: the thought unknown—that is, those vague "thoughts", feelings or hunches we have that inform our work; and the unthought unknown—that is, our reflexes, "gut feelings", visceral sensations and so on, which we would conceptualise as either somatic present-centred relating or somatic co-transferential relating.

Interestingly, Berne (1962/1977d) considered intuition to be "an archeopsychic phenomenon", which is the origin of, and rational for, the intuitive "Little Professor" being the Adult in the Child (A_1). However, as Cornell and Landaiche III (2008) have pointed out, "in his early writings, Berne did not consider intuitive, nonconscious decision making to be necessarily problematic" (p. 203)—which is why we consider intuition as an aspect of the neopsyche (see Chapter Two).

In his early work, Berne (1949/1977c) not only defined intuition—as "knowledge based on experience and acquired through sensory contact with the subject" (p. 4)—he also described the process for the person being intuitive (the "intuitor") "without … being able to formulate to himself or others exactly how he came to his conclusion … It is [therefore] knowledge acquired by means of preverbal unconscious or preconscious functions" (p. 4). Later on in the same article he suggested that the intuitive function is: "part of a series of perceptive processes which work above and below the level of consciousness in an apparently integrated fashion, with shifting emphasis according to special conditions" (p. 30). Thus Berne viewed intuition and intuiting as operating at/in all levels of consciousness. Such sensing, judging, processing and functioning is, of course, fine-tuned by experience and training. Commenting on Berne's work on intuition, Schmid (1984) suggested that: "When therapists are trained to use a particular vocabulary and theory, their intuition makes more and more use of theoretical concepts, technical jargon and symbolic schemes, enabling them to place the observed phenomena in a particular frame" (p. 64). This also echoes the etymology of the word, from the Latin *intuitio*, meaning a looking at, consideration.

Clearly, Berne viewed intuition as important to the work of the therapist; and we think that his work on this supports our own views about the value of implicit and tacit knowing that cannot be accessed by analysis alone.

Applications

Whilst, in some ways, the development of co-creative transactional analysis was informed primarily by our experiences as psychotherapists, it was also informed by our experience as trainees (i.e., in education); our experience in and of other theoretical approaches (specifically the person-centred approach and gestalt psychology); our interest in social context (encompassing social work, social psychology, field theory, politics, and social constructivism); and our interest in critical theory. In that sense, unlike some other traditions in transactional analysis; for instance, the Cathexis tradition, which was originally exclusively concerned with therapeutic work in therapeutic communities, co-creative transactional analysis was and is not field-specific. Its principles and its analysis are applicable across all fields of application. We acknowledge that there are differences between each of the four fields and that exponents in these fields will understand and apply different aspects of co-creative transactional analysis in different ways, and, indeed, we are both heartened and humbled that it has been cited and developed by practitioners in all fields: in the clinical field—that is, counselling and psychotherapy, by Hawkes (2003), and Widdowson (2008), as well as Hawkes, Mazzetti and Hargaden in Chapter Eight; in the educational field, by Newton (2003), and Newton and Wong (2003), as well as Newton in Chapter Eight; and in the organisational field by Mountain and Davidson (2005); as well as by colleagues developing theory— Grégoire (2004, 2007), van Beekum (2005, 2006, 2009), Newton (2007), Erskine (2009), and Napper (2009); discussing supervision across all fields (Chandran, 2007; Newton & Napper, 2007); writing about groups (van Beekum & Laverty, 2007); and commenting about the social world (Allen, 2006; Newton, 2007, as well as Mazzetti in Chapter Eight).

Given our own experience and critique of psychotherapy training, we are particularly pleased that co-creative transactional analysis, with its emphasis on Adult–Adult relating, expansiveness, creativity, and possibilities, is having an impact in the postgraduate education and "training" of the next generation of transactional analysts.

There is one other "application", which we want to mention briefly, that is a different form of or forum for work—that is, group work.

Group work

We see great potential for the co-creative approach to groups and working with and through groups. Each of us was drawn to transactional analysis partly because it was presented as a *group* therapy, and we had considerable experience of being clients in therapy groups as well as running groups—which was probably more true for practitioners in the early/mid 1980s than it is nowadays. One advantage of working with individuals in groups, and especially if the therapist/facilitator/conductor/consultant works with a group *as a group*, is that it supports them as group/social beings as a part of something rather apart from it—whether the group, their family, tribe, community, or, ultimately, society. Another advantage of working with individuals in and through the group is that the therapist sees them in a social context, one that provides more opportunities for more transactions and more analysis of transactions (than with one-to-one therapy), as well as greater opportunities for both rupture and repair: more possibility for enactment and more possibility for—well, more and different possibilities. In this sense, the group may be viewed as a container, matrix or temenos (space) for co-creativity; indeed, eight out of the twelve therapeutic factors identified by Yalom (1995) are, in effect, co-created, and rely on co-creativity.

- Universality—the idea that we are not unique, alone or isolated in our "wretchedness", which, by definition, depends on another or others.
- Altruism—the concept that people also receive through giving support, reassurance, suggestions, insight, etc., which, again, depends on others.
- The corrective recapitulation of the primary family group—for which the group provides possibilities that individual therapy does not.
- The development of socialising techniques—which also involves others, not least on which and with whom to practice.
- Imitative behavior—which, as with socialising techniques, may be integrated from the environment (see Berne, 1961/1975a, and Chapter Two), and which may be introjected; either way, this can be more effectively processed in a group.

- Interpersonal learning—which, according to Yalom, is gained primarily through transference and insight, to which we would add present-centred and co-transferential relating and learning.
- Group cohesiveness—which, according to Yalom, *"must encompass the patient's relationship ... to the other group members and to the group as a whole"* (p. 48, original emphasis), which, by definition, can only be experienced and explored in a group.
- Existential factors—including responsibility and contingency, to which we would add belonging, community, merger, submission, and much more; interestingly, the majority of the existential factors that Yalom identified were concerned with the individual (isolation, mortality, etc.), which reflects the inherent narcissism of existentialism, at least in its Western, modernist form, for critique of which see Loewenthal (2011).

In terms of methodology, we consider that the co-creative approach is particularly suitable to working *with, through* and even with individuals *in* groups. For example, if we think about the principles of co-creativity (see Chapter One), especially those of "we"ness and of shared responsibility, but also that of present-centred development, then groups are the ideal place and space for working co-creatively and for fostering and facilitating the co-creativity of others (see Giesekus & Mente, 1986).

Some years ago, as part of the background work for a book he wrote on groups (Tudor, 1999a), Keith conducted some research based on Yalom's own research on therapeutic factors, using a Q-sort method of sixty items clustered into twelve groups of therapeutic factors (see above). In Yalom's study (Yalom, Tinklenberg, & Gilula, 1968) seven out of the first eight ranked items represented some form of catharsis or of insight. Keith's own research into one ongoing weekly group (which ran for some seven years), comprising eight members, found that five out of the first six ranked items concerned group cohesion and interpersonal learning. To some or even a great extent, these different findings reflect the different aims of the relative group and, no doubt, the different styles of the group facilitators. As Yalom (1995) himself observed:

> these research findings pertain to a specific kind of therapy group:
> an interactionally based group with the ambitious goals of symptom relief and behavioral and characterological change. Other

groups with different goals may capitalize on a different set of therapeutic factors. (p. 80)

Whilst we have not written more (than this) about the co-creative approach to therapeutic groups, we anticipate more could be done, said and, hopefully, researched and written about this application of the approach.

Possibilities

Co-creative transactional analysis is a transactional analysis of relational possibilities; of a moving and expanding neopsyche; of a developing personality co-created by and through relationships and discourse; of a changing personal, social and cultural identity, which we can define and redefine; of transactional patterns, which we can use to confirm healthy and enhancing senses of self and to regulate ourselves and others. It is a transactional analysis in all fields of application that acknowledges and works through the limitations of the past and the present to enhance people's present to ensure their futures. In short, it is a transactional analysis of possibilities, about which we offer the following questions—as much for ourselves as the reader.

- What words do you use to describe how open you are to experience and your experiencing of life?
- What words do you use to describe fixed patterns that you and/or others use?
- What questions might be implied and generated by viewing transactional analysis from this co-creative perspective?
- What further questions do you have when you think about transactional analysis and/or your own work and life from a co-creative perspective?
- What aspects of transactional analysis or your work do you consider are not amenable or compatible to a co-creative approach or "reading"?
- What would you consider as the next development in co-creative transactional analysis?
- What's the next development in your own co-creativity?

AFTERWORD

Graeme Summers

As this book draws to a close I feel both appreciative and relieved. Playing with ideas has always been a source of pleasure for me, expressed mostly through reading, conversation and, in various forms, teaching. I am, however, much more ambivalent about writing. With some degree of predictability, I have often found my creative flow interspersed with frustrated attempts to find the right, or even approximately right, words. So I am both proud and relieved to be sharing my concluding thoughts. I am also deeply appreciative of everyone who has been directly and indirectly involved in bringing this project to fruition.

For me transactional analysis is not just a theory, it is also a community, which I have now been part of for over thirty years. In that time, conferences, training and supervision networks, professional examinations, committees, peer groups and publications have all provided touch points for people to connect, influence and witness each other as colleagues and often as friends. This has been, and still is, important to me.

In recent years the International Association of Relational Transactional Analysis has hosted twice yearly online colloquia. These have been professional forums consisting of: a presented paper, international panelists, and discussions mediated by email. This virtual "meeting place" has provided a format that lies somewhere between informal emails and published articles, and is one in which participants encourage each other to share, discuss and test ideas. As discussed above, this forum helped me test out my thinking that led to the "Dynamic Ego States" paper (Summers, 2011, Chapter Four).

The intersubjective theme of "ongoing mutual influence" is core to our original reformulation of transactional analysis concepts. I wonder if this focus emerged, in part, because of how I experience my professional community. Of course, I don't know if this is true, but it's another plausible hypothesis that resonates with me.

The models presented in this book, developed with Keith, are my internal guides imbued and informed by many experiences and influences. If I explicitly share any of these models with clients then I usually present the core idea within a few minutes. This accessible "front end" of this theory (see Appendix One) can then become a shared resource to which the client and I refer as needed.

In addition to recognising and building upon Adult strengths, clients often gain insight into problematic patterns, identifying defensive reactions in themselves or others. I aim to create a relational context in which we can be non-defensive about our defences so that, where possible, they can be compassionately acknowledged and reflected upon rather than reinforced. Paradoxically, being open about defences builds trust, which often leads to deeply intimate coaching conversations even within very formal organisational settings.

This is not however as easy as it sounds. I remember one encounter in particular.

CLIENT: I get feedback that I am not empathic but I don't know why people see me that way.

COACH: Do you want some feedback from me?

CLIENT: OK.

COACH: You arrived late. Then you left for a while because you had forgotten something. Then, back in the group, you were looking at your Blackberry [phone] when someone else was talking. These behaviours could give the impression that you don't care about others.

We held eye contact in tense silence for a few seconds (that felt like minutes) until he relaxed his posture and nodded respectfully. At our next meeting he arrived early and, with a beaming smile, shook my hand. We both laughed knowingly together.

I, therefore, use psychological theory in two ways: 1. as an internal framework for making meaning and considering how to intervene; and 2. as a shareable resource with coaching clients. Transactional analysis theory has proven extremely valuable for both of these purposes. For my part, our co-creative interpretation, articulated in this book, reflects my need to update transactional analysis constructs in order to account for my personal and professional experiences and my reading about developments in related disciplines. It, therefore, represents my own ongoing need to find and make meaning and is not intended to be either definitive or conclusive. Hollis (2009) has stated:

> Yes, there are multitudes of people running around shouting the Truth, that is, their fractal purchase on subjective prejudice, but their agitation betrays an old confession that fervor is a defense against doubt, and doubt is experienced as an enemy to be suppressed. (p. xiv)

I, too, am passionate about theory, which I think is important because the theories we explicitly and implicitly employ shape our perceptions and how we relate. However, our theory is just a plausible story that seems to make sense to me/us at this point in time and is open to refinement or revision over time. I think passion and doubt can and should co-exist.

Thank you, the reader, for your interest in my/our perspectives. I hope that, at least in some ways, they resonate meaningfully with some of your own.

AFTERWORD

Keith Tudor

Past present

Putting together, editing and writing this book with Graeme has been a thoroughly enjoyable project for me, and, as it has entailed reviewing and revising previously published material and revisiting with each other some of our own history as well as the history of co-creative transactional analysis, and presenting, re-presenting and representing our work to others and taking it forward; as such it has also had something of a "back to the future" feel to it. I have also enjoyed the opportunity the book has created for me to identify with this approach and to present this material in my new homeland of Aotearoa New Zealand. In terms of making this a coherent book, I am also pleased that we have made and taken the opportunity, as it were, to push the "Refresh" button on the previously published material by revising the four original co-creative papers, as well as developing and inviting new material. In the same spirit, it seems appropriate to return to the first word, foreword, or, in this case, my Introduction, to consider whether this book has fulfilled its aims with regard to addressing some of the concerns that I had about transactional analysis.

- *With regard to some of the language and ideas of transactional analysis*

    I think that co-creative transactional analysis, as an approach to, or reading of, transactional analysis has updated both the language and some of the key concepts of transactional analysis and, in doing so, has developed and continues to propose a language of process, of the present, of wholes and holism, of integration, and of possibility.

- *With regard to jargon*

    I think, for the most part, that we have avoided jargon, although I accept that, for some, the language of process, for example, "co-creative transferential relating" might appear a bit of a mouthful. On the whole, however, I think that our attention to the meaning and the implications of the use of language is helpful, especially in making the constructivist point that language and discourse creates systems. I look forward to further work on this in the tradition and spirit of deconstruction, reconstruction and, of course, co-construction.

- *With regard to a more psychological and relational dynamic*

    Co-creative transactional analysis has certainly contributed to the "relational turn" in transactional analysis, and specifically with regard to a different way of understanding the therapeutic relationship and the impact of past- and present-centred "ways-of-being-with". I have particularly appreciated Graeme's input, our dialogue on the unconscious and the non-conscious (if not the preconscious!), as well as Helena's contribution of the analytic third to co-creative transactional analysis, which I consider to be a rich one, and one worthy of further development.

- *With regard to exploring multiple and constructed meanings (as distinct from simply naming things)*

    With its roots in social constructivism, co-creative transactional analysis represents, as it were, the psychological wing or manifestation of this sociological theory, and, as such, represents the subjectivist approach to social and psychological science with its nominalist ontology, voluntaristic views of human nature, anti-positivist epistemology, ideographic methodology and, by and large, its qualitative methods (see Burrell & Morgan, 1979).

- *With regard to the impact of the social/political world on clients*

    As we draw on *social* constructivism and on field theory, co-creative transactional analysis is highly contextual and, in its practice, accounts for context more than most other schools, traditions or approaches within transactional analysis. As someone who is culturally intentional, interested in, and, I hope, sensitive to questions and issues of culture, I appreciate Marco's contribution, applying co-creativity to working cross-culturally. In my own context of living in a country that is based on a bicultural relationship between Māori and non-Māori (see the Waitangi Tribunal, 2013) and that is grappling with diversity within the Māori world and multiculturalism within the non-Māori world, as well as different responses to biculturalism (on the negative spectrum, from ignorance, through apathy, ambivalence, and avoidance, to outright hostility), I anticipate that one of my own developments will be to consider how co-creativity can inform cultural relationships that are also impacted by asymmetrical power dynamics against a (relatively recent) history of colonisation.

• *With regard to the conservatism of transactional analysis*

As with most other approaches or modalities in clinical, educational and organisational fields, transactional analysis is a "broad church" and not only encompasses practitioners across the political spectrum but also comprises theories that may be viewed as conservative, liberal, or radical (see Fay, 2008; Tudor, 2010c). I think that we have demonstrated some clear links between co-creative transactional analysis and the radical psychiatry tradition with the result that, hopefully, there may be more interest in the concept of alienation as the basis of psychopathology (see Tudor & Worrall, 2006) and in psychotherapy as a form of personal and interpersonal liberation. In terms of my own journey, I began training in transactional analysis when I very much identified as a political activist and was a member of a left wing political organisation. My journey with psychotherapy and politics has not been an easy one (in either world) and, although I have not been as politically active as I once was, I have remained political. For many years this has taken the form of being concerned with the politics of education in counselling and psychotherapy. I have been involved with the journal *Psychotherapy and Politics International* (http://onlinelibrary.wiley.com/journal/10.1002/(ISSN)1556–9195) since its inception and, for the past three years, as its editor. Here in Aotearoa New Zealand, I am a member of Nga Ao e Rua (the Two Worlds), a bicultural group of Māori and non-Māori psychotherapists, counsellors, health care providers, and students. If anything, I am as, if not more, politically active as ever: the struggle does, indeed, continue (see Walker, 1990).

• *With regard to critique and critical capacity*

   With its intellectual roots in constructivism, which encompasses deconstruction; its values of curiosity and openness; its emphasis on questioning and possibilities; and our positioning of it as an *approach* to or a *reading* of transactional analysis, I think that co-creative transactional analysis both offers a critical analysis of transactional analysis and challenges transactional analysts to be reflective and critical (reflexive)—and more critical. I make no apology for being critical, and I challenge uncritical moves to pathologise criticism. If we are operating at postgraduate levels of education, training, and activity, as are, for example, psychotherapists the world over, it is an expected capacity and competence; if you are academic, working in a university (as I am) it is required, for instance, the New Zealand *Education Amendment Act 1990* defines one of the characteristics of a university as being "a critic and conscience of society"; and, if you are at all political, it is a necessity.

• *With regard to adult development*

   With its emphasis on the neopsyche/integrating Adult, expanding Adult, and self-Adulting, co-creative transactional analysis represents andragogy (as distinct from pedagogy), an approach to education and, by extension and application, to clinical practice and organisation consultancy, in which adult clients, students or colleagues are viewed and treated as adults, and encouraged to learn, critique, develop and progress as such. This provides the philosophical base of our views on personal—that is, interpersonal, and psychological development in the present. Whilst this offers a very different paradigm from the assumed and more common pedagogic and Parental one (with regard to both education and personal development), I think there is much more work to be done to challenge the hegemonic view in psychotherapy and especially in psychotherapy training of adult learners as pseudo children or less than adults.

• *With regard to marginalised and oppressed peoples and clients*

   Following on from the previous point, I would say that, to paraphrase Freire (1970/1972), co-creative transactional analysis practices represent a practice of an *andragogy* of the oppressed. That said,

I would hope that, in the next fifteen years, we will see more application of co-creativity in this area and more publication of such work.

Co- & co

Whilst Graeme and I coined the term "co-creative transactional analysis", we did not invent co-creativity. As we were putting the finishing touches to this book, I googled "co-creative", a search that returned over half a million results or "hits", including (on the first page alone):

- A sustainable living centre—the Hummingbird Centre for a Co-creative World in Mexico, founded in 1996 (see www.humming birdcenterforacocreativeworld.com/).
- A definition of co-creation as a form of marketing or business strategy—Interestingly, one of the key works cited in this Wikipedia (2013) entry was by Prahalad and Ramaswamy (2000) on "Co-opting customer competence", which, expressed in the language of business, echoes something of our emphasis on the client's health; another point they make about the co-creation of value by the firm and the customer resonates not only with our emphasis on participation but also represents transactional theory and practice about contracts that require mutual consent and valid consideration (Steiner & Cassidy, 1969).
- A production studio in Hawaii, established in 2006 (http:// cocreativetv.squarespace.com/).
- An article on co-creative labour—This article by Banks and Deuze (2009) introduced a special issue of the *International Journal of Cultural Studies* on the subject of co-creative labour, which the authors described as "the phenomenon of consumers increasingly participating in the process of making and circulating media content and experiences" (p. 419). That these activities are viewed as a form of labour and as generating value echoes the emphasis in co-creative transactional analysis on the participation of the client and of the value of the therapy not only being co-created but also ultimately assessed by the client.
- An international co-creative symposium—The advert for this symposium, which was aimed at visionaries and leaders (and which took place in Aotearoa New Zealand), talked about a new way of being in the world, living "from a unified field—a shift from head to heart,

[and] from duality to unity consciousness." (see www.thespiritguide. net/main/event/1050).

• A presentation about co-creative organisation (Coates & Peters, n.d.)—In which the authors stated that "Co-creation *will* become a way of being" www.slideshare.net/nickcoates/the-co-creative-organization-of-the-future (Slide 21).

Although, when we were developing our ideas about co-creativity, we were not reading or researching very much outside our field of psychotherapy, looking back I wonder if we were picking up something of a zeitgeist, which has developed over the past twenty years in a number of fields. Since the publication of our article in 2000, I have become more aware not only of the use and application of the words co-creative and co-creativity, but also of other words and concepts with the suffix "co-". Here I refer briefly to four of them.

Co-regulation

We have referred to this throughout our work and, by now, the reader will be aware that both Graeme and I have been hugely influenced by the work of Daniel Stern (1934–2013) and his perspective on the interpersonal world of the infant and the co-construction of various senses of self—and domains of relatedness. Largely through my wife Louise Embleton Tudor, who knows a lot more about this than I do (see Embleton Tudor, 2009, 2011), I have also been influenced by the work of the neuropsychologist and psychotherapist Allan Schore, whose major work on affect regulation and dysregulation (Schore, 1994, 2003a, 2003b) includes references to the mutuality of the mother–infant dyad and the reciprocity of mutual influences, as well as of dyadic misattunements. This work, as well as my own experience as a parent, has helped me understand the power of co-influence in asymmetrical relationships. It is clear that we are hardwired for co-creativity; the work of Stern, Schore and others, notably Damasio (1994/1996, 2010), Pally (2000) and Cozolino (2002) provides us with the neuroscientific, neurobiological, and developmental psychological base of and for co-creativity—and my reading and learning continues!

The concept of co-regulation has also been developed in the field of communication by Fogel (1993), who has described communication as a continuous and dynamic process, which we may think of as representing a genuinely two-person psychology, as distinct from communication as the exchange of discrete information, which represents a more separate one-person-plus-one-person psychology.

Co-intelligence

I recently came across the concept of co-intelligence, which, in many ways, follows on from what Shore (2003b) has referred to as "the interacting brain", which, interestingly, he views as reflecting a two-person psychology. The Co-Intelligence Institute (2013) takes the view that "Healthy communities, institutions and societies—perhaps even our collective survival—depend on our ability to organize our collective affairs more wisely, in tune with each other and nature." In the sense that the whole is greater than the sum of its parts, and that two heads are better than one, the Institute refers to people being wiser together as co-intelligence. In the same spirit as Gardener's (1983) work on multiple intelligences (musical, visual, verbal, etc.), the Institute suggests a number of co-intelligences: collaborative, collective, wisdom, resonant, and universal (i.e., not only human). Co-creative transactional analysis and, not least, its expression in the creation of, and ideas in, this book certainly represents a collaborative intelligence.

Co-operative enquiry

Also known as collaborative inquiry, this approach to research was first proposed by John Heron in 1971 and later developed, appropriately enough, in collaboration with Peter Reason (Reason & Rowan, 1981).[1] It is an approach that researches "with" rather than on or about the subject that is people, and thus emphasises that all active participants are fully involved in research decisions as co-researchers. Co-operative enquiry creates—co-creates—a research cycle involving different types of knowledge or knowing: propositional, practical, experiential, and presentational. This kind of enquiry is entirely compatible with our co-creative approach and I would like to hope that, if we are to research co-creative transactional analysis, we would base our method in this enquiry. Given a political and professional context, which is demanding more evidence and justification of psychotherapy through research and the emerging interest in "practice-based evidence" (Morgan & Juriansz, 2002) (as distinct from "evidence-based practice"), I would like to enquire more into co-operative enquiry.

Co-operacy

This refers to the technology of collective or consensus decision-making, as distinct from a parliamentary democracy in which voters vote once in a while for a representative who then votes on issues, usually following party lines. Co-operacy is a philosophy or a methodology that informed the consensus decision-making process at the various Occupy protests, which took place in 2011 and 2012 all over the world (see, for instance, Land, 2012). As a concept and a practice, it has been developed by New Zealand authors and consultants Hunter, Bailey and Taylor (1998), who have described it as an approach to the organisation as a community.

I refer to these four "co-"s—concerning, respectively, attachment/regulation, emerging intelligence(s); a specific research method; and a political—and, potentially, professional—model of organisation and a way of organising—as I think they both reflect and represent something of a wider co-creativity in the social world, and areas of development for co-creative transactional analysis.

Finishing, not ending

Sometime it's hard to let go of an idea or a piece of writing. As the Roman lyric poet Horace (65 BCE–8 BCE) put it in one of his Epistles: "Es semel emissum volat irrevocabile verbum" (Once released a word flies off without recall) (Horace, *Epistolae 18*). Whilst the words in this book have now flown off our keyboards and the press, and, in that sense, can no longer be recalled, I hope that they fly and land, and, in doing so, stimulate, evoke and provoke response, discussion, and dialogue, and, in this sense, that the co-creative project in and beyond transactional analysis continues.

Note

1. Since moving to Aotearoa New Zealand, I have had the great privilege of meeting John, who, I was delighted to discover, lives less than an hour away from me. I have come to regard John not only as a mentor but as a friend; as a comrade in the struggle to keep humanism on the map in a professional world, at least in psychotherapy, which is dominated by psychoanalytic and psychodynamic thinking—and as a co-conspirator in indulging our sweet tooths!

Introducing co-creative transactional analysis

Graeme Summers and Keith Tudor

What is co-creative transactional analysis?

Transactional analysis (TA) is a way of understanding what happens within and between people. Since its conception in the 1950s by Eric Berne (1910–1970) it has evolved well-established applications in the fields of psychotherapy, education, and organisational development.

Co-creative TA is a contemporary interpretation of TA that integrates recent developments in philosophy and psychology. Our original article (Summers & Tudor, 2000, Chapter One) was re-published in *From Transactions to Relations* (Cornell & Hargaden, 2005), an edited volume that plots the development of a new relational paradigm in TA psychotherapy. In this paper we outline a "user friendly" summary of our approach written for anyone interested in understanding and improving their personal and/or working relationships, in a user-friendly way by addressing "you" the reader directly. It will also be of interest to practitioners in the fields of educational and organisational development seeking a generic, coherent and accessible theoretical framework for learning and change.

Co-creative TA updates the four core concepts of TA theory—ego states, transactions, games and scripts—to provide models of:

- Personality—a way of understanding yourself and others;
- Relationship—ways of initiating or maintaining creative contact with other people;
- Confirmation—understanding and influencing repeating patterns of positive or negative interactions and their predictable outcomes; and
- Identity—ways of understanding yourself in the context of your past and present culture and shaping the "stories" you construct about yourself, others, and life.

These four models interact to give a clear and consistent framework for understanding what happens within and between people. Each model describes healthy and dysfunctional patterns and can be used to generate effective strategies to support personal and professional development. We now explore each model in turn.

Model 1. Ego states: co-creative personality

Personality can be thought of as our "sense of self", created through movement within and between ego states.

Ego states

An ego state is a set of feelings, attitudes, and behaviours. It is a possible state of self—a potential way of being or relating that is co-created through our interactions with others (see Figure A1.1).

The development of ego states

In the course of healthy human development we integrate experience throughout life. From infancy onwards we are naturally proactive and, with adequate support, will get what we need and reject what we don't need, or negotiate "good enough" compromises. We are innately motivated to be curious and seek attachment, competence, and mutual recognition. Much of this can be achieved through the vitality of healthy interdependent relationships, which help to regulate our feelings and

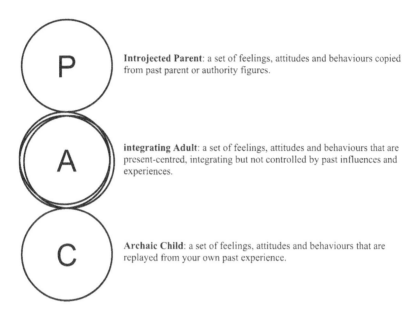

Figure A1.1. Three types of ego states.

needs. Healthy interactions include "rough and tumble" and recovery from difficult or traumatic experiences. With repetition, these interactions become generalised and encoded in emotional memory. These emotional memories support us to use and create sets of feelings, attitudes and behaviours that are effective in dealing with the challenges and opportunities that life presents. These are integrating Adult ego states.

However, most of us will have had situations in which we were not helped to manage particular feelings and needs. When our experience becomes unmanageable we can split our "sense of self", creating two sets of feelings, attitudes and behaviours that are disconnected from our usual sense of who we are. This is an attempt to manage the mismatch between our need for support and the lack of appropriate response from a significant other. We simultaneously create a Parent and Child ego state. The Child ego state is like a "snapshot" of ourselves attempting to cope with more than we could manage. The Parent ego state is a set of feelings, attitudes and behaviours "copied" from the parent figure or other person we were relating to at the time.

Ego states in everyday life

Parent, Adult and Child are not "people" inside us. They are possible (and probable) ways of being and relating that are influenced by our choices, our expectations based on past experience, and our present situation.

Consider a time when you dealt with a problem or challenging situation creatively. You probably accessed resources from within yourself as well as accessing resources around you. Even though you may have been profoundly challenged or emotionally distressed, you were responsive, resourceful, and creative. What did you feel? What attitude did you have? What did you do? At such moments you are probably in Adult "flow"—in good contact with yourself and your environment.

Now consider a situation in which you got "stuck". In hindsight you recognise that the set of feelings, attitudes and behaviours you brought to that situation were not useful. Perhaps at a different time you might have managed the situation much more effectively. The probability here is that you were approaching the situation from a Parent or Child ego state—a familiar but ultimately unhelpful set of feelings, attitudes, and behaviours.

It is not surprising that people tend to "go into" Parent or Child at times of stress or anxiety, since these are familiar ways of attempting to manage difficult experiences. These "regressive" ego states are often at the heart of problematic or unfulfilling relationships at home and work.

Using ego states

1. Develop awareness

Knowing "where you're coming from" is enormously useful. Sometimes this awareness alone is sufficient to help you interrupt a defensive Parent or Child response and approach a situation from Adult instead. There are four clues that you can use to help identify which ego state you (or others) may be using at any given point in time:

- Behavioural—are you behaving in a parental or childlike way, for example, "telling someone off" (Parent) or "sulking" (Child)?
- Social—are others around you behaving in a complementary fashion? If others are being childlike, this might indicate that you are operating from a Parent ego state.

- Historical—does your attitude or behaviour remind you of one of your parent figures, or yourself when you were younger?
- Felt sense—do you "feel" as if you are one of your parent figures, or as if you are younger than you actually are?

Note that "in" Adult we may behave in a parent or childlike way because it is appropriate, effective, or just good fun. This is different from compulsively responding from Parent or Child, which is usually ineffective, defensive, and limiting. You can use the four questions above to help identify which ego state you (or others) are coming from. Notice the situations in which you are more likely to move into each of the three types of ego state.

2. Strengthen and expand your integrating Adult

Our greatest potential for personal and professional development lies in developing our strengths rather than improving our weaknesses. It is important to know and exercise your natural and cultivated strengths. In which situations do you thrive? What triggers your Adult ego state? In what conditions do you enjoy and maintain Adult "flow"? Which sets of feelings, attitudes and behaviours do you use?

The answers to these questions will be very personal, reflecting your uniqueness as an individual. These are important questions because they help us focus on health, strength, and vitality. It is also essential to draw on healthy Adult resources in order to manage our areas of weakness and our potential to use Parent or Child defences.

When in Adult "flow" we naturally explore and expand our range of being and relating because we are curious about ourselves, others, and life. We invent and test new possibilities, expanding our relational, emotional, intellectual or technical capacities. At times this may involve managing and "working through" our Parent and Child defences against the fear and excitement this new learning might provoke.

3. Manage or "work through" Parent or Child defences

It is important to stay respectful of yourself even when you notice that you compulsively move into Parent or Child ego states. Recognise that you created these ego states (out of awareness) as an attempt to manage what felt unmanageable at the time. You might still use these ego states in the present for the same reason. It may be that adopting this compassionate attitude towards yourself (and others) helps you move out of Parent and Child more quickly.

"Working through" means learning how to tolerate more of your experience with fresh support, which, previously, was unavailable. Interestingly, learning to feel intense pleasure or excitement can be as challenging as feeling anger, fear, and sadness. This healing process is one of expanding your Adult capacity to experience and manage previously repressed feelings, needs and desires so reducing the compulsion to use Parent and Child defences at times of difficulty or change.

Model 2. Transactions: co-creative relationship(s)

A transaction is an "exchange" between people that consists of a "stimulus" and a "response". It is the building block of relationship. From a TA perspective there are three main types of transaction: parallel, crossed, and ulterior. Each type of transaction leads to a corresponding rule of communication (Berne, 1966).

Parallel transactions

These are when:

- The "vectors" of communication are parallel (see Figure A1.2); and
- The ego state that is addressed is the one that responds.

From a co-creative perspective, healthy present-centred relating consists of Adult–Adult transactions. Problematic or unhealthy relating consists of transactions involving Parent and Child ego states, a common example of which is the Parent–Child transaction. Both these types of transactions are parallel, yet each build very different kinds of relationship. Nevertheless, as Berne (1966) put it, the first rule of communication is: "as long as the vectors are parallel, communication can proceed indefinitely" (p. 223).

Crossed transactions

With crossed transactions:

- The vectors are no longer parallel; and
- The ego state that is addressed is not the one that responds.

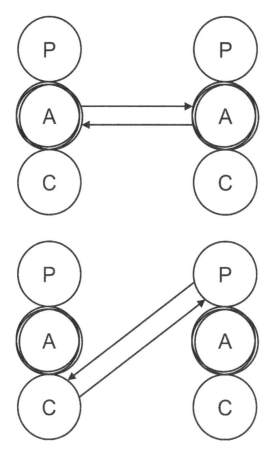

Figure A1.2. Parallel transactions: two types.

The crossed transaction is the "agent of change". It is a way of switching from healthy to unhealthy relating or vice versa. This is summarised in the second rule of communication: "When a transaction is crossed, a break in communication results and one or both individuals will need to shift ego-states in order for communication to be re-established" (Stewart & Joines, 1987, p. 65).

Ulterior transactions

Here we distinguish between "social" and "psychological" level messages to conceptualise the ulterior transaction (see Figure A1.4) in which the social level messages are explicit and represented by solid arrows;

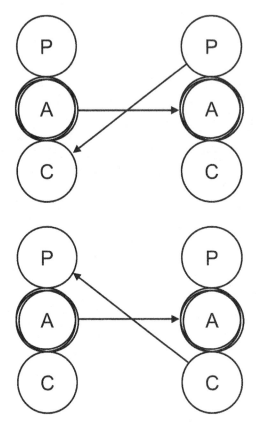

Figure A1.3. Crossed transactions: two types.

and the psychological level messages are implicit and represented by dashed arrows.

The non-verbal messages we give and receive often have the most impact. We can give and receive healthy (Adult) and unhealthy (Parent or Child) ulterior messages. Parent or Child psychological messages are often hidden by apparent Adult–Adult social level messages. This is reflected in the third rule of communication: "The behavioural outcome of an ulterior transaction is determined at the psychological and not at the social level" (Berne, 1966, p. 227).

Recognition

Any transaction involves an exchange of recognition between people. This is significant because it is a powerful motivation for people to

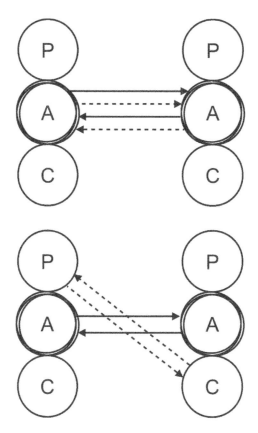

Figure A1.4. Ulterior transactions: two types.

interact. Recognition may vary in intensity or significance and be verbal or non-verbal, positive or negative, and conditional or unconditional.

Using transactions

1. Build Adult–Adult relationships

Discover and use Adult triggers. Enjoy Adult–Adult transactions. Use positive ulteriors. Negotiate for what you want. Develop secure attachments.

2. Cross-problem transactions

Use your own impulses to respond from Parent or Child as information about the other person. Reject invitations to respond from these ego states.

Respond from Adult ego state. Tolerate the discomfort of temporarily breaking communication. Allow the other person time to move to Adult. Validate old realities. Create and support new possibilities.

3. Use positive and useful recognition

Catch yourself and others doing things right. Give, ask for and receive positive and useful feedback. Reject unhelpful feedback.

Model 3. Games: co-creative confirmation

A game is a pattern of transactions that is used to confirm positive or negative feelings and beliefs about self or others. It is "an ongoing series of complementary ulterior transactions progressing to a well-defined predictable outcome" (Berne, 1964/1968a, p. 44). We "play" games in order to confirm our script.

Structure of games

The structure of a positive or negative game can be described using the game plan (James, 1973; with the addition of two "mystery questions" by Lawrence Collinson):

1. What keeps happening to me over and over again?
2. How does it start?
3. What happens next?
4. (Mystery question)
5. And then?
6. (Mystery question)
7. How does it end?
8a. How do I feel?
8b. How do I think the other person feels?

The feelings and attitudes created at the end of a game are described as the game "pay-off".

Positive games

Consider a relationship with someone you know that is consistently satisfying. Now use the above game plan to map out the sequence of the pattern you manage to co-create with this person "over and over again". Finally consider the mystery questions:

4. What is my secret message to the other person?
6. What is the other person's secret message to me?

Typical responses to this approach are that such patterns start with a sense of anticipation, welcoming, and reconnection. The middle phase often involves sharing, exploring, honesty, and creative co-operation. Such patterns often end with satisfaction, confirmation, and well-being. Common ulteriors include: "I like you", "I trust you", and "I respect you". In satisfying relationships such patterns create a framework for intimate and productive contact.

Negative games I

Now use the above game plan to consider a repetitive negative pattern that occurs "over and over" with another person. Here you are describing the structure of a game where the "pay-off" is to end up with familiar negative feelings and attitudes towards yourself and/or others.

The drama triangle

The structure of a negative game can also be described using the drama triangle (Karpman, 1968).

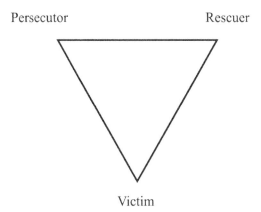

Persecutor   Rescuer

Victim

Figure A1.5. The drama triangle (Karpman, 1968).

All three game roles are inauthentic and are played from Parent or Child ego states.

Negative games II

Negative games often involve a "switch" in game roles as the game is played out. Examples of negative games include:

- "Now I've got you"—exploiting other people's mistakes or weakness for psychological gain.
- "Kick me"—doing things wrong until eventually people feel obliged to put you down.
- "Why don't you?"—offering unsolicited advice, which often leads to …
- "Yes, but"—acting as if you needed help and then refusing every suggestion.
- "After all I've done for you"—doing too much and then feeling resentful.

Characteristics of negative games

Negative games are repetitive, involve negative ulterior transactions, often include a moment of surprise or confusion, and end with the players experiencing familiar bad feelings and attitudes. They can be played at different degrees of intensity.

Advantages of games

People play positive and negative games to regulate feelings, structure time, confirm beliefs about self and others, get recognition, and maintain connected to other people.

Using game theory

1. Develop and savour positive games

Pay attention to relationships that work well. Understand your explicit and implicit contribution to positive outcomes. Savour satisfaction and ask yourself "How can I repeat this in other areas of my life?"

2. Change negative games

Celebrate awareness as you use hindsight, mid sight, insight and foresight to become aware of and name negative games. Disinvest in the negative pay-off. Use the "winners' triangle" (Choy, 1990) to respond from Adult instead of Parent or Child—that is, be assertive instead of Persecutory, responsive instead of Rescuing, and proactively vulnerable instead of being a Victim. Adjust or reaffirm goals, agreements, and positive aspects of relationship. Learn from the game. Create alternative forms of structure, stimulation, and recognition.

Model 4. Scripts: co-creative identity

Our script is the set of beliefs we make about ourselves, others and life and the decisions we make based on these beliefs. It is a way of understanding how we define ourselves within the context of past and present cultural influence. As Cornell (1988) put it: "Life script is the ongoing process of a self-defining and sometimes self-limiting psychological construction of reality" (p. 281).

Script messages

Our "psychological construction" influences and is influenced by messages we receive from others and the culture and subcultures within which we live. These messages may be positive or negative in intent or impact and can be classified in five main ways:

- Attributions—for example, "You are …"—that is, characteristics ascribed to you by others such as shy, clever, stupid, likeable;
- Injunctions—for example, "Don't …"—that is, prohibitive messages (often non-verbal);
- Permissions—for example, "You can …"—that is, messages that encourage/support options;
- Counter-injunctions—for example, "You should …"—that is, prescriptive messages, usually given directly, such as "Work hard", "Be good", "Do your best", etc.; and
- Modelling—for example, "Here's how to …"—that is, intentional modelling by others showing how to fulfil other script messages.

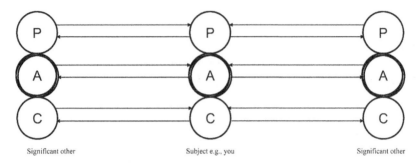

Figure A1.6. Co-creative script matrix (Summers & Tudor, 2000).

Co-creative script matrix

The matrix above (Figure A1.6) helps map script messages to and from significant others. This can be used to reflect on formative influences earlier in life or to reflect on current relationships.

Whilst the significant others might be two parents, this matrix can also be used to map influences in terms of any social construct important to you; for example, regarding gender, class, race, age, etc. What messages do people give to you? What messages do you give others?

Script responses

The messages we receive from different people, and sometimes the same person, may be contradictory. In addition, we are not passive recipients and will therefore respond to messages we receive with our own creative and adaptive capacities. This means that, even in difficult circumstances, we have scope for forming our own conclusions and making personal decisions. Sometimes these beliefs and decisions are not cognitive or even conscious but can be characterised as emotional, instinctive or intuitive responses to our opportunities and limitations in a given situation. As you reflect on your experience, consider what beliefs and decisions have you made (in or out of awareness) in response to script messages? Are there any you have already changed or want to change? Also, script formation is a two-way process ... so what influence do you want to have on others or your culture?

Using script theory

1. Identify script messages and responses

Identify past and present script messages—that is, attributions, injunctions, permissions, counter-injunctions, and modelling. Use the script matrix to map these out in terms of significant relationships and broader cultural patterns. Identify and infer the beliefs and decisions you have made in the context of these influences.

2. Update script messages, beliefs, and decisions

Experiment with alternative beliefs and decisions about you and your life. Take into account your natural strengths, interests, and your social identity. Notice what happens when you define yourself differently. Seek and use messages and relationships that support the beliefs and decisions that feel right for you. See the bigger picture—understand that your personal change may be emotional, cognitive, and behavioural, as well as being part of broader social, political and spiritual processes.

A co-creative "TA 101": notes on the syllabus

Keith Tudor

The "TA 101" is the official introduction to transactional analysis, and although its stated purpose is "to provide consistent and accurate information about TA concepts" (Training and Certification Council (T&CC, 2010, Section 4.1), as many if not most of these concepts are defined differently by different transactional analysts; there is a healthy diversity about TA 101s. Here, I follow those Sections of the TA 101 Introductory Course as laid down as essential and mandatory by the T&CC in its *Training and Examinations Handbook* and offer an outline and notes on the way I tend to teach this.

Being able to teach elements of this curriculum, almost literally, at the drop of a hat, is one of the requirements of the TSTA qualifying Teaching Exam (see T&CC, 2010, Section 11) in which candidates pick an (unseen) topic out of a hat; these notes may, therefore, be helpful for candidates preparing for that particular exam. As there is emphasis placed on the coherence of the candidate's training philosophy, preferred theoretical models of learning, and choice of teaching methods, it seems entirely proper that a TA 101 should be taught coherently, based on the trainer's philosophy of education and practice in whatever field of application. I also include in these notes—and, indeed, in my presentations—an element of critique, as I support the development of critical thinking and capacity (see my Afterword p. 230).

C. Definition and underlying values of transactional analysis and its areas of application[1]

1. Definition of transactional analysis

Transactional analysis is: "1. an easily understandable yet sophisticated psychological theory about people's thinking, feelings, and behaviour and, 2. a contemporary and effective system of psychotherapy, education, organizational and socio-cultural analysis and social psychiatry" (ITAA, 2013).

A theory of personality (of people, groups, and systems)
A theory of child development and psychopathology
A theory of communication (between people, groups, and systems)
A rich and diverse body of theories centred on the analysis of transactions or relations between people.

2. Value base

People are OK: "I'm OK, You're OK".

– From existentialism and humanism (Note the difference)
– The three-handed position and "They're OK" (Berne, 1972/1975b).

Everyone has the capacity to think—link with autonomy

– NB regarding homonomy (or belonging) (Angyal, 1941); and relational needs (Erskine, 1998a).
  People can decide their own destiny
– Autonomy
– Decision and redecision
– Change and the contractual method.

3. Definitions of autonomy

Definition: autonomy "is manifested by the release or recovery of three capacities: awareness, spontaneity and intimacy" (Berne, 1964/1968a, p. 158).

- The aim/goal of TA in all its applications
- Autonomy is Adult, "characterized by an autonomous set of feelings, attitudes, and behavior patterns which are adapted to the current reality" (Berne, 1961/1975a, p. 76).

Critique: autonomy as *self*-determination represents an individualistic view, as distinct from a more relational and collective approach, which is represented by homonomy (Angyal, 1941), and, in transactional analysis, the concept of relational needs (Erskine, 1998a).

4. Contractual method

Context: in the tradition of Jean-Jacques Rousseau (1712–1778) and the social contract—that is, we can be free *and* members of society, as distinct from Thomas Hobbes' (1588–1679) view that man is free *or* a member of society.

It is the *methodology* or philosophy of transactional analysis, which involves:

- A mutually agreed statement of change (NB valid, ethical, legal)
- Open communication, for example, regarding client case conferences (see Berne, 1968b).

Contracts

Definition: "an explicit bilateral agreement to a well-defined *course* of action" (Berne, 1966, p. 362); it is, therefore, a contract about *process*, more than outcome.

Features: bilateral, social (and, therefore, co-created if not co-creative), observable/behavioural, and finishable.

Critiques:

- Making and having a contract may set up a false expectation of certainty, control, and individual achievement
- Philosophically, contracts are "a modernist conceit" (Tudor, 2006, p. 119).

5. Areas of application—differences in process

Clinical (now Psychotherapy and Counselling), Education(al), Organisations (Organisational).

History (linked to Berne's publications and developments):

- Clinical: *Mind in Action* (Berne, 1947), *Transactional Analysis in Psychotherapy* (Berne, 1961/1975a)
- Organisational: *Structure and Dynamics of Organisations and Groups* (Berne, 1963), *Principles of Group Treatment* (Berne, 1966)
- Educational (chapter in *Principles of Group Treatment*), in practice and other, later contributions.

NB The problem of "translation" across fields; field-specific theory; and metatheory and "readings" across transactional analysis.

Differences

Table A2.1. Differences between the four fields of application in transactional analysis.

Application	Contact	Contract	Process	"Cure"/Goal
Counselling	1:1, group, direct	Bilateral, multilateral	Counselling (different approaches) Psychoeducational work	Autonomy—and homonomy
Psychotherapy	1:1, group, direct	Bilateral, multilateral	Psychotherapeutic (different approaches)	Autonomy—and homonomy
Educational	1:1, group direct, indirect	Multilateral	Teaching Facilitating Consultancy	Learning process and outcomes
Organisational	1:1, group direct, indirect	Multilateral	Coaching Consultancy Organisational development	Profit, productivity, internal homonomy, autonomy in relation to the external world

D. Brief overview of the development
of transactional analysis

1. Eric Berne

The development of his ideas and bibliography
   Perspective: All theory is autobiographical, and all theory is contextual (NB Link this to the context of the particular "TA 101").

Timeline:

1910	Is born in Montreal
1921	Age 11, father dies of tuberculosis (aged 38)
1936	Moves to New York
1938	Changes his name
1941	First appointment; begins training as psychoanalyst; analysand of Paul Federn
1943	Joins US Medical Army Corp
1944–46	Practices group therapy; intuition experiments
1947	*The Mind in Action* is published (later revised and republished as *The Layman's Guide to Psychiatry and Psychoanalysis*); analysand of Erik Erikson; moves to California
1956	Formal application to San Francisco Psychoanalytic Institute is turned down
1958	First article on transactional analysis is published; San Francisco Social Psychiatry Seminars begin
1961	*Transactional Analysis Psychotherapy* is published
1962	First issue of *Transactional Analysis Bulletin* is published
1963	*Structure and Dynamics of Organizations and Groups* is published
1964	*Games People Play* is published
1966	*Principles of Group Treatment* is published
1968	*The Happy Valley* is published
1970	*Sex in Human Loving* is published; dies
1972	*What Do You Say After You Say Hello?* is published (posthumously)
1977	*Ego States and Intuition* is published
2011	*A Montreal Childhood* is published.

2. Development of transactional analysis

Evolution of transactional analysis theory and methodology post Berne.

From "Schools" (Classical, Cathexis, and Redecision) to a number of traditions or approaches: Classical (psychoanalytic); Classical (cognitive-behavioural); Cathexis; Radical Psychiatry; Redecision; Integrative; Constructivist (see Tudor & Hobbes, 1996).

The "relational turn".

Eric Berne Memorial Awards and award-winning publications (referred to throughout and given as a handout).

3. Transactional analysis organisations

TA worldwide: national, regional, transnational and international TA associations (handout).

E. Theory of personality—ego states

1. Motivational theory—structure, stimulus, and recognition hungers
    Question: What do you "hunger" for?
    Hungers—from *Sex in Human Loving* (Berne, 1970/1973)

– *Stimulus*—sensory stimulation
– Contact—for example, touch
– *Recognition*—fuels our self-concept and self-esteem NB strokes
– Sexual—stimulation of sexual organs and fulfilment of sexual appetite
– *Structure*—certainty and security; for example, time
– Incident—destabilisation

Question (to reflect on): How do you get these hungers met?

2. Definition of ego states
3. Structural model of ego states
4. Contamination
5. Behavioural descriptions of ego states
See Appendix One.

F. Theory of communication—transactional analysis proper

1. Transactions

See Appendix One.

2. Strokes

Definitions: "the fundamental unit of social action" (Berne, 1964/1968a, p. 15) or a unit of recognition.

Based on our human hunger for recognition—and to recognise (link to relational needs).

1. Strokes reinforce behaviour
2. We may seek negative strokes rather than none
3. This knowledge may help us to seek positive strokes
4. The quality and intensity of strokes are important—and are experienced differently and subjectively.

Types of strokes:

– Verbal or non-verbal
– Positive or negative
– Conditional or unconditional.

Stroke economy:

History from theory of alienation (see Steiner, 2000).
Analogy with rules of financial economy.
Rules (Steiner, 1966):

– Don't give strokes when we have them to give
– Don't ask for strokes when we need them
– Don't accept strokes if we want them
– Don't reject strokes when we don't want them
– Don't give ourselves strokes.

3. Social time structuring

Structure hunger

– Responds to need for certainty and security
– Structure hunger is a way of understanding our need to experience levels of recognition
– Time structuring as a subset of structure hunger.

Time structuring in groups (Berne, 1970/1973):

▲ Intimacy
  Play (Boyd & Boyd, 1980)
  Psychological games
  Activity
  Pastiming
  Ritual
  Withdrawal

The model describes the experience of recognition in groups, the order reflects degrees of intensity (from most to more) and, therefore, emphasises the relational dimension.

Critiques:

– Based on certain assumptions about the value of intimacy
– Discounts the importance of withdrawal.

G. Theory of life patterns—script

1. Game analysis

a. Definitions of games
b. Ways of describing the process of games
See Appendix One.

2. Racket analysis

a. Definitions of rackets and their pay-offs

A racket is a substitute, inauthentic feeling.
A racket is a *process* in which someone sets up to feel a racket feeling (Stewart & Joines, 1997).
NB regarding protection racket.

b. Significance of internal/intrapsychic processes

Any time you experience a racket feeling you're in script and you leave a situation unfinished or open. This goes back to feelings repressed at the time of the script decision and gives rise to beliefs people have about ourselves, others, and the world.

c. Relationship of rackets to transactions, games, and script

If (in the context of the TSTA exam), in response to drawing this subject out of the hat, I think "I'm stupid" I could be in a "racket"—that is, a set of scripty behaviours, outside awareness and entailing a "racket feeling"—that is, *"a familiar emotion, learned and encouraged in childhood, experienced in many different stress situations, and maladaptive as an adult means of problem-solving"* (Stewart & Joines, 1987, p. 209, original emphasis).

One way of thinking about this is: Racket + Transaction $\rightarrow$ Game $\rightarrow$ Script—that is, an (individual) racket + (interpersonal) transaction $\rightarrow$ game (interpersonal over time) $\rightarrow$ script (individual/contextual); for example, "I'm stupid" + acting stupid $\rightarrow$ invites Rescuing $\rightarrow$ "See, I told you so."

3. Script analysis

a. Life positions

Definition: "represent fundamental stances a person takes up about the essential *value* he perceives in himself and others" (Stewart & Joines, 1987, p. 117).

History:

– "Position" (Klein): paranoid (I+ U-), depressive (I- U+), schizoid (I-U-)
– Additions: I+ U+ (Berne), and I+ U+ They+ (Berne, 1972), inspired by Satir's "I count, you count, context counts".

Critique: It conflates humanism (OKness) with existentialism ("is"ness).

Relationship to script

A script is "A life plan based on a decision made in childhood, reinforced by the parents, justified by subsequent events, and culminating in a chosen alternative" (Berne, 1972/1975b, p. 445).

The relationship between life positions and script is dialogic—that is, if someone is paranoid they will tend to justify events in terms of people being out to get them, and vice versa.

b. Script

1. Definitions of script
2. Origin of script in child's experiences
3. Process of script development
See Appendix One.

H. Transactional analysis methodology

Table A2.2. Transactional methodology and method (from Tudor, 1999).

TA—Philosophy (methodology), method and therapeutic attitude	Implications for the practitioner's attitude to the therapeutic relationship
Basic philosophy	
• People are OK[2]	Positive and mutual regard/respect (I'm OK, You're OK)[3]
• Everyone has the capacity to think	… and a belief in self-responsibility
• People decide their own destiny and these decision can be changed	A belief in personal responsibility and autonomy[4]
Therapeutic slogans (Berne, 1966)	
• *Primum non nocere*—Above all do no harm	The principle from moral philosophy and ethics of non-maleficence
• *Vis medicatrix naturae*—the curative power of nature	Respect for the client's health, potential for health and for developmental obstructions to health; for example, defences
• *Je le pensay, et Dieu le guarist*—I treat them and God cures them[5]	A factual (not false) humility[6]
Therapeutic method	
• Contractual method (a mutually agreed statement of change)	Commitment to a clearly defined relationship in which there is joint responsibility for the process of change
• Open communication	Commitment to open communication; for example, regarding client case notes, case conferences, references, etc.

(Continued)

Table A2.2. Continued.

TA—Philosophy (methodology), method and therapeutic attitude	Implications for the practitioner's attitude to the therapeutic relationship
Therapeutic attitudes (Berne, 1966) A fresh frame of mind:	
• In good health, physically and psychologically	Respect for self and others
• Well prepared, clear and open	Authenticity *as a therapist* (as distinct from as a friend)

Notes

1. Section A is a heading "Statement of the purpose of the TA101 course" and Section B is the projected outcomes of the 101.
2. A shorthand statement describing the positive essence of people.
3. In his last book, Berne (1972/1975b) developed this into three-handed life positions: "I'm OK, You're OK, They're OK", etc.—thereby giving eight possible life positions.
4. Defined within transactional analysis as "the release or recovery of three capacities: awareness, spontaneity and intimacy" (Berne, 1964/1968a, p. 158).
5. Although Berne (1966) defined this as "getting the patient ready for the cure to happen today" (p. 63), this slogan contradicts much of Berne's other writing on the subject of cure.
6. Berne also reminded us that "the professional therapist's job is to use his [sic] knowledge *therapeutically*; if the patient is going to be cured by love, that should be left to a lover" (p. 63, emphasis added).

GLOSSARY

Keith Tudor and Graeme Summers

Transactional analysis has a long tradition, dating back to Berne's (1947) "Word List" in *The Mind in Action*, providing a glossary, vocabulary, or clavis (key) of words or terms, especially of those within a particular book that are specialised, uncommon, or new. From a co-creative perspective, which is based on social constructivism and which values flow, fluidity, and change, there may appear to be a certain irony and tension in defining things. However, as we know, definitions can be redefined! Money (1997) identified three *modes* of defining: stipulative (prescriptive and authoritative), reportive (reflecting common usage), and mythogenic (expressing radical reconceptualisations of concepts); as well as three *strategies* of defining—that is, using words (verbally), pointing (ostensively), and doing (performatively), the latter echoing Wittgenstein's (1922/1974) view or proposition that the meaning of a word is the *way* in which it is used. Thus, we offer this glossary principally in the mythogenic mode, using all three strategies, in that we are writing down our verbal use of words and terms and, thereby, pointing to different and possible usages, and demonstrating different ways of doing things, in this case transactional analysis—or design.

(the) Adult ego state—a metaphor for any experience that is not defensively organised.

Adulting (see **integrating**).

(the) archaeopsyche—A system aimed at organising unconscious archaic and unintegrated instinctual drives, basic needs and primary emotional experiences.

bullseye transaction—a stimulus and response that has the impact and effect of expanding the neopsyche/integrating Adult.

(the) Child ego state—a metaphor for archaic experiences that are fixated.

co-creative confirmation—a healthy affirmation of self or other that concludes a positive game—that is, a positive game pay-off.

co-creative empathic transacting—the process of communicating and receiving empathy (see Figure 6.1, p. 132).

co-creative identity—a sense or senses of self, based on past and present constructed narratives, influenced by significant others and the social/cultural context of the individual, co- and re-created in the present, culminating in a fluid self-definition and sometimes a limiting self-definition.

co-creative personality—the enduring sense of self, which, in transactional analysis, is conceptualised in terms of the metaphor Parent, Adult and Child aspects of self, each of which are psychic systems created and co-created through transactions and discourse (see also **ego state**).

co-creative reality—the co-construction of meaning through dialogue by means of a series of interactions or transactions between people as well as within the individual.

(the) co-creative script helix—a diagram that describes multiple script matrixes based on specific constructions that are significant to the subject (see Figure 1.4, p. 24).

(the) co-creative script matrix—a diagram that emphasises ongoing mutual influence between the subject and significant others (see Figure 1.3, p. 23 and Figure 10.2, p. 206).

co-creative transactional analysis—a contemporary interpretation of core transactional analysis concepts of ego states, transactions, games, and script, informed by field theory and social constructivism.

contamination(s)—Parent and Child ego states (see Figure 7.4, p. 153).

co-transference—the psychological field co-created by the archaic/introjected ego states of both therapist and client.

diagnosis—the co-constructed and shared knowing of the client and her or his processes as they change over time.

dynamic ego states—a variation of the co-creative ego state model, which ascribes levels of consciousness to different ego states.

ego state—a metaphor for a state or a coherent aspect of personality (see **co-creative identity**).

ego state models—various ways of framing and diagramming a transactional understanding of personality (for a summary of which, see Tudor, 2010b).

expanding Adult/expansion of the Adult—(a way of conceptualising) ongoing, self-generated or facilitated growth, including healing of past trauma.

(the) exteropsyche—a system aimed at organising introjected psychic material.

flow—"the holistic experience that people feel when they act with total involvement" (Csikszentmihalyi, 1975, p. 36).

game—"an ongoing series of complementary ulterior transactions progressing to a well-defined, predictable outcome" (Berne, 1964/1968a, p. 44; see also **co-creative confirmation**).

impasse, interpersonal—a stalemate conflict between two people where each person adopts a polarised stance in relation to the other.

impasse, intersubjective—a stalemate conflict between two shared but different psychological fields, each of which are co-created by both people.

impasse, intrapsychic—a stalemate conflict within the person between different ego states.

(the) Integrated Adult—1. a person exhibiting three kinds of tendencies: "personal attractiveness and responsiveness [pathos], objective data processing [logos], and ethical responsibility [ethos]" (Berne, 1961/1975a, p. 195); 2. Integrated Adult ego states are developed by "People moving towards autonomy [who] expand their personal capacities for awareness, spontaneity, and intimacy" (James & Jongeward, 1971, p. 297); 3. the healthy ego "in which the Adult ego state, with full neopsychic functioning, is in charge and has integrated (assimilated) archeopsychic and exteropsychic content and experiences" (Erskine, 1988, p. 19).

integrating—the process whereby humans take in material either through some internal process (such as reflection) or directly from the environment (such as feedback or appreciation).

(the) integrating Adult—1. an ego state that is "fully in contact both internally and externally" (Trautmann & Erskine, (1999, p. 16); 2. a metaphor for that aspect of the personality, which, being the neopsyche, is new in that it is constantly updating information derived from processing external stimuli, and internal experience, whether consciously, unconsciously, or non-consciously.

integration—the concept or state of integrating.

intuition—reflex imitation; thinking through subjective experience (see Berne, 1949/1977c).

life script (see **script**).

method—practice.

methodology—the philosophy, philosophical underpinnings and process of practice.

(the) neo–archaeopsyche two ego state model—a model that represents the distinction between, on the one hand, the present or "neo" aspects of the psyche, and, on the other, past, introjected and archaic states, in a binary—as distinct from the more familiar tripartite—model of the personality.

(the) neopsyche—An elaborative—and integrating—system that processes the mental-emotional analysis of the here-and-now.

(the) one ego state model of health—the model in which the Adult ego state is considered healthy and the Parent and Child ego states are considered to be defensive (for a review of which, see Tudor 2010b).

physis—"the force for Nature, which eternally strives to make things grow and to make growing things more perfect" (Berne, 1957/1981, p. 98).

pseudo physis—"a narcissistic, archaic Child or Parent defence" (Summers, personal communication, 2002; see p. 56).

relational transactional analysis—a development within transactional analysis that emphasises working in and with the relationship between therapist/practitioner and client; which emphasises intersubjectivity and, thereby, represents one-and-a-half and two-person psychologies (as distinct from one-person psychology) (see Stark, 1999), and, which, whilst drawing on different theoretical influences, operates on certain common principles (as elaborated by the International Association of Relational Transactional Analysis, 2010; see also Fowlie & Sills, 2011).

script—"the ongoing process of a self-defining and sometimes self-limiting psychological construction of reality" (Cornell, 1988, p. 281; see also **co-creative identity**).

self-Adulting (see **Adulting**).

(the) therapeutic contract—"an explicit bilateral agreement to a well-defined course of action" (Berne, 1966, p. 362).

three ego state model of personality—the model in which all ego states are considered as potentially healthy aspects of personality (for a review of which, see Tudor 2010b).

transaction (see **co-creative relationship**).

unitary—not defensively split.

REFERENCES

Agel, J. (Ed.) (1971). *The Radical Therapist*. New York: Ballantine.

Allen, J. R. (2006). Oklahoma City ten years later: Positive psychology, transactional analysis and the transformation of trauma from a terrorist attack. *Transactional Analysis Journal, 36*(2): 120–133.

Allen, J. R. (2010). The neurosciences, psychotherapy and transactional analysis: A second look [Posting]. In: C. Shadbolt (Moderator), *International Association of Relational Transactional Analysis. Online Colloquium, No. 2*. www.relationalta.com [last accessed 30/10/2010].

Allen, J. R., & Allen, B. A. (1991). Concepts of transference: A critique, a typology, an alternative hypothesis, and some proposals. *Transactional Analysis Journal, 21*: 77–91.

Allen, J. R., & Allen, B. A. (1995). Narrative theory, redecision therapy, and postmodernism. *Transactional Analysis Journal, 25*: 327–334.

Allen, J. R., & Allen, B. A. (1997). A new type of transactional analysis and one version of script work with a constructivist sensibility. *Transactional Analysis Journal, 27*: 89–98.

Amundson, J. K., & Parry, T. A. (1979). The willing Adult. *Transactional Analysis Journal, 9*(1): 20–5.

Angyal, A. (1939). The structure of wholes. *Philosophy of Science, 6*(1): 25–37.

Angyal, A. (1941). *Foundations for a Science of Personality*. New York: Commonwealth Fund.

Angyal, A. (1973). *Neurosis and Treatment: A Holistic Theory*. New York: Wiley [original work published 1965].

Antonovsky, A. (1979). *Health, Stress and Coping: New Perspectives on Mental and Physical Well-Being*. San Francisco, CA: Jossey-Bass.

Antonovsky, A. (1987). The salutogenetic perspective: Toward a new view of health and illness. *Advances, 4*: 47.

Ariely, D., Loewenstein, G., & Prelec, D. (2003). Coherent arbitrariness: Stable demand curves without stable preferences. *The Quarterly Journal of Economics, 118*(1): 73–106.

Aron, L. (1996). *A Meeting of Minds: Mutuality in Psychoanalysis*. Hillsdale, NJ: Analytic Press.

Atkinson, D., Morton, G., & Sue, D. W. (1989). *Counseling American Minorities: A Cross Cultural Perspective*. Dubuque, IA: William C. Brown.

Atwood, G. E., & Stolorow, R. D. (1984). *Structures of Subjectivity*. Hillsdale, NJ: Analytic Press.

Atwood, G., & Stolorow, R. (1996). The intersubjective perspective. *Psychoanalytic Review, 83*: 181–194.

Bale, A. (1999). Prenatal personality formation and ego states. *Transactional Analysis Journal, 29*(1): 59–63.

Banks, J., & Deuze, M. (2009). Co-creative labour. *International Journal of Cultural Studies, 12*(5): 419–431.

Barnes, G. (2004). Homosexuality in the first three decades of transactional analysis: A study of theory in the practice of transactional analysis psychotherapy. *Transactional Analysis Journal, 34*(2): 126–155.

Barnes, G. (2007). Not without the couch: Eric Berne on basic differences between transactional analysis and psychoanalysis. *Transactional Analysis Journal, 37*(1): 41–50.

Barr, J. (1987). The therapeutic relationship model: Perspectives on the core of the healing process. *Transactional Analysis Journal, 17*: 134–140.

Barrett-Lennard, G. (1985). The helping relationship: Crisis and advance in theory and research. *The Counseling Psychologist, 13*(2): 279–294.

Bazzano, M. (2011). The Buddha as a fully functioning person: Toward a person-centered perspective on mindfulness. *Person-Centered & Experiential Psychotherapies, 10*(2): 116–128.

Bergin, A. E., & Lambert, M. J. (1978). The evaluation of therapeutic outcomes. In: S. L. Garfield & A. E. Bergin (Eds.), *Handbook of Psychotherapy and Behavior Change* (2nd edition) (pp. 139–190). New York: Wiley.

Berne, E. (1947). *The Mind in Action*. New York: Simon & Schuster.

Berne, E. (1963). *The Structure and Dynamics of Organisations and Groups*. New York: Grove Press.

Berne, E. (1966). *Principles of Group Treatment*. New York: Grove Press.

Berne, E. (1968a). *Games People Play: The Psychology of Human Relationships*. Harmondsworth, UK: Penguin (original work published 1964).

Berne, E. (1968b). Staff–Patient staff conferences. *American Journal of Psychiatry, 125*(3): 286–293.

Berne, E. (1973). *Sex in Human Loving*. Harmondsworth, UK: Penguin (original work published 1970).

Berne, E. (1975a). *Transactional Analysis in Psychotherapy: A Systematic Individual and Social Psychiatry*. London: Souvenir Press [original work published 1961].

Berne, E. (1975b). *What Do You Say After You Say Hello? The Psychology of Human Destiny*. London: Corgi [original work published 1972].

Berne, E. (1977a). *Intuition and Ego States: The Origins of Transactional Analysis* (P. McCormick, Ed.). San Francisco, CA: TA Press.

Berne, E. (1977b). Primal images and primal judgement. In: P. McCormick (Ed.), *Intuition and Ego States: The Origins of Transactional Analysis* (pp. 67–97). San Francisco, CA: TA Press [original work published 1955].

Berne, E. (1977c). The nature of intuition. In: P. McCormick (Ed.), *Intuition and Ego States: The Origins of Transactional Analysis* (pp. 1–31). San Francisco, CA: TA Press [original work published 1949].

Berne, E. (1977d). The psychodynamics of intuition. In: P. McCormick (Ed.), *Intuition and Ego States: The Origins of Transactional Analysis* (pp. 159–166). San Francisco, CA: TA Press [original work published 1962].

Berne, E. (1981). *A Layman's Guide to Psychiatry and Psychoanalysis*. Harmondsworth, UK: Penguin [original work published 1957].

Blackstone, P. (1993). The dynamic Child: Integration of second-order structure, object relations, and self psychology. *Transactional Analysis Journal, 23*(4): 216–234.

Bleuler, J. (1914). Die Kritik der Schizophrenien [Criticisms of [Freud's paper on] schizophrenia], *Zeitschrift für die Gesamte Neurologie und Psychiatrie, 22*: 19–44.

Bohart, A. C., & Tallman, K. (1999). *How Clients Make Therapy Work: The Process of Active Self-Healing*. Washington, DC: American Psychological Association.

Bollas, C. (1987). *The Shadow of the Object: Psychoanalysis of the Unthought Unknown*. New York: Columbia University Press.

Boston Change Process Study Group. (2010). *Change in Psychotherapy*. New York: W. W. Norton.

Boyd, L. W., & Boyd, H. S. (1980). Caring and intimacy as a time structure. *Transactional Analysis Journal, 10*(4): 281–283.

Brady, F. N. (1980). Philosophical links to TA: Kant and the concept of Reason in the Adult ego state. *Transactional Analysis Journal, 10*(3): 252–254.

Brah, A. (1992). Difference, diversity and differentiation. In: J. Donald & A. Rattansi (Eds.), *Race, Culture and Difference* (pp. 126–145). London: Sage.

Brodley, B. T. (1999). The actualizing tendency concept in client-centered theory. *The Person-Centered Journal, 6*(2): 108–120.

Bruner, J. (1986). *Actual Minds, Possible Worlds*. Cambridge, MA: Harvard University Press.

Buber, M. (1937). *I and Thou* (R. G. Smith, Trans.). Edinburgh, UK: T & T Clark [original work published 1923].

Bucci, W. (1997). *Psychoanalysis and Cognitive Science: A Multiple Code Theory*. New York: Guilford Press.

Burrell, G., & Morgan, G. (1979). *Sociological Paradigms and Organisational Analysis*. London: Heinemann.

Chandran, S. (2007). Connecting with the guru within: Supervision in the Indian context. *Transactional Analysis Journal, 37*(3): 218–226.

Cheney, W. D. (1971). Eric Berne: Biographical sketch. *Transactional Analysis Journal, 1*(1): 14–22.

Chinnock, K. (2011). Relational transactional analysis supervision. *Transactional Analysis Journal, 41*(4): 336–350.

Choy, A. (1990). The winner's triangle. *Transactional Analysis Journal, 20*(1): 40–46.

Clark, B. D. (1991). Empathic transactions in the deconfusion of the child ego states. *Transactional Analysis Journal, 21*(2): 92–98.

Clarkson, P. (1987). The bystander role. *Transactional Analysis Journal, 17*(3): 82–87.

Clarkson, P. (1990). A multiplicity of psychotherapeutic relationships. *British Journal of Psychotherapy, 7*: 148–163.

Clarkson, P. (1992a). Physis in transactional analysis. *Transactional Analysis Journal, 22*(4): 202–209.

Clarkson, P. (1992b). *Transactional Analysis Psychotherapy: An Integrated Approach*. London: Routledge.

Clarkson, P. (1995). *The Therapeutic Relationship*. London: Whurr.

Clarkson, P., & Fish, S. (1988). Rechilding: Creating a new past in the present as a support for the future. *Transactional Analysis Journal, 18*(1): 51–59.

Clarkson, P., & Gilbert, M. (1988). Berne's original model of ego states. *Transactional Analysis Journal, 18*(1): 20–29.

Clarkson, P., & Gilbert, M. (1991). The training of counsellor trainers and supervisors. In: W. Dryden & B. Thorne (Eds.), *Training and Supervision for Counselling in Action* (pp. 143–169). London: Sage.

Coates, N., & Peters, A. (n.d.). *The Co-creative Organization of the Future* [Slide presentation]. www.slideshare.net/nickcoates/the-co-creative-organization-of-the-future [last accessed 23/07/2013].

Cornell, W. F. (1988). Life script theory: A critical review from a developmental perspective. *Transactional Analysis Journal, 18*: 270–282.

Cornell, W. F. (2000). If Berne met Winnicott: Transactional analysis and relational analysis. *Transactional Analysis Journal, 30*(4): 270–275.

Cornell, W. F. (2003). Brains, babies and bodies: Somatic foundation of the Child. In: C. Sills & H. Hargaden (Eds.), *Ego States. Key Concepts in Transactional Analysis: Contemporary Views* (pp. 28–54). London: Worth.

Cornell, W. F., & Hargaden, H. (Eds.), (2005). *From Transactions to Relations: The Emergence of a Relational Tradition in Transactional Analysis.* Chadlington, UK: Haddon Press.

Cornell, W. F., & Landaiche III, M. N. (2006). Impasse theory and intimacy: Applying Berne's concept of script protocol. *Transactional Analysis Journal, 36*(3): 196–213.

Cornell. W. F., & Landaiche III, N. M. (2008). Nonconscious processes and self-development: Key concepts from Eric Berne and Christopher Bollas. *Transactional Analysis Journal, 38*(3): 200–218.

Cornell, W. F. (Ed.), Hargaden, H., Allen, J. R., Erskine, R., Moiso, C., Sills, C., Summers, G., & Tudor, K. (2006). Roundtable on the ethics of relational transactional analysis. *Transactional Analysis Journal, 36*: 105–119.

Cozolino, L. (2002). *The Neuroscience of Psychotherapy: Building and Rebuilding the Human Brain.* New York: W. W. Norton.

Csikszentmihalyi, M. (1975). *Beyond Boredom and Anxiety.* San Francisco, CA: Jossey-Bass.

Csikszentmihalyi, M. (1990). *Flow: The Psychology of Optimal Experience.* New York: Harper & Row.

Damasio, A. (1996). *Descartes' Error: Emotion, Reason and the Human Brain.* New York: Harper Collins [original work published 1994].

Damasio, A. (2010). *Self Comes to Mind: Constructing the Conscious Brain.* New York: Pantheon.

Dashiell, S. R. (1978). The parent resolution process: Reprogramming psychic incorporations in the parent. *Transactional Analysis Journal, 8*(4): 289–295.

de Bono, E. (1992). *Serious Creativity.* London: HarperCollins.

Drego, P. (2000). Toward an ethic of ego states. *Transactional Analysis Journal, 30*(3): 192–206.

Duncan, B. L., & Moynihan, D. W. (1994). Applying outcome research: Intentional utilization of the client's frame of reference. *Psychotherapy, 31*(2): 294–301.

Duncan, B. L., Miller, S. D., Wampold, B. E., & Hubble, M. A. (2010). *The Heart and Soul of Change: Delivering What Works in Therapy* (2nd edition). Washington, DC: American Psychological Association.

Dylan, B. (1975). Lily, Rosemary and the Jack of Hearts. *Blood on the Tracks* [Album]. New York: Columbia Records.

Edelman, G. M. (1989). *The Remembered Present: A Biological Theory of Consciousness.* New York: Basic.

Embleton Tudor, L. (2010). *Dissociation: A Fragile Process*. A talk given to the New Zealand Association of Psychotherapists (Northern Branch) meeting, Auckland, Aotearoa New Zealand.

Embleton Tudor, L. (2011). The neuroscience and politics of regulation. In: K. Tudor (Ed.), *The Turning Tide: Pluralism and Partnership in Psychotherapy in Aotearoa New Zealand* (pp. 167–176). Auckland, Aotearoa New Zealand: LC Publications.

Embleton Tudor, L., & Tudor, K. (2009). Past present: Person-centred therapy with trauma and enactment. In: D. Mann & V. Cunningham (Eds.), *The Past in the Present: Therapy Enactments and the Return of Trauma* (pp. 136–154). London: Routledge.

Embleton Tudor, L., Keemar, K., Tudor, K., Valentine, J., & Worrall, M. (2004). *The Person-Centred Approach: A Contemporary Introduction*. Basingstoke, UK: Palgrave.

English, F. (1975). The three-cornered contract. *Transactional Analysis Journal*, 5(4): 383–384.

English, F. (1977). What shall I do tomorrow? Reconceptualising transactional analysis. In: G. Barnes (Ed.), *Transactional Analysis after Eric Berne: Teachings and Practices of Three TA Schools* (pp. 287–350). New York: Harper's College Press.

Erikson, E. (1965). *Childhood and Society*. New York: W. W. Norton [original work published 1950].

Erikson, E. (1968). *Identity, Youth and Crisis*. New York: W. W. Norton.

Erskine, R. G. (1974). Therapeutic interventions: Disconnecting rubberbands. *Transactional Analysis Journal*, 4(1): 7–8.

Erskine, R. G. (1988). Ego structure, intrapsychic function, and defense mechanisms: A commentary on Eric Berne's original theoretical concepts. *Transactional Analysis Journal*, 18(1): 15–19.

Erskine, R. G. (1991). Transference and transactions: Critique from an intrapsychic and integrative perspective. *Transactional Analysis Journal*, 21(1): 63–76.

Erskine, R. G. (1993). Inquiry, attunement, and involvement in the psychotherapy of dissociation. *Transactional Analysis Journal*, 23(4): 184–190.

Erskine, R. G. (1998a). Attunement and involvement: Therapeutic responses to relational needs. *International Journal of Psychotherapy*, 3(3): 235–243.

Erskine, R. G. (1998b). The therapeutic relationship: Integrating motivation and personality theories. *Transactional Analysis Journal*, 28(2): 132–141.

Erskine, R. G. (2009). The culture of transactional analysis: Theory, methods, and evolving practice. *Transactional Analysis Journal*, 39(1): 14–21.

Erskine, R. G., & Moursund, J. P. (1988). *Integrative Psychotherapy in Action*. Newbury Park, CA: Sage.

Erskine, R. G., & Trautmann, R. L. (1996). Methods of an integrative psychotherapy. *Transactional Analysis Journal, 26*(4): 316–329.

European Association of Transactional Analysis. (2013). Oral examination CTA psychotherapy scoring sheet. *EATA Training and Examination Handbook* [Form 12.7.12]. Konstanz, Germany: EATA.

Eusden, S. (2011). Minding the gap: Ethical considerations for therapeutic engagement. *Transactional Analysis Journal, 41*(2): 101–113.

Eusden, S., & Summers, G. (2008). *Vital Rhythms*. [Pre-conference institute]. The Australasian Transactional Analysis Conference, Rotorua, Aotearoa New Zealand.

Fairbairn, W. R. D. (1952). *Psychological Studies of the Personality*. London: Routledge & Kegan Paul.

Fay, J. (2008). Conservative, liberal and radical psychotherapy. *Forum* [the Journal of the New Zealand Association of Psychotherapists], *14*: 103–110.

Federn, P. (1928). Narcissism in the structure of the ego. *International Journal of Psycho-Analysis, 9*: 401–419.

Federn, P. (1932). Ego feeling in dreams. *Psychoanalytic Quarterly, 1*: 511–542.

Federn, P. (1952a). *Ego Psychology and the Psychoses* (E. Weiss, Ed.). New York: Basic.

Federn, P. (1952b). The ego as subject and object in narcissism. In: E. Weiss (Ed.), *Ego psychology and the psychoses* (pp. 283–322). New York: Basic [original work published 1929].

Fogel, A. (1993). *Developing Through Relationships: Origins of Communication, Self, and Culture*. Chicago, IL: University of Chicago Press.

Fosshage, J. (2010). Implicit and explicit pathways to psychoanalytic change. In: J. Petrucelli (Ed.), *Knowing, Not-Knowing and Sort of Knowing: Psychoanalysis and the Spirit of Uncertainty* (pp. 215–224). London: Karnac.

Fowlie, H. (2005). Confusion and introjection: A model for understanding the defensive structures of the parent and child ego states. *Transactional Analysis Journal, 35*(2): 192–204.

Fowlie, H., & Sills, C. (Eds.), (2011). *Relational Transactional Analysis: Principles in Practice*. London: Karnac.

Fredrickson, B. (2009). *Positivity: Groundbreaking Research Reveals How to Embrace the Hidden Strength of Positive Emotions, Overcome Negativity, and Thrive*. New York: Crown Publications.

Freire, E. S. (2006). Randomized controlled clinical trial in psychotherapy research: An epistemological controversy. *Journal of Humanistic Psychology, 46*(3): 322–335.

Freire, P. (1972). *The Pedagogy of the Oppressed* (M. B. Ramos, Trans.). Harmondsworth, UK: Penguin [original work published 1970].

Freud, S. (1900a). *The Interpretation of Dreams* (first part). *S. E.* 4: xxiii–338. London: Hogarth Press.

Freud, S. (1915e). *The Unconscious. S. E.* 14: 166–215. London: Hogarth Press.

Freud, S. (1923b). *The Ego and the Id. S. E.* 19: 13–27. London: Hogarth Press.

Fromm, E. (1968). *The Revolution of Hope.* New York: Bantam.

Gardener, H. (1983). *Frames of Mind: The Theory of Multiple Intelligences.* New York: Basic.

Gelso, C. J., & Carter, J. A. (1985). The relationship in counseling and psychotherapy: Components, consequences and theoretical antecedents. *The Counseling Psychologist, 13*(2): 155–243.

Gergin, K. J. (1985). The social constructionist movement in psychology. *American Psychologist, 40*: 266–275.

Gergen, K. J. (1991). *The Saturated Self.* New York: Basic.

Giesekus, U., & Mente, A. (1986). Client empathic understanding in client-centered therapy. *Person-Centered Review, 1*(2): 163–171.

Gildebrand, K. (2003). An introduction to the brain and the early development of the Child ego state. In: C. Sills & H. Hargaden (Eds.), *Ego States. Key Concepts in Transactional Analysis: Contemporary Views* (pp. 1–27). London: Worth.

Glover, E. (1955). *The Technique of Psychoanalysis* (revised edition). London: Baillière, Tindall & Cox.

Goldstein, K. (1995). *The Organism.* New York: Zone Books [original work published 1934].

Gordon, D. (1978). *Therapeutic Metaphors.* Cupertino, CA: Meta Publications.

Goulding, M. M., & Goulding, R. L. (1979). *Changing Lives through Redecision Therapy.* New York: Brunner/Mazel.

Goulding, R. L., & Goulding, M. M. (1976). Injunctions, decisions, and redecisions. *Transactional Analysis Journal, 6*(1): 41–48.

Goulding, R. L., & Goulding, M. M. (1978). *The Power is in the Patient: A TA/Gestalt Approach to Psychotherapy* (P. McCormick, Ed.). San Francisco, CA: TA Press.

Greenson, R. R. (1967). *The Technique and Practice of Psychoanalysis. Vol. 1.* New York: International Universities Press.

Grégoire, J. (2004). Ego states as living links between past and current experiences. *Transactional Analysis Journal, 34*(1): 10–29.

Grégoire, J. (2007). *Les Orientations Récentes de L'analyse Transactionnelle* [The Recent Orientations of Transactional Analysis]. Lyon, France: Les Éditions d'Analyse Transactionnelle.

Hagehülsmann, H. (1984). The "Menschenbild" in transactional analysis: Conceptions of human nature. In: E. Stern (Ed.), *TA: The State of the Art.*

A European Contribution (pp. 39–59). Dordrecht, The Netherlands: Foris Publications.

Hall, C., & Lindzey, G. (1970). *Theories of Personality*. New York: Wiley.

Hall, C., & Lindzey, G. (1978). *Theories of Personality* (3rd edition). New York: Wiley.

Hall, S. (2008). *Anger, Rage and Relationship: An Empathic Approach to Anger Management*. London: Routledge.

Hargaden, H. (2001). There ain't no cure for love: The psychotherapy of an erotic transference. *Transactional Analysis Journal, 31*(4): 213–219.

Hargaden, H., & Fenton, B. (2005). An analysis of nonverbal transactions drawing on theories of intersubjectivity. *Transactional Analysis Journal, 35*(2): 173–186.

Hargaden, H., & Sills, C. (2001). Deconfusion of the child ego state: A relational perspective. *Transactional Analysis Journal, 31*(1): 55–70.

Hargaden, H., & Sills, C. (2002). *Transactional Analysis: A Relational Perspective*. London: Routledge.

Harré, R. (1983). *Personal Being*. Oxford, UK: Blackwell.

Hartmann, H. (1958). *Ego Psychology and the Problem of Adaptation*. London: Imago [original work published 1939].

Hawkes, L. (2003). The tango of therapy: A dancing group. *Transactional Analysis Journal, 33*(4): 288–301.

Helms, J. E. (1984). Towards a theoretical model of the effects of race on counseling: A black and white model. *The Counseling Psychologist, 12*: 153–165.

Heron, J. (1971). *Experience and Method*. Human potential research project, University of Surrey, Guildford, UK.

Hill, C. E. (1989). *Therapist Techniques and Client Outcomes*. Newbury Park, CA: Sage.

Hine, J. (1997). Mind structure and ego states. *Transactional Analysis Journal, 27*(4): 278–289.

Hirsch, I. (2008). *Coasting in the Countertransference: Conflicts of Self-Interest Between Analyst and Patient*. New York: Analytic Press.

Hoffman, L. (1993). A reflective stance for family therapy. In: S. McNamee & K. J. Gergen (Eds.), *Therapy as Social Construction* (pp. 7–24). London: Sage.

Hofmann, S. G., & Weinberger, J. (2006). *The Art and Science of Psychotherapy*. London: Routledge.

Hollis, J. (2009). *What Matters Most: Living a More Considered Life*. New York: Gotham.

Holloway, W. (1977). Transactional analysis: An integrative view. In: G. Barnes (Ed.), *Transactional Analysis after Eric Berne* (pp. 169–221). New York: Harper's College Press.

Holmes, J. (1993). *John Bowlby and Attachment Theory*. London: Routledge.

House, R., Kalich, D., & Maidman, J. (Eds.), (2013). Carl Rogers' new challenge [Special issue]. *Self & Society: An International Journal for Humanistic Psychology*, 40.

Hudson-Allez, G. (2008). *Infant losses, adult searches: A neural and developmental perspective on psychopathology and sexual offending*. London: Karnac.

Hunter, D., Bailey, A., & Taylor, B. (1998). *Co-Operacy: A New Way of Being at Work*. Cambridge, MA: Da Capo Press.

Institute of Transactional Analysis. (2013). *Code of Practice for Psychotherapy Trainers and Training Establishments*. Cambridge, UK: ITA.

International Association for Relational Transactional Analysis. (2010). *Relational Transactional Analysis (RTA)—An Introduction*. www.relationalta. com/what_is_rta.php [last accessed 30/11/2010].

Ivey, A. E., Ivey, M. B., & Simek-Morgan, L. (1993). *Counseling and Psychotherapy* (3rd edition). Boston, MA: Allyn & Bacon.

Jackson, P. Z., & McKergow, M. (2007). *The Solutions Focus*. London: Nicholas Brealey.

Jackson, P. Z., & Summers, G. (2010). Constructive games people play: e-Organisations and people. *Association for Management Education and Development*, 17(1): 41–45.

Jacobs, A. (2000). Psychic organs, ego states, and visual metaphors: Speculation on Berne's integration of ego states. *Transactional Analysis Journal*, 30(1): 10–22.

Jahoda, M. (1958). *Current Concepts of Positive Mental Health*. New York: Basic.

James, J. (1973). The game plan. *Transactional Analysis Journal*, 3(4): 194–197.

James, M., & Jongeward, D. (1971). *Born to Win: Transactional Analysis with Gestalt Experiments*. Reading, MA: Addison-Wesley.

Jorgenson, E. W., & Jorgenson, H. I. (1984). *Eric Berne: Master Gamesman*. New York: Grove Press.

Kabat-Zinn, J. (1994). *Wherever You Go, There You Are: Mindfulness Meditation in Everyday Life*. New York: Hyperion.

Kahn, M. (1997). *Between Therapist and Client: The New Relationship*. New York: W. H. Freeman.

Kantor, J. R. (1924a). *Principles of Psychology. Vol.1*. New York: Knopf.

Kantor, J. R. (1924b). *Principles of Psychology. Vol.2*. New York: Knopf.

Karpman, S. (1968). Fairy tales and script drama analysis. *Transactional Analysis Bulletin*, 7(26): 39–43.

Kennard, D., & Lees, J. (2001). A checklist of standards for democratic therapeutic communities. *Therapeutic Communities*, 22(2): 143–151.

Kirsher, I. (Director), (1980). *The Empire Strikes Back* [Film]. Los Angeles, CA: Twentieth Century Fox.

Klein, Mavis. (1980). *Lives People Live*. London: Wiley.

Klein, Melanie. (1960). On mental health. *British Journal of Medical Psychology, 33*: 237–241.

Kohlrieser, G. (2006). *Hostage at the Table: How Leaders Can Overcome Conflict, Influence Others, and Raise Performance*. San Francisco, CA: Jossey-Bass.

Kohut, H. (1971). *The Analysis of the Self*. New York: International Universities Press.

Kohut, H. (1977). *The Restoration of the Self: A Systematic Approach to the Psychoanalytic Treatment of Narcissistic Personality Disorder*. New York: International Universities Press.

Kopp, S. (1971). *If You Meet the Buddha on the Road, Kill Him!* London: Sheldon.

Krumper, M. (1977). Sub-dividing the Adult: Ac and Aa. *Transactional Analysis Journal, 7*(4): 298–299.

Kujit, J. (1980). Differentiation of the Adult ego state. *Transactional Analysis Journal, 10*(3): 232–237.

Lake, F. (1980). *Studies in Constricted Confusion: Exploration of a Pre- and Perinatal Paradigm*. Nottingham, UK: The Clinical Theology Association.

Lambert, M. J. (1992). Psychotherapy outcome research: Implications for integrative and eclectic therapists. In: J. Norcross & M. R. Goldfried (Eds.), *Handbook of Psychotherapy Integration* (pp. 94–129). New York: Basic.

Land, C. (2012). Occupy Auckland. *Psychotherapy and Politics International, 10*(1): 79–82.

Lapworth, P., & Sills, C. (2011). *Transactional Analysis Counselling: Helping People Change*. London: Sage.

Lapworth, P., Sills, C., & Fish, S. (1993). *Transactional Analysis Counselling*. Bicester, UK: Winslow.

LeDoux, J. (1998). *The Emotional Brain*. London: Weidenfeld & Nicolson.

Lee, A. (1997). Process contracts. In: C. Sills (Ed.), *Contracts in Counselling* (pp. 94–112). London: Sage.

Levin, P. (1974). *Becoming The Way We Are: A Transactional Analysis Guide to Personal Development*. Berkeley, CA: Transactional Publications.

Levin-Landheer, P. (1982). The cycle of development. *Transactional Analysis Journal, 12*(2): 129–139.

Lewin, K. (1952). *Field Theory in Social Science*. London: Tavistock.

Little, R. (2001). Schizoid processes: Working with the defenses of the withdrawn child ego state. *Transactional Analysis Journal, 31*(1): 33–43.

Little, R. (2006). Ego state relational units and resistance to change. *Transactional Analysis Journal, 36*(1): 7–19.

Little, R. (2011). Impasse clarification within the transference-countertransference matrix. *Transactional Analysis Journal, 41*(1): 23–38.

Loewenthal, D. (2011). *Post-existentialism and the Psychological Therapies: Towards a Therapy without Foundations.* London: Karnac.

Lorenzer, A. (1970). *Sprachzerstörung und Rekonstruktion* [The Destruction of Language and its Reconstruction]. Frankfurt, Germany: Suhrkamp.

Loria, B. R. (1990). Epistemology and the reification of metaphor in transactional analysis. *Transactional Analysis Journal, 20*(3): 152–161.

Luborsky, L., Crits-Christoph, P., Alexander, L., Margolis, M., & Cohen, M. (1983). Two helping alliance methods for predicting outcome of psychotherapy. *Journal of Nervous and Mental Disease, 171*: 480–491.

Lyons-Ruth, K., Bruschweiler-Stern, N., Harrison, A. M., Morgan, A. C., Nahum, J. P., Sander, L., & Tronick, E. Z. (1998). Implicit relational knowing: Its role in development and psychoanalytic treatment. *Infant Mental Health Journal, 19*(3): 282–289.

Magner, V. (1985). *Series of Comparative Charts of Psychological Theory No.1: Child Development.* Available from Metanoia Institute, 13 North Common Road, London W5, UK.

Maslow, A. H. (1954). *Motivation and Personality.* New York: Harper & Row.

Maslow, A. H. (1993). Self-actualization and beyond. In: A. H. Maslow, *The Farther Reaches of Human Nature* (pp. 40–51). London: Arkana [original work published 1967].

Mattingly, C. (1991). What is clinical reasoning? *The American Journal of Occupational Therapy, 45*(11): 979–986.

Matze, M. G. (1991). Commentary on transactions in the context of transference. *Transactional Analysis Journal, 21*(3): 141–143.

McNeel, J. R. (1976). The parent interview. *Transactional Analysis Journal, 6*(1); 61–68.

Mead, G. H. (1980). *The Philosophy of the Present* (A. E. Murphy, Ed.). Chicago, IL: University of Chicago Press [original work published 1932].

Mearns, D. (1994). The dance of psychotherapy. *Person-Centred Practice, 2*(2): 5–13.

Mearns, D., & Schmid, P. F. (2006). Being-with and being-counter: Relational depth: The challenge of fully meeting the client. *Person-Centered & Experiential Psychotherapies, 5*(4): 255–265.

Mehrabian, A. (1981). *Silent Messages: Implicit Communication of Emotions and Attitudes* (2nd edition). Belmont, CA: Wadsworth.

Mellor, K. (1980). Impasses: A developmental and structural understanding. *Transactional Analysis Journal, 10*(3): 213–220.

Mellor, K., & Andrewartha, G. (1980). Reparenting the parent in support of redecisions. *Transactional Analysis Journal, 10*(3): 197–203.

Menaker, E. (1995). *The Freedom to Inquire*. Northvale, NJ: Jason Aronson.

Mlodinow, L. (2013). *Subliminal: How Your Unconscious Mind Rules Your Behavior*. New York: Vintage.

Modell, A. H. (2003). *Imagination and the Meaningful Brain*. Cambridge, MA: Massachusetts Institute of Technology.

Mohr, G. (2011). *Individual and Organisational TA for the 21st Century*. Berlin, Germany: Pro Business Publishers.

Moiso, C., & Novellino, M. (2000). An overview of the psychodynamic school of transactional analysis and its epistemological foundations. *Transactional Analysis Journal, 30*(3): 182–187.

Money, M. (1997). Defining mental health—What do we think we're doing? In: M. Money & L. Buckley (Eds.), *Positive Mental Health and its Promotion* (pp. 13–15). Liverpool, UK: Institute for Health, John Moores University.

Moreno, J. L. (1977). *Psychodrama* (Vol. 1; 5th edition). New York: Beacon House.

Morgan, S., & Juriansz, D. (2002). Practice-based evidence. *OpenMind, 114*: 12–13.

Mountain, A., & Davidson, C. (2005). Assessing systems and processes in organizations. *Transactional Analysis Journal, 35*(4): 336–345.

Moursund, J. P., & Erskine, R. G. (2004). *Integrative Psychotherapy: The Art and Science of Relationship*. New York: Brooks/Cole.

Moustakas, C. (1990). *Heuristic Research: Design, Methodology and Applications*. London: Sage.

Murakami, H. (2006). Aeroplane: Or, how he talked to himself as if reciting poetry. In: H. Murakami, *Blind Willow, Sleeping Woman* (J. Rubin, Trans.; pp. 45–53). London, UK: Harvill Secker.

Murphy, G. (1947). *Personality: A Biosocial Approach to Origins and Structure*. New York: Harper.

Napper, R. (2009). Positive psychology and transactional analysis. *Transactional Analysis Journal, 39*(1): 61–74.

Naughton, M., & Tudor, K. (2006). Being white. *Transactional Analysis Journal, 36*(2): 159–171.

Neugarten, B. L. (1968). *Middle Age and Ageing*. Chicago: Chicago University Press.

Newton, T. (2003). Identifying educational philosophy and practice through imagoes in transactional analysis training groups. *Transactional Analysis Journal, 33*(4): 321–331.

Newton, T. (Ed.), (2004). Transactional analysis and education [Special issue]. *Transactional Analysis Journal, 34*(3).

Newton, T. (2007). The health system: Metaphor and meaning. *Transactional Analysis Journal, 37*(3): 195–205.

Newton, N., & Napper, R. (2007). The bigger picture: Supervision as an educational framework for all fields. *Transactional Analysis Journal, 37*(2): 150–158.

Newton, N., & Napper, R. (Eds.), (2009). Transactional analysis training [Special issue]. *Transactional Analysis Journal, 39*(4).

Newton, N., & Wong, G. (2003). A chance to thrive: Enabling change in a nursery school. *Transactional Analysis Journal, 33*(1): 79–88.

Novellino, M. (1993). On closer analysis: A psychodynamic revision of the rules of communication within the framework of transactional psychoanalysis. In: C. Sills & H. Hargaden (Eds.), *Ego States. Key Concepts in Transactional Analysis: Contemporary Views* (pp. 149–168). London: Worth.

Novellino, M. (2012). *The Transactional Analyst in Action: Clinical Seminars.* London: Karnac.

Novey, T. B., Porter-Steele, N., Gobes, N., & Massey, R. F. (1993). Ego states and the self-concept: A panel presentation and discussion. *Transactional Analysis Journal, 23*(3): 123–138.

Ogden, T. (1994). The analytic third: Working with intersubjective clinical facts. *International Journal of Psycho-Analysis, 75*(1): 3–20.

O'Hara, M. (1997). Relational empathy: Beyond modernist geocentricism to postmodern holistic contextualism. In: A. C. Bohart & L. S. Greenberg (Eds.), *Empathy Reconsidered: New Directions in Psychotherapy* (pp. 295–319). Washington, DC: American Psychological Association.

O'Hara, M. (1999). Moments of eternity: Carl Rogers and the contemporary demand for brief therapy. In: I. Fairhurst (Ed.), *Women Writing in the Person-Centred Approach* (pp. 63–77). Ross-on-Wye, UK: PCCS.

Ohlsson, T. (1988). Two ways of doing regressive therapy: Using transactional analysis proper and using expressive techniques. *Transactional Analysis Journal, 28*(1): 83–87.

Orange, D. M., Atwood, G. E., & Stolorow, R. D. (1997). *Working Intersubjectively: Contextualism in Psychoanalytic Practice.* Hillsdale, NJ: Analytic Press.

Pally, R. (2000). *The Mind–Brain Relationship.* London: Karnac.

Panksepp, J. (1998). *Affective Neuroscience: The Foundations of Human and Animal Emotions.* Oxford, UK: Oxford University Press.

Parlett, M. (1991). Reflections on field theory. *The British Gestalt Journal, 1*: 69–81.

Perls, F. S. (1971). *Gestalt Therapy Verbatim* (J. O. Stevens, Comp. & Ed.). New York: Bantam [original work published 1969].

Perls, F. S., Hefferline, & Goodman. (1996). *Gestalt Therapy.* Highland, NJ: Gestalt Journal Press[original work published 1951].

Petriglieri, G. (2007). Stuck in a moment: A developmental perspective on impasses. *Transactional Analysis Journal, 37*(3): 185–194.

Phelan, B. N., & Phelan, P. E. (1978). The fully functioning adult. *Transactional Analysis Journal, 8*(2): 123–126.

Philippson, P. (2009). *Self in Relation*. Highland, NY: Gestalt Journal Press.

Phillips, A. (1988). *Winnicott*. London: Fontana.

Pine, F. (1990). *Drive, Ego, Object and Self*. New York: Basic.

Piontelli, A. (1992). *From Fetus to Child*. London: Tavistock/Routledge.

Prahalad, C. K., & Ramaswamy, V. (2000). Co-opting customer competence. *Harvard Business Review, 78*(1): 79–88.

Reason, P., & Rowan, J. (1981). *Human Inquiry: A Sourcebook of New Paradigm Research*. London: Wiley.

Riebel, L. (1996). Self-sealing doctrines, the misuse of power, and recovered memory. *Transactional Analysis Journal, 26*(1): 40–45.

Ringstrom, P. (2010). Meeting Mitchell's challenge: A comparison of relational psychoanalysis and intersubjective systems theory. *Psychoanalytic Dialogues, 20*(2): 196–218.

Rogers, C. R. (1942). *Counseling and Psychotherapy: Newer Concepts in Practice*. Boston, MA: Houghton Mifflin.

Rogers, C. R. (1951). *Client-Centered Therapy: Its Current Practice, Implications, and Theory*. London: Constable.

Rogers, C. R. (1957). The necessary and sufficient conditions of therapeutic personality change. *Journal of Consulting Psychology, 21*: 95–103.

Rogers, C. R. (1959). A theory of therapy, personality and interpersonal relationships, as developed in the client-centered framework. In: S. Koch (Ed.), *Psychology: A Study of Science, Vol. 3: Formulation of the Person and the Social Context* (pp. 184–256). New York: McGraw-Hill.

Rogers, C. R. (1961). *On Becoming a Person*. London: Constable.

Rogers, C. R. (1967a). A process conception of psychotherapy. In: C. R. Rogers, *On Becoming a Person: A Therapist's View of Psychotherapy* (pp. 125–159). London: Constable [original work published 1958].

Rogers, C. R. (1967b). Some of the directions evident in therapy. In: C. R. Rogers, *On Becoming a Person: A Therapist's View of Psychotherapy* (pp. 73–106). London: Constable [original work published 1953].

Rogers, C. R. (1973). Some new challenges. *American Psychologist, 28*(5): 379–387.

Rogers, C. R. (1978). *Carl Rogers on Personal Power*. London: Constable.

Rogers, C. R. (1980a). *A Way of Being*. London: Constable.

Rogers, C. R. (1980b). Empathic: An unappreciated way of being. In: C. R. Rogers, *A Way of Being* (pp. 137–163). Boston, MA: Houghton Mifflin [original work published 1975].

Roy, B., & Steiner, C. (Eds.), (1988). *Radical Psychiatry: The Second Decade* [unpublished manuscript]. www.emotional-literacy.com/self.htm [last accessed 30/11/2013].

Royal Commission on Social Policy. (1988). *The April Report*. Wellington, Aotearoa New Zealand: RCSP.

Rubens, R. L. (1994). Fairbairn's structural theory. In: J. S. Grotstein & D. B. Rinsley (Eds.), *Fairbairn and the Origins of Object Relations* (pp. 151–173). London: Free Association.

Samuels, A. (1997). Pluralism and psychotherapy: What is good training? In: R. House & N. Totton (Eds.), *Implausible Professions: Arguments for Pluralism and Autonomy in Counselling and Psychotherapy* (pp. 199–214). Ross-on-Wye, UK: PCCS.

Samuels, A., & Williams, R. (2001). Andrew Samuels in conversation with Ruth Williams. *Transformations, 13* (Supplement): 1–8.

Sanders, P., & Tudor, K. (2001). This is therapy: A person-centred critique of the contemporary psychiatric system. In: C. Newnes, G. Holmes, & C. Dunn (Eds.), *This is Madness Too: Critical Perspectives on Mental Health Services* (pp. 147–160). Ross-on-Wye, UK: PCCS.

Saner, R. (1989). Culture bias of gestalt therapy: Made-in-USA. *The Gestalt Journal, 12*(2): 57–73.

Sapriel, L. (1998). Can gestalt therapy, self-psychology and intersubjectivity theory be integrated? *The British Gestalt Journal, 7*(1): 33–44.

Satir, V. (1978). *Conjoint Family Therapy*. London: Souvenir Press [original work published 1967].

Schafer, R. (1983). *The Analytic Attitude*. New York: Basic.

Schiff, J. (1969). Reparenting schizophrenics. *Transactional Analysis Bulletin, 8*(31): 47–63.

Schiff, J. L., Schiff, A. W., Mellor, K., Schiff, E., Schiff, S., Richman, D., Fishman, J., Wolz, L., Fishman, C., & Momb, D. (1975). *Cathexis Reader: Transactional Analysis Treatment of Psychosis*. New York: Harper & Row.

Schmid, B. (1984). Theory, language and intuition. In: E. Stern (Ed.), *TA: The State of the Art. A European Contribution* (pp. 61–65). Dordrecht, The Netherlands: Foris Publications.

Schmid, B. (1991). Intuition of the possible and the transactional creation of realities. *Transactional Analysis Journal, 21*(3): 144–154.

Schon, D. A. (1983). *The Reflective Practitioner: How Professionals Think in Action*. New York: Basic.

Schore, A. N. (1994). *Affect Regulation and the Origin of the Self: The Neurobiology of Emotional Development*. Hillsdale, NJ: Lawrence Erlbaum.

Schore, A. N. (2003a). *Affect Dysregulation and Disorders of the Self*. New York: W. W. Norton.

Schore, A. N. (2003b). *Affect Regulation and the Repair of the Self*. New York: W. W. Norton.

Schore, A. N. (2010). The right brain implicit self: A central mechanism of the psychotherapy change process. In: J. Petrucelli (Ed.), *Knowing,*

Not-Knowing and Sort of Knowing: Psychoanalysis and the Spirit of Uncertainty (pp. 177–202). London: Karnac.

Schore, A. N. (2012). *The Science of the Art of Psychotherapy.* New York: W. W. Norton.

Seligman, M. E. P. (2003). *Authentic Happiness.* London: Nicholas Brealey.

Shakespeare, W. (1985). *Hamlet.* Cambridge, UK: Cambridge University Press [original work published 1603].

Shmukler, D. (1991). Transference and transaction: Perspectives from developmental theory, object relations, and transformational processes. *Transactional Analysis Journal, 21*(1): 94–102.

Shweder, R. A. (1990). Cultural psychology—What is it? In: J. W. Stigler, R. A. Shweder, & G. Herdt (Eds.), *Cultural Psychology: Essays on Comparative Human Development* (pp. 1–43). Cambridge, UK: Cambridge University Press.

Sills, C., & Hargaden, H. (Eds.), (2003a). *Ego States. Key Concepts in Transactional Analysis: Contemporary Views.* London: Worth.

Sills, C., & Hargaden, H. (2003b). Introduction. In: C. Sills & H. Hargaden (Eds.), *Ego states. Key Concepts in Transactional Analysis: Contemporary Views* (pp. ix–xxiii). London: Worth.

Singh, J., & Tudor, K. (1997). Cultural conditions of therapy. *The Person-Centered Journal, 4*(2): 32–46.

Smith, J. B. (2011). Licensing of psychotherapists in the United States: Evidence of societal regression? *Transactional Analysis Journal, 41*(2): 147–150.

Smuts, J. (1987). *Holism and Evolution.* New York: Macmillan [original work published 1926].

Spinelli, E. (1989). *The Interpreted World: An Introduction to Phenomenological Psychology.* Newbury Park, CA: Sage.

Sprietsma, L. C. (1982). Adult ego state analysis with apologies to "Mr Spock". *Transactional Analysis Journal, 12*(3): 227–231.

Stark, M. (1999). *Modes of Therapeutic Action.* Northvale, NJ: Jason Aronson.

Steiner, C. (1971a). Radical psychiatry manifesto. In: J. Agel (Ed.), *The Radical Therapist* (pp. 280–282). New York: Ballantine.

Steiner, C. (1971b). The stroke economy. *Transactional Analysis Journal, 1*(3): 9–15.

Steiner, C. (1981). *The Other Side of Power.* New York: Grove Press.

Steiner, C. (2000). Radical psychiatry. In: R. J. Corsini (Ed.), *Handbook of Innovative Therapy* (pp. 578–586). Chichester, UK: Wiley.

Steiner, C., & Cassidy, W. (1969). Therapeutic contracts in group treatment. *Transactional Analysis Bulletin, 8*(3): 29–31.

Steiner, C., Wyckoff, H., Golstine, D., Lariviere, P., Schwebel, R., Marcus, J., and Members of the Radical Psychiatry Center. (1975). *Readings in Radical Psychiatry.* New York: Grove Press.

Stern, D. N. (1985). *The Interpersonal World of the Infant: A View from Psychoanalysis and Developmental Psychology*. New York: Basic.

Stern, D. N. (1992). *Diary of a Baby*. New York: Basic.

Stern, D. N. (1998). *The Interpersonal World of the Infant: A View from Psychoanalysis and Developmental Psychology* (revised edition). New York: Basic.

Stern, D. N. (2004). *The Present Moment: In Psychotherapy and Everyday Life*. New York: W. W. Norton.

Stewart, I. (1992). *Eric Berne*. London: Sage.

Stewart, I. (1996). *Developing Transactional Analysis Counselling*. London: Sage.

Stewart, I. (2001). Ego states and the theory of theory: The strange case of the little professor. *Transactional Analysis Journal, 31*(2): 133–147.

Stewart, I., & Joines, V. (1987). *TA Today: A New Introduction to Transactional Analysis*. Nottingham, UK: Lifespace Publishing.

Stewart, I., & Joines, V. (2012). *TA Today: A new Introduction to Transactional Analysis* (2nd edition). Nottingham, UK: Lifespace Publishing.

Stolorow, R. D., & Atwood, G. E. (1992). *Contexts of Being: The Intersubjective Foundations of Psychological Life*. Hillsdale, NJ: Analytic Press.

Stolorow, R. D., Atwood, G. E., & Orange, D. M. (2002). *Worlds of Experience: Interweaving Philosophical and Clinical Dimensions in Psychoanalysis*. New York: Basic.

Stuthridge, J. (2010). Script or scripture? In: R. G. Erskine (Ed.), *Life Scripts: A Transactional Analysis of Unconscious Relational Patterns* (pp. 73–100). London: Karnac.

Sullivan, H. S. (1964). A note on the implications of psychiatry, the study of interpersonal relations, for investigations in the social sciences. In: H. S. Sullivan, *The Fusion of Psychiatry and Social Science* (pp. 15–29). New York: W. W. Norton [original work published 1937].

Summers, G. (2008). *The Unfolding Future: A Co-creative TA Vision*. Keynote speech at the Australasian Transactional Analysis Conference, Rotorua, New Zealand.

Summers, G. (2010). [Posting]. In: C. Shadbolt (Moderator), *International Association of Relational Transactional Analysis. Online Colloquium No. 1*. http://lists.topica.com/lista/iarta/2010/read [last accessed 04/03/2010].

Summers, G. (2011). Dynamic ego states. In: H. Fowlie, & C. Sills (Eds.), *Relational Transactional Analysis: Principles in Practice* (pp. 59–67). London: Karnac.

Summers, G., & Tudor, K. (2000). Co-creative transactional analysis. *Transactional Analysis Journal, 30*(1): 23–40.

Summers, G., & Tudor, K. (2001). Une analyse transactionelle co-créative [Co-creative transactional analysis]. *Actualities En Analyse Transactionelle, 25*(100): 137–154.

Summers, G., & Tudor, K. (2005a). Co-creative transactional analysis. In: B. Cornell & H. Hargaden (Eds.), *From Transactions to Relations: The Emergence of a Relational Tradition in Transactional Analysis* (pp. 103–128). Chadlington, UK: Haddon Press [original work published 2000].

Summers, G., & Tudor, K. (2005b). Introducing co-creative TA. www.co-creativity.com [last accessed 30/11/2005].

Summers, G., & Tudor, K. (2005c). *Predstavljanje Ko-kreativne TA* [*Introducing Co-creative TA*]. www.sata.co.rs/files/introducing_co-creativa_ta_in_serbian.pdf [last accessed 30/11/2013].

Summers, G., & Tudor, K. (2007). In: K. Tudor (Ed.), *The Adult is Parent to the Child: Transactional Analysis with Children and Young People*. Lyme Regis, UK: Russell House Publications.

Summers, G., & Tudor, K. (2012). *Análisis Transaccional Co-creativo* [*Co-creative Transactional Analysis*] (O. E. V. Zafra, Trans.). Unpublished manuscript.

Taft, J. (1933). *The Dynamics of Therapy in a Controlled Relationship*. New York: Macmillan.

Tangolo, A. E. (2010). *Psicoterapia Psicodinamica con L'analisi Transazionale: Un'esperienza* [*Psychodynamic Psychotherapy with Transactional Analysis: An Experience*] Ghezzano, Italy: Felici Editore.

Temple, S. (1999). Functional fluency for educational transactional analysts. *Transactional Analysis Journal, 29*(3): 164–174.

Temple, S. (2004). Update on the functional fluency model in education. *Transactional Analysis Journal, 34*(3): 197–204.

The Co-Intelligence Institute. (2013). *The Co-Intelligence Institute* [Homepage]. www.co-intelligence.org/ [last accessed 23/07/2013].

The International Transactional Analysis Association. (2013). A compilation of core concepts. www.itaaworld.org/index.php/about-ta/ta-core-concepts [last accessed 31/ 07/2013].

Tophoff, M. M. (2006). Sensory awareness as a method of mindfulness training within the perspective of person-centered psychotherapy. *Person-Centered & Experiential Psychotherapies, 5*(2): 127–137.

Training and Certification Council of Transactional Analysis. (2004). Oral examination CTA psychotherapy scoring sheet. In: *T&CC Training and Examination Handbook* [Form 12.7.12]. Pleasanton, CA: T&CCTA.

Training and Certification Council of Transactional Analysis. (2010). *T&CC Training and Examination Handbook*. Pleasanton, CA: T&CCTA.

Trautmann, R. L., & Erskine, R. G. (1999). A matrix of relationships: Acceptance speech for the 1998 Eric Berne memorial award. *Transactional Analysis Journal, 29*(1): 14–17.

Tudor, K. (1991). Children's groups: Integrating TA and gestalt perspectives. *Transactional Analysis Journal, 21*(1): 12–20.

Tudor, K. (1996a). *Mental Health Promotion*. London: Routledge.

Tudor, K. (1996b). Transactional analysis integration: A metatheoretical analysis for practice. *Transactional Analysis Journal, 26*: 329–340.

Tudor, K. (1997). Being at dis-ease with ourselves: Alienation and psychotherapy. *Changes, 22*(2): 143–150.

Tudor, K. (1999a). *Group Counselling*. London: Sage.

Tudor, K. (1999b). I'm OK, you're OK—and they're OK: Therapeutic relationships in transactional analysis. In: C. Feltham (Ed.), *Understanding the Counselling Relationship* (pp. 90–119). London: Sage.

Tudor, K. (2002). Introduction. In: K. Tudor (Ed.), *Transactional Approaches to Brief Therapy or What Do You Say Between Saying Hello and Goodbye?* (pp. 1–18). London: Sage.

Tudor, K. (2003). The neopsyche: The integrating adult ego state. In: C. Sills & H. Hargaden (Eds.), *Ego States. Key Concepts in Transactional Analysis: Contemporary Views* (pp. 201–231). London: Worth.

Tudor, K. (2004). Mental health promotion. In: I. Norman & I. Rylie (Eds.), *Mental Health Nursing*. Buckingham, UK: Open University Press.

Tudor, K. (2005). Die neo-psyche: der integrierende Erwachsenen-ich-zustand [The neopsyche: The integrating Adult ego state]. *Zeitschrift Für Transaktionsanalyse, 3*: 168–186.

Tudor, K. (2006). Contracts, complexity and challenge. In: C. Sills (Ed.), *Contracts in Counselling and Psychotherapy* (2nd edition) (pp. 119–136). London: Sage.

Tudor, K. (2007a). Geestelijk gezond; autonoom én homonoom [Psychological health: Autonomy and homonomy]. *Tijdschrift Cliëntgerichte Psychotherapie, 45*(1): 5–18.

Tudor, K. (2007b). *On Dogma*. Paper presented at the Institute of Transactional Analysis Annual Conference, York, UK.

Tudor, K. (Ed.), (2007c). *The Adult is Parent to the Child: Transactional Analysis with Children and Young People*. Lyme Regis, UK: Russell House.

Tudor, K. (2007d). Working with the individual child using transactional analysis. In: K. Tudor (Ed.), *The Adult is Parent to the Child: Transactional Analysis with Children and Young People* (pp. 89–103). Lyme Regis, UK: Russell House.

Tudor, K. (2008a). Psychological health: Autonomy and homonomy. In: B. Levitt (Ed.), *Reflections on Human Potential: Bridging the Person-Centered Approach and Positive Psychology* (pp. 161–174). Ross-on-Wye, UK: PCCS.

Tudor, K. (2008b). "Take it": A sixth driver. *Transactional Analysis Journal, 38*(1): 43–57.

Tudor, K. (2008c). Therapy is a verb. *Therapy Today, 19*(1): 35–37.

Tudor, K. (2008d). Verbal being: From being human to human being. In: B. E. Levitt (Ed.), *Reflections on Human Potential: Bridging the Person-Centered Approach and Positive Psychology* (pp. 68–83). Ross-on-Wye, UK: PCCS.

Tudor, K. (2010a). *The Fight for Health: A Heuristic Enquiry into Psychological Well-being*. Unpublished context statement for PhD in Psychotherapy by Public (Published) Works, School of Health and Social Sciences, Middlesex University, London, UK.

Tudor, K. (2010b). The state of the ego: Then and now. *Transactional Analysis Journal, 40*(4): 261–277.

Tudor, K. (2010c). Transactional Analysis: A little liberal, a little conservative, and a little radical. *The Psychotherapist, 46*: 17–20.

Tudor, K. (2011a). Empathy: A co-creative perspective. *Transactional Analysis Journal, 41*(4): 322–335.

Tudor, K. (2011b). Rogers' therapeutic conditions: A relational conceptualisation. *Person-Centered & Experiential Psychotherapies, 10*(3): 165–180.

Tudor, K. (2011c). There ain't no license that protects: Bowen theory and the regulation of psychotherapy. *Transactional Analysis Journal, 41*(2): 154–161.

Tudor, K. (2011d). Understanding empathy. *Transactional Analysis Journal, 41*(1): 39–57.

Tudor, K. (2012). *Enmity, Rivalry, and Alliance: Psychoanalysis, Behaviourism, and Humanistic Psychologies*. Paper/workshop given at the Australian Centre for Integrative Studies Conference: Allies and enemies: The role of real and metaphoric siblings in our psychological worlds. Sydney, Australia.

Tudor, K. (2013). Back to the future: Carl Rogers' "new challenge" reviewed and renewed. *Self & Society: An International Journal for Humanistic Psychology, 40*: 17–24.

Tudor, K., & Hargaden, H. (2002). The couch and the ballot box: The contribution and potential of psychotherapy in enhancing citizenship. In: C. Feltham (Ed.), *What's the Good of Counselling and Psychotherapy? The Benefits Explained* (pp. 156–178). London: Sage.

Tudor, K., & Hobbes, R. (2007). Transactional analysis. In: W. Dryden (Ed.), *The Handbook of Individual Therapy* (5th editon, pp. 256–286). London: Sage.

Tudor, K., & Widdowson, M. (2008). From client process to therapeutic relating: A critique of the process model and personality adaptations. *Transactional Analysis Journal, 38*(3): 218–232.

Tudor, K., & Worrall, M. (2006). *Person-Centred Therapy: A Clinical Philosophy*. London: Routledge.

Van Beekum, S. (2005). The therapist as a new object. *Transactional Analysis Journal, 35*(2): 187–191.

Van Beekum, S. (2006). The relational consultant. *Transactional Analysis Journal, 36*(4): 318–329.

Van Beekum, S. (2009). Siblings, aggression, and sexuality: Adding the lateral. *Transactional Analysis Journal, 39*(2): 129–135.

Van Beekum, S., & Krijgsman, B. (2000). From autonomy to contact. *Transactional Analysis Journal, 30*(1): 52–57.

Van Beekum, S., & Laverty, K. (2007). Social dreaming in a transactional analysis context. *Transactional Analysis Journal, 37*(3): 237–234.

Van Rijn, B., & Wild, C. (2013). Humanistic and integrative therapies for anxiety and depression: Practice-based evaluation of transactional analysis, gestalt, and integrative psychotherapies and person-centered counseling. *Transactional Analysis Journal, 43*(2): 150–163.

von Foerster, H. (1984). On construing a reality. In: P. Watzlawick (Ed.), *The Invented Reality: How Do We Know What We Believe We Know?* (pp. 41–61). New York: W. W. Norton [original work published 1981].

Waitangi Tribunal. (2013). The Treaty of Waitangi. www.waitangi-tribunal. govt.nz/treaty/ [last accessed 05/31/2013].

Walker, R. (1990). *Ka Whawhai Tonu Matou: Struggle Without End.* Auckland, Aotearoa New Zealand: Penguin.

Wallen, R. (1970). Gestalt therapy and gestalt psychology. In: J. Fagan & I. L. Shepherd (Eds.), *Gestalt Therapy Now* (pp. 8–13). New York: Harper & Row.

Weiss, E. (1937). Psychic defence and the technique of its analysis. *International Journal of Psychoanalysis, 23*: 69–80.

Weiss, E. (1950). *Principles of Psychodynamics.* New York: Grune & Stratton.

Weiss, E. (1952). Introduction. In: E. Weiss, *Ego Psychology and the Psychoses* (pp. 1–21). New York: Basic.

Wells, M. (2012). From fiction to freedom: Our true nature beyond life script. *Transactional Analysis Journal, 42*(2): 143–151.

Werner, H. (1948). *Comparative Psychology of Mental Development* (revised edition). Chicago, IL: Follett.

Wheeler, R. H. (1940). *The Science of Psychology* (2nd edition). New York: Crowell.

White, J. D., & White, T. (1975). Cultural scripting. *Transactional Analysis Journal, 5*(1): 12–23.

White. T. (2001). The contact contract. *Transactional Analysis Journal, 31*(3): 194–198.

White, T. (2008). The two ego state model. WPATA [Western Pacific Association of Transactional Analysis] *Bulletin, 1*: 45–55.

Whitehead, A. N. (1920). *The Concept of Nature*. Cambridge, UK: Cambridge University Press.

Whitehead, A. N. (1978). *Process and Reality* (D. R. Griffin & D. W. Sherburne, Eds., corrected edition). New York: The Free Press [original work published 1929].

Widdowson, M. (2008). Metacommunicative transactions. *Transactional Analysis Journal, 38*(1): 58–71.

Widdowson, M. (2009). *Transactional Analysis: 100 Key Points and Techniques*. London: Routledge.

Winnicott, D. W. (1952). Anxiety associated with insecurity. In: D. W. Winnicott, *Through Paediatrics to Psycho-Analysis: Collected Papers* (pp. 97–100). New York: Brunner/Mazel.

Winnicott, D. W. (1971). *Playing and Reality*. Harmondsworth, UK: Penguin [original work published 1967].

Wittgenstein, L. (1974). *Philosophical Investigations*. Oxford, UK: Blackwell [original work published 1922].

Woodworth, R. S., & Sheehan, M. (1965). *Contemporary Schools of Psychology* (3rd edition). New York: The Ronald Press Company [original work published 1931].

Woollams, S., & Brown, M. (1978). *Transactional Analysis*. Dexter, MI: Huron Valley Institute Press.

Wyckoff, H. (Ed.), (1976). *Love, Therapy and Politics*. New York: Grove Press.

Yalom, I. D. (1995). *The Theory and Practice of Group Psychotherapy* (4th edition). New York: Basic.

Yalom, I. D., Tinklenberg, J., & Gilula, M. (1968). *Curative Factors in Group Therapy*. Unpublished study, Department of Psychiatry, Stanford University, Stanford, California, USA.

Yontef, G. (1976). Gestalt therapy: Clinical phenomenology. In: V. Binder, A. Binder, & B. Rimland (Eds.), *Modern Therapies*. Englewood Cliffs, NJ: Prentice-Hall.

Zimmerman, J., with Coyle, V. (1996). *The Way of Council*. Las Vegas, NV: Bramble Books.

Žvelc, G. (2002). From withdrawal to relational contact: The psychotherapy of self-destructiveness. *Transactional Analysis Journal, 32*(4): 243–255.

Žvelc, G. (2010). Relational schemas theory and transactional analysis. *Transactional Analysis Journal, 40*(1): 8–22.

Žvelc, G., Černetič, M., & Košak, M. (2011). Mindfulness-based transactional analysis. *Transactional Analysis Journal, 41*(3): 241–254.

INDEX

Numbers in italics refer to where the subject is diagrammed; numbers in bold to where the subject is defined.

A_0 87–*88*

A_1 34, 56–57, 87, 108, 217

A_2 34, 42–*43*, *51*, *56*, 86, *88*, 108, *132*, *151*

A_a 45

A_c 45

adaptability 48–49

adaptation 57, 60, 66, 72, 81, 109, 174, 194

   reciprocal 162

Adult (ego state) xxii, xxiv–xxv, xxvii–xxviii, xxxiii–xxxv, xxxvii, 14, 16–19, 30–36, 73–76, 85–88, 90–91, 93–99, 101, 108–113, 116, 120–121, 126, 133–134, 136–137, 149, 153–154, 190–*191*, 197, 199, 203, 206, 213, 238–239, 244, 247, 253, **264**, 267

   adaptability of 48–49, 75

   conscious xxxvi, 96

   critical 57

   definition(s) of 35–36, 44, 47, 51, 109, 133, **264**

   epigenetic origins of 35, 43–44, 57, 74, 108

   executive power of 48–49

   expanding 58–64, 77–79, 90, 93, 97, 101, 130–131, 192, 230, **265**

   fully functioning 45

   Integrated xxii, 17, 31, 43–44, 84, 86, 109–110, 120, 133–134, **266**

   integrating xxv, xxviii, xxxiv, 29–67, *51*, *57*, 69–79, 85–86, 93, 97, 101, 108–109, 112, 114, 120–121, 129, 131, 133–134, 137, 144, *150*, 152–*153*,

165–170, 174, 190, 192–193, 200, 230, 237, 239, 264, **266**
features of 51–54, 76–77, 166
and mindfulness 166–170
organisational implications of 64–66, 79
and relational schema 165–168, 192
structural analysis of *43*
theoretical implications of 54–58
mindful 166–167, 190, 192
non-conscious xxxvi, 145, 187
present-centred 54, 64, 165
rebellious 57
structural analysis of 42–45
in transactional analysis 44–45
Adulting 129, **264**
Agel, J. 212
Alexander, L. 5
Allen, B. A. 2–3, 5, 10–11, 21–22, 24, 36, 125
Allen, J. G. 157–158
Allen, J. R. 2–3, 5, 10–11, 21–22, 24, 36, 96, 125, 218
"Alì", 162–164, 186–188
Amundson, J. K. 54
Andrewartha, G. 19
Angyal, A. xxiv, 81, 126, 252–253
Antonovsky, A. 17, 59
Aotearoa New Zealand 125, 147, 189, 229, 234n.1
A$_p$ *88*
applications, fields of (in TA) xiv, xxvi, 41, 139, 195–196, 218, 221, 235, 251–254, *254*
archaeopsyche 17, 33, 35, 49, 55–56, 60, 86, 87–88, 133, 144, 202, **264**
Ariely, D. 70
Aron, L. 188, 212
Atkinson, D. 23
attachment 15–16, 96, 157, 234, 236, 243

theory 15, 21
Atwood, G. E. 13, 73, 76, 130, 146, 168, 207
autonomy xxiv, xxxiv, 49, 51–52, 60, 65–67, 76, 79, 82–83, 166, 174, 193, 252–254, 260, 266

Bailey, A. 234
Bale, A. 35
Banks, J. 231
Barnes, G. xx, 108
Barr, J. 5–6
Barrett-Lennard, G. 6
Barrow, G. 159, 174
Bazzano, M. 193
Bellah, R. N. 172
Benjamin, J. 175
Bergin, A. E. 5
Berne, E. xx, xxii, xxvii–xxviii, xxxii, xxxvi, 4–5, 8, 10, 13, 17–20, 25, 27, 30–38, 40–45, 47–49, 51–52, 54–55, 60, 62–63, 67n.6, 72–73, 76, 85, 89, 95–96, 99, 104, 107–109, 124, 127, 130, 133, 149, 167, 202, 206, 213–217, 219, 240, 242, 244, 252, 258–263, 265–267
biological fluidity 47–49, 75
black 28n.3
Blackstone, P. 91
Bleuler, J. 105
Bohart, A. C. 103, 131
Bollas, C. 136, 175, 217
Boston Change Process Study Group 71, 89
Boyd, H. S. 158, 258
Boyd, L. W. 258
Brady, F. N. 52
Brah, A. 28n.3
(the) brain 45, 50, 52, 111, 233
Britton, R. 175
Brodley, B. T. 49
brown 28n.3

Brown, M. 14, 35, 56
Bruner, J. 5
Buber, M. 12
Bucci, W. 77
bullseye transaction, *see* transaction, bullseye
Burrell, G. 120, 228

C_0 57
C_1 34, *88*, 108
C_2 34, *51*, *132*, *151*
Carter, J. A. 6
Cassidy, W. 231
Černetič, M. 166–167, 192
Certified Transactional Analyst xx, 66
Chandran, S. 218
Chasseguet-Smirgel, J. 175
Cheney, W. D. 108
Child (ego state) xxxiii, xxxv, 12, 14–15, 18, 30, 32–35, 42, 49, 55, 57, 60, 64, 76, 86, 90–91, 95, 98, 112, 129, 131, 133, 136, 144–145, 153, 167, 193, 202, 206–207, 237–240, **246**, 265, 267
    Archaic 18, 55–57, 60, 64, 96, 109, 126, 129, 131, 133, 136, 144–145, 153, 204, 267
    Free 45
    Inner 14, 19–20, 50, 64
    Rebellious 53
    structural analysis of 34–35, 57
Chinnock, K. 173
Choy, A. 215, 247
Clark, B. D. 104
Clarkson, P. 5–6, 19, 25, 40, 49, 67n.6, 108, 215
client-centred perspective 122–123, 125, 141, 185
co- xix, 231
Coates, N. 232
co-created unconscious relational third 175–178

co-creative
    confirmations xii, 5, 25–26, 213–215, 244–247, **264**–265
    identity xxii, 5, 21–24, 120, 247–249, **264**–267
    method 120–121, 127, 144–145, 129–132
    methodology 125, 127–129, 143–144
    personality xxii, 5, 17–21, 190, 236–240, **264**
    reality xxii, 5–17, 190, **264**
    relating 83
    script helix **264**
    script matrix **264**
    transactional analysis *see* transactional analysis, co-creative
    transactional relating 152
co-creativity xxvii, xxxiii–xxxiv, 168, 183–184, 195, 211, 215, 219–220, 229, 231–234, 264
    the roots of 2–3
Cohen, M. 5
co-intelligence 233
communication
    non-verbal 103, 142
    rules of xxxvi, 8, 10, 15, 72, 240–242
    theory of 252, 256–258
conformity 65, 111, 155, 185, 195
(the) conscious 13, 66, 75, 89, 94–97, 101–102, 105–107, 114, 147, 155
consciousness 76–79, 89–98, 101–107, 11, 113–114, 116–117, 165, 217, 232, 265
    Adult xxxvi
    critical 31, 53–54, 60, 65, 93, 101, 166, 194
    different 101–103

domains of 101
reflective 49, 52, 95, 114, 116–117,
    166, 170
unity 232
see also conscious, preconscious,
    unconscious
constructivism 2, 21, 122, 124–125,
    141, 202, 230
and narrative 124–125
principles of 3
social xxii, 1–3, 21, 122, 125, 134,
    136, 218, 228, 263, 265
contact xxxiii, 12, 14, 46, 54, 61, 63,
    77–78, 120, 123, 126–127,
    134, 141, 159, 167, 183–184,
    187–188, 190, 197–198, 202,
    236, 238, 245, 254, 256, 266
Adult–Adult 12, 197, 203,
    207, 209
healthy 191
making 61, 78
present-centred 61
sensory 217
contamination(s) 43–44, 54, 95, 108,
    152, 153–154, 256, 265
double 152
context, social/cultural 3, 18, 32, 78,
    122–123, 173, 218–219, 264
contract, therapeutic 267
co-operacy 234
co-operative enquiry 233
co-regulation xxxii, 94, 96, 232–233
medium of 213–215
Cornell, W. F. xxii, xxv, 14, 17, 21–23,
    40, 76, 131, 135, 146, 155,
    160, 185, 188, 203, 216–217,
    235, 247, 267
co-transference 8, 11, 13, 16–17,
    20, 96, 113, 130, 206–207,
    265; see also relating,
    co-transferential therapeutic
counterinjunction(s) 21

countertransference 10–11, 62–63,
    135, 177, 209, 216
cultural 161–163, 186, 188
Coyle, V. 147
Cozolino, L. 110, 232
creativity 56, 79, 91, 138, 168, 184, 218
Crits-Christoph, P. 5
cross-cultural 161–165
Csikszentmihalyi, M. 75, 83, 265
culture(s) 19, 23, 73, 83, 92, 123, 126,
    134, 172, 176, 186, 189, 229,
    236, 247–248
of enquiry 65
"we" 3
see also cross-cultural
cure xxi, 36, 38, 60–61, 84–85, 245, 261

Damasio, A. 98, 111, 232
Dashiell, S. R. 19
Davidson, C. 218
de Bono, E. 194
decision(s) 21, 148, 217, 247–249, 252,
    258–260
deconfusion 14, 16, 64, 136, 152–154,
    203
decontamination 60, 95, 108, 152–154,
    202–203
defences 15, 18, 153, 190, 204–205,
    224, 240
Child xxxiv, 239–240
Parent xxxiv, 239–240
depth
psychology 105
psychotherapy 14–15
designers, transactional 21, 170–174,
    194
Deuze, M. 231
development
adult xxi, 35, 48, 230
Adult 7, 144
ego state xxxiii, 56–57, 108
healthy 21, 74, 236

human 3, 16, 47, 49, 80, 93, 108,
        134–135, 172, 236
    present-centred 4–5, 14–16, 128,
        161, 164, 167, 186–187, 220
diagnosis 20, 38, 41, 48, 54, 57, 59,
        61–63, 78, 148, 159, **265**
disconcerting 149
dis-integration 199
disturbance 75, 114, 149, 209, 212
Donald, M. 231
drama triangle 25, 215, *245*
Drego, P. 37, 41–42, 49
driver(s) 21, 23, 195
Duncan, B. L. 5
Dylan, B. 198
dynamic
    co-created 177–178, 197
    ego states *see* ego states, dynamic
    psychological and relational xxi,
        228
    repression 113
dynamics 45, 65, 100, 113, 168, 198
    Adult–Adult 17
    Child 206
    oppressive 213
    Parent–Child 75, 115, 206, 209
    power 210, 213, 229
    relational xxxvi

Edelman, G. M. 50
(the) educational field (of TA)
        170–174, 195–196 *see also*
        applications, fields of
ego
    conceptualisations of 17–21, 57,
        87–88, 91, 93, 100, 190
    healthy 52, 133, 266–267
ego state(s) **265**
    development xxxiii, 56–57, 108
    dynamic 89–*90*, 91–98, 224, **265**
    metaphor 14, 33
        structural 19–20

models of 35, 39, *43–44*, *51, 57,*
        87–88, 90, 154, *237*, **265**
    properties 47–50, 75–76
    types of 75, *237*, 239
    see also Adult, Child, Parent
Embleton Tudor, L. 122, 126, 128,
        196, 232
empathy
    a co-creative perspective 119–139
    and co-operation 172
    and narrative 172
    and play 172
English, F. 22, 124
enquiry
    culture of 65
    intersubjective 207
    three domains of 203–210
Erikson, E. 44, 108, 126
Erskine, R. G. xxii, xxxiii, 5–6, 17–19,
        31, 40, 42, 45, 51, 61, 79, 86,
        93, 110, 119–120, 122, 131,
        133–134, 160, 165, 169, 190,
        218, 252–253, 266
ethos 17, 42, 64, 266
European Association of
        Transactional Analysis
        184–185
Eusden, S. xxxvi, 95, 208–209
exteropsyche 17, 33, 35, 49, 55, 60,
        86–87, 133, 144, 202, **265**

Fairbairn, W. R. D. xxxiii, 72, 74, 92,
        146, 204
Fay, J. 229
Federn, P. 33, 36, 108–109, 118n.1
Fenton, B. 72, 135
field theory xxii, 1–2, 73, 121, 134,
        136, 218, 228
Fish, S. 10, 19, 31
flow 48, 75, 83, 97, 112, 137, 175,
        183, 185, 209, 223, 238–239,
        263, **265**

fluidity xxxiii, 48, 75, 83, 112, 263
    see also biological fluidity
Fogel, A. 232
Fonagy, P. 157–158
Fosshage, J. 77
Fowlie, H. xxiii, xxv, 72, 89, 99, 135,
        139, 146, 154, 267
Fredrickson, B. 96
Freire, E. S. 138
Freire, P. 59, 171–173, 213, 230
Freud, S. 74, 90, 92, 94, 100, 105
Fromm, E. 10

game(s) xx, xxii, xxvii–xxviii, xxxii,
        4–5, 10, 14, 25–26, 72,
        120–121, 130, 168, 213–215,
        244–247, 258–259, **265**
    analysis 258
    antithesis xxxii
    as (a) healthy process 25–26
    "good" 25, 214
    negative 213–214, 244–247
    plan 25–26, 213, 215, 244–245
    positive 213–215, 244–246, 264
    theory(ies) 25–26, 48, 130,
        214–215, 246
        analysed 214–215
Gardener, H. 233
Gelso, C. J. 6
Gergen, K. J. 2, 125
Gerson, S. 175, 178
gestalt xxii, xxxiii, 39, 61, 78, 94, 104,
        126, 136, 160, 218
    therapy xx, xxxiii, 2, 143
Giesekus, U. 220
Gildebrand, K. 49, 76
Gilula, M. 220
Glover, E. 109, 118n.1
Gobes, N. 33, 35, 44, 56–57, 72, 120
Goldstein, K. 39, 80
Gordon, D. 37
Goulding, M. M. 12, 25, 135, 215

Goulding, R. L. 12, 25, 135, 215
Greenson, R. R. 6
Grégoire, J. xxiv, xxvi, 185, 218
group work xxxii, 71, 195, 201, 219–221

Hagehülsmann, H. 39, 134
Hall, C. 39–40, 49, 80–81
Hall, S. xxv
Hargaden, H. xxii, xxv, 33, 39, 50, 57,
        61, 72, 119–120, 122–123, 129,
        131, 135–137, 146, 151, 193,
        203, 235
Harré, R. 52
Hartmann, H. 109, 118n.1
Hawkes, L. 218
healing xxxvi, 12–13, 38, 34, 65, 78,
        84, 91, 94, 96, 117, 134, 167,
        169, 190, 193, 240, 265
health 73–74, 76–78, 84–87, 91, 97,
        106–107, 109, 114, 134, 173,
        188, 190–*191*, 202, 209, 221,
        231, 233, 236, 239, 260–261
    assuming 59–60
    one ego state model of 72, 76, 93,
        116, 145, 160, **267**
    three ego state model of 72, 76, 160
healthy ego *see* ego, healthy
Helms, J. E. 23
Heron, J. 233
heuristic research *see* research,
        heuristic
Hill, C. E. 5
Hine, J. 35, 41, 56
Hirsch, I. xxxvi, 209
Hobbes, R. 185, 256
Hoffman, L. 124
Hofmann, S. G. 185
Hollis, J. 225
Holloway, W. 34
Holmes, J. 15
House, R. 196
Hubble, M. A. 5

Hudson-Allez, G. 96
Hunter, D. 234

imagination 20, 54, 61, 166
impasse(s) 12, 175, 177–178, 197
    and impasse theory 203–210
    interpersonal 205–206, *206*–207,
        265
    intersubjective *207–208*, 209–210,
        265
    intrapsychic 12, 203–204,
        204–205, **265**
    Past–Present impasse 204–206
    resolution 12, 203
    Type(s) of 12
improvisation/al 157–160, 183–184,
    197, 208
injunction(s) 21, 23, 247, 249
(The UK) Institute of Transactional
    Analysis 67n.7
Integrated Adult, *see* Adult, Integrated
integrating xxii, 31, 49–51, 76–77,
        110–112, 116–118, 133, 137,
        170, 199, 230, 264, **266**
    Adult, *see* Adult, integrating
integration 14–15, 40–41, 43, 47, 50–52,
        54–*56*, 58, 63–64, 73–77, 81,
        84–85, 93, 101, 107–112,
        116–118, 130, 133–134, 138,
        150, 165–167, 169–170, 192,
        199, 208, 228, **266**
    Adult xxii, 17–18, 133
    and physis *56*
interaction(s)
    healthy xxxvi, 237
    that have been generalised,
        representations of (RIGS)
        91, 106, 190, 192
inter-adaptability 48, 75
internalisations 91
(The) International Association of
    Relational Transactional

Analysis xxixn.1, 138,
    223, 267
(The) International Transactional
    Analysis Association 252
interruptions xxxiii, 130–131, 141, 197
intersubjective xxxv, 15, 18–20, 47–48,
        72–75, 77–78, 102, 146, 168,
        175, 198, 203, 224
    domain(s) 203, 207, 209
    field(s) xxxv, 73, 78, 168
        intrapsychic mode within
            168–169
        relationship mode within
            168–169
    see also enquiry, intersubjective;
            impasse, intersubjective
intersubjectivity 12–14, 18, 113, 134,
        196, 216, 267
intrapsychic loop, defensive *191*
intuition 20–21, 30, 54, 56–57, 104,
        186, 215–218, 255, **266**
I–Thou 28n.2
Ivey, A. E. 189
Ivey, M. B. 189

Jackson, P. Z. 97, 215
Jacobs, A. 33, 36–37, 39
Jahoda, M. 50, 52
James, J. 25, 213–215, 244
James, M. xxii, 17, 31, 35, 42, 44, 56,
        59, 86, 109, 120, 266
Joines, V. xxiv, 8, 25, 185, 241, 258–259
Jongeward, D. xxii, 17, 31, 35, 42, 44,
        56, 59, 86, 109, 120, 266
Jorgenson, E. W. 108
Jorgenson, H. I. 108
Juriansz, D. 233

Kabat-Zinn, J. 166, 192
Kahn, M. 5
Kalich, D. 196
Kantor, J. R. 80

Karenina, Anna 175–178, 197–199
Karpman, S. 25, 215, 245
Keemar, K. 196
Kennard, D. 65
Kirsher, I. 82
Klein, M. (Mavis) 35, 108
Klein, M. (Melanie) 107, 110, 137,
    199, 259
knowing 58–59, 233, 265
    implicit xxxvi, 71, 78, 92, 103–105,
        114–115
    tacit 103–105, 216, 218
knowledge 5–6, 23, 41, 45, 77, 94, 104,
        120, 125, 163, 171, 186, 199,
        216–217, 233, 261n.6
    empathic 130–131, 145
    experiential 130, 189
    implicit 114, 131, 145
    see also intuition
Kohlrieser, G. 79
Kohut, H. 52
Kolb, D. 174
Kopp, S. 37–38
Krijgsman, B. 52, 61
Krumper, M. 29, 45, 55
Kujit, J. 45, 55

Lacan, J. 175
Lake, F. 35
Lambert, M. J. 5
Land, C. 234
Landaiche III, M. N. 203,
    216–217
language xx, xxviii, 13, 38, 100–101,
        109, 111, 118, 155, 163, 171,
        178, 189, 192, 201–203,
        228, 231
Lapworth, P. xxiv–xxv, 10, 31
Laverty, K. 218
learning xxxvi, 4, 12, 48, 59, 65, 73,
        77–78, 94, 109, 115, 117, 134,
        159–160, 170–174, 186–189,

        192–193, 195–196, 220, 232,
        235, 239–240, 251, 254
    designing 174
    interpersonal 220
    to design 174
LeDoux, J. 104
Lee, A. 63
Lees, J. 65
Levin, P. 35, 108
Levin-Landheer, P. 35
Lewin, K. 2
life
    patterns, theory of 258–260
    position(s) 13, 124
    script(s) *see* script(s)
"Lily" 175–178, 197–199, 205
Lindzey, G. 39–40, 80–81
Little, R. 72, 204, 207
Loewenstein, G. 70
Loewenthal, D. 220
Lorenzer, A. 131
Loria, B. R. 20, 36
Luborsky, L. 5
Lyons-Ruth, K. 71

Magner, V. 35
Maidman, J. 196
Margolis, M. 5
Maslow, A. H. 40, 110
Massey, R. F. 33, 35, 44, 56–57, 72, 120
Mattingly, C. 104
maturity 50, 53–54, 166
Matze, M. G. 18–19
Mazzetti, M. 161, 163, 173
McKergow, M. 97
McNeel, J. R. 19
Mead, G. H. 122
meaning 3–4, 11, 20, 22, 26, 55,
        70–71, 94, 103–104, 112–113,
        123–125, 142, 163, 165,
        172–174, 176, 192, 198, 211,
        225, 228, 263–264

Mearns, D. 125, 185
Mehrabian, A. 103
Mellor, K. 12, 19
Menaker, E. 136
Mente, A. 220
messages,
    healthy 242
    non-verbal 242, 247
metanoia 57
Metanoia (Psychotherapy Training)
        Institute xix–xx, xxiii,
        xxvi–xxvii
metaphor(s) 2, 14, 19–20, 32–33, 35,
        36–39, 69–72, 74–77, 81,
        83–84, 97, 115, 134, 136, 154,
        166, 175, 190, 194, 202, 208,
        211, 214, 264–266
    conflation of 35, 72
    of possibility/possibilities
        19, 134
metatheory 39–42, 73, 254
method **266**
methodology **266**
migration 162–164, 189
Miller, S. D. 5
(the) mind 52, 71, 76, 98, 105–106,
        111, 125, 127, 167, 169, 176,
        261
mindfulness xxxvi, 165–170,
        189–190, 192–193
Mlodinow, L. 114
Modell, A. H. 71, 77
Mohr, G. xxv
Moiso, C. 64
Money, M. 263
Moreno, J. L. 12, 197
Morgan, G. 120, 228
Morgan, S. 233
Morton, G. 23
motivation xxi, 39, 49, 53–55,
        106–107, 137, 166
Mountain, A. 218

Moursund, J. P. 31, 40, 119, 122,
        131, 169
Moustakas, C. 104
Moynihan, D. W. 5
Murakami, H. 126
Murphy, G. 80
mutuality 4, 22, 172–173, 188,
        193–194, 196, 211–213, 232

Napper, R. 97, 218
narrative(s) 1–3, 5, 17, 22, 24, 117,
        121, 125, 148, 163, 202
    constructivism and 124–125
    and empathy 172
    implicit and explicit 147–149
    turn 5, 26, 110
Naughton, M. 188
neo–archaeopsyche 86–*88*, 202, **266**
neopsyche 29–76, 69–88, 93, 95,
        99, 108, 112–113, 118–119,
        121, 131, 133–134, 137, 166,
        192, 202, 216–217, 221, 230,
        264, **266**
    present-centred 49, 128–129, 133,
        143–144
neopsychic functioning 52, 120,
        128–130, 133, 143–144, 266
    expanding 150–152
Neugarten, B. L. 48
neuroscience 44, 49, 52, 89, 104, 110
Newton, T. 196, 213, 218
New Zealand *see* Aotearoa New
        Zealand
non-conscious xxxv, 66, 75, 89, 91–94,
        98, 102, 105–108, 116, 155,
        193, 198, 209, 216, 228
    Adult xxxvi, 145, 187
    co- 197
    life plan 187; *see also* script
    patterns xxxv, 138
    process(es) 98, 110, 114, 116, 137,
        144, 165, 217

(the) non-verbal 103, 193
not knowing 59, 94, 114
Novellino, M. xxv, 64, 72
novelty xxxiii, 71, 75, 79, 183–184
Novey, T. B. 33, 35, 44, 56, 57,
        72, 120

Ogden, T. 175, 198
O'Hara, M. 129
Ohlsson, T. 34
OKness 13, 259
oppression 194, 212
Orange, D. M. 73, 175
(the) organisational field (of TA)
        xxxviii, 37, 131, 195, 202,
        218, 229, 235 *see also* Adult,
        integrating, organisational
        implications of
organism 39–41, 53–54, 59, 78,
        80–84, 94, 104, 107, 111,
        121, 169, 193
organismic psychology 32, 39–40, 50,
        73, 80–81, 104, 134
otherness 187, 189

P$_0$ *88*
P$_1$ 34, *88*, 108
P$_2$ 34, 51, 86, 108, *132*, *151*
Pally, R. 50, 232
Panksepp, J. 95–96
Parent (ego state) xxxiii–xxxv,
        14, 18–19, 29–30, 32–36,
        39–40, 48–49, 58, 60, 62,
        74, 76–77, 86, 88, 90–91,
        93–97, 100, 106, 112–113,
        115, 117, 129–130, 145, 149,
        151–154, 165–167, 177, 190,
        193, 202–203, 205–207, 210,
        237–240, 242–243, 246–247,
        264–265, 267
    Critical 45, 53, 57, 85
    inner 19–20

Introjected 55, 57, 60, 64, 131, 133,
        136, 144–145, 153, 204
    messages 85–87
    Nurturing 57
    Pig 212
    structural analysis of 42
    transactional analysis 66
Parlett, M. 2
Parry, T. A. 54
Past
    I 8, 13
    –Present impasse 204–206
    You 8, 13, 27n.1
pathologising xxi
pathology xxxii, 17, 23, 60, 77–78, 84,
        86, 134, 173, 184, 187, 190
pathos 17, 42, 266
pattern(s) 27, 33, 35, 47, 56, 90, 95–96,
        104, 109, 111, 130, 143, 154,
        184, 194, 212, 214, 221, 224,
        236, 245, 249, 253
    conscious 89, 138
    defensive 90, 113, 190
    healthy 25–26, 212, 236
    life 258–260
    negative 213
    non conscious xxxv, 89, 138
    pathological xxxvi, 73
    positive 213
    repetitive 215 *see also* game(s)
    unconscious xxxv, 89, 138
    unhealthy 212
Perls, F. S. 78, 133
personality
    model of 57, 116, **267**
        one ego state 72, 85–86, 93,
            116–117, 145, **267**
        three ego state 72, 76, 80,
            85, 108, 116, 136, 145, *152*,
            154, **267**
        two ego state 86, *87–88*,
            202–203, **266**

person-centred 86–87
person-centred psychology
      xx, 80, 193
perspective, third person 167, 193
Peters, A. 232
Petriglieri, G. 210
Phelan, B. N. 45, 55
Phelan, P. E. 45, 55
phenomenology 128–129
   intersubjective 18, 47, 72, 76
   systematic 18–19, 38, 49, 57, 60,
      72, 75–76
Philippson, P. xxxiii
Phillips, A. 84
physis (or phusis) 41, 49, 55–56,
      67n.6, 107, 109, 164, 187, **267**
   pseudo 56, **267**
Piaget, J. 172
Pine, F. 39, 73
Piontelli, A. 35
play xxxii, xxxvi–xxxvii, 50, 58–59,
      130, 157, 172, 174, 178, 186,
      195, 208, 214, 258
Porter-Steele, N. 33, 35, 44, 56–57,
      72, 120
possibility/possibilities xxxvii, 3,
      11, 19–21, 58, 63, 70, 116,
      134, 142, 145–146, 148, 155,
      171, 174–175, 183, 194–195,
      201–202, 218–219, 221, 228,
      230, 239, 244
   metaphor of 19, 134
   named 142, 148
   present/present-centred 11, 204
   relational 19–20, 63, 78, 90, 98,
      131, 134, 137, 145, 221
      new 98, 107, 131, 148, 153, 204
   unnamed 142, 148
power 23, 48, 135, 153, 171, 196,
      210–213, 229, 232
   executive 47–49
   personal 48, 66

Prahalad, C. K. 231
preconscious 75, 89, 94–98, 102, 105,
      107, 115–116, 187, 216–217,
      228
Prelec, D. 70
present 8, 10, 12–19, 21, 23–24, 53,
      62, 64, 78, 92–93, 96, 101,
      104–105, 108, 112, 114, 117,
      122, 128, 159, 166–168, 172,
      221, 228, 230, 236, 239, 247,
      249, 264, 266
   -centred(ness) 18–19, 26, 50, 61,
      142, 171; *see also* Adult,
      integrating; relating,
      present-centred; therapeutic,
      relationship(s), present-
      centred
   moment 70, 122, 125–128,
      158–159, 166–167, 174
   process(es) 3
   self 39, 57
   work(ing) with(in) the 128–129,
      137, 143, 163, 168, 187, 193
   see also development, present-
      centred; relating, present-
      centred; relationship(s),
      present-centred
Present
   I 8, 12–14, 16, 27n.1
   You 8, 12–14, 16, 27n.1
process(es)
   healthy 25
   present-centred 130–131
programme(s) 21, 23
psychic organs 33–34, 37, 41, 47,
      49, 202
psychoanalysis xxv, 6, 47, 105, 170, 187

Ramaswamy, V. 231
Reason, P. 233
reciprocity 13, 232
relatedness 178, 197

domains of 102, 114, 232
relating
    Adult–Adult xxxv, 4, 7–8, 15–16,
        19, 60, 165, 207, 218
    co-transferential therapeutic
        11–17
    the duality of 14, 144, 208
    healthy 241
    patterns of 18, 212
    present-centred 7–8, 12, 14–16,
        20, 32, 60, 86, 120, 134, 144,
        217, 220
    therapeutic 1, 8, 11–17, 64, 131,
        134
        co-creative 7
    unhealthy 240–241
    ways of 7–8, 10–12, 20–21,
        137, 160
relational
    field 135, 146, 161, 173, 188–189,
        207, 210
    knowing xxxvi, 71, 78, 92
    needs 52, 166, 252–253, 257
    possibility/possibilities 19–20,
        63, 78, 90, 98, 131, 134, 137,
        145, 221
    principles xxvi, xxixn.1, 138–139
    schemas 71, 153, 165–170, 190, 192
    third 175–178
    "turn" xxv, 107, 138, 228, 256
relationship(s)
    present-centred 12–14
    therapeutic xxi, xxvi, 1–11, 13, 17,
        20, 26, 61–64, 96, 130, 136,
        175, 212, 228, 260–261
        co-creative 9, 16
repression dynamic 113
research, heuristic xxiv, 41, 104
responsibility, shared 4, 6, 8, 48, 122,
        144, 161, 186, 211, 213, 220
Riebel, L. 116
Ringstrom, P. 146

Robinson, W. L. 159
Rogers, C. R. 8, 41, 48–49, 53–54,
        61–62, 67n.5, 80, 83, 107,
        112, 122–123, 128, 130, 137,
        148–149, 172, 188–189,
        192, 196
Rowan, J. 233
Roy, B. 212
Royal Commission on Social Policy
        189
Rubens, R. L. 190

Samuels, A. xxi, 53, 155
Sanders, P. 37–38, 123
Saner, R. 3
Sapriel, L. 11
Satir, V. 25
Schafer, R. 124
Schiff, J. L. 19, 35, 56
Schmid, B. 21, 217
Schmid, P. F. 28n.2, 125
Schon, D. A. 52
Schore, A. N. 76, 81–82, 111, 185, 232
script(s)/life script(s) **266**
    analysis 170, 259–260
    helix 24, 161, 171, 211
        co-creative **264**
    matrix xxviii, 22, 160
        co-creative 23–24, 210–211,
        248–249, **264**
    theory 2, 5, 21–24, 125, 188, 202,
        249
        critical review of 21–22
scripting, cultural 22
self
    Adulting 129, 230, **267**
    sense(s) of 74, 93, 102, 264
        core 15, 102, 114, 221, 232
        emergent 15, 102
        intersubjective 15, 102
        narrative 102
        present-centred 57

true 82
   verbal 15, 102
Seligman, M. E. P. 96
Shakespeare, W. 54
Sheehan, M. 39
Shmukler, D. 129
Shweder, R. A. 189
Sills, C. xxii–xxvi, 10, 31, 33, 39, 50,
        57, 61, 89, 99, 119–120, 122,
        129, 131, 135–136, 139, 146,
        151, 154, 173, 193, 267
Simek-Morgan, L. 189
Singh, J. 123
Smith, J. B. 67n.7
Smuts, J. 81
social
   constructivism xxii, 1–2, 121,
        125, 134, 136, 218, 228, 263,
        265
   science 5, 45, 47, 81, 120–121
   time structuring 257–258
sociocentric 123, 142
Spinelli, E. xxxiv
Sprietsma, L. C. 35
Stark, M. 127–129, 134, 143,
        168, 267
Steiner, C. 53, 61, 67n.4, 210, 212,
        231, 257
Stern, D. N. xxxv, 15, 21, 35, 44,
        70–72, 74, 77–78, 82, 89, 91,
        92–93, 97, 101–102, 105–106,
        110, 112, 122, 126, 128, 143,
        190, 192
Stewart, I. xxiv, 5, 8, 25, 36, 44, 108,
        195, 241, 258–259
Stolorow, R. D. 13, 73, 76, 130, 146,
        168, 207
strokes 67n.4, 85, 256–257
Stuthridge, J. 74
subjectivity 72, 138
Sue, D. W. 23
Sullivan, H. S. 107

Summers, G. (work other than that
        reproduced in this book)
        27n.1, 55, 90, 95, 112, 119,
        175, 267

Taft, J. 67n.5
Tallman, K. 103, 131
Tangolo, A. E. xxiv
Taylor, B. 234
technics 42
Temple, S. 97
The Co-Intelligence Institute 233
therapeutic
   contract **267**
   relating 1, 8, 12–14, 16, 64,
        131, 134
      co-creative 7
      co-transferential 11–17
      and intersubjectivity 12–14
      present-centred 12–14
   relationship(s) xxi, xxvi, 1–13,
        16–17, 20, 26, 61–64, 96,
        130, 136, 175, 212, 228,
        260–261
      co-creative 9, 16
      present-centred 63
therapy
   present-centred 126
   the tango of 157–160
The Transactional Analyst 67n.8
third, relational 175–178, 197
thirdness 175, 178
Thou–I 28n.2
Tinklenberg, J. 220
(te) Tiriti o Waitangi | The Treaty of
        Waitangi 189
Tolstoy, L. 177
Tophoff, M. M. 193
Training and Certification Council
        of Transactional Analysis
        184–185, 251
transacting

Adult–Adult 150
co-creative empathic *132, 151,* **264**
transaction(s) **267**
bullseye 188, 200n.1, 202, **264**
co-transferential 12
countertransference 72
crossed 8–9, 15–16, 197, 206–207,
    240–*242*
empathic 16, 121, 129–131,
    136–137, 151–152
parallel 205, 210, 240–*241*
social *150*
transference/transferential, xxxiii
    7–8, 18
co- 12
partial 7–8, 16–17
ulterior xxxv, 10, 16–17, 25–26,
    129, 144–145, *150*, 193, 214,
    241–242, *243–244*, 246, 265
transactional
designers 21, 170–174, 194, 196
relating 121, 131, 137
transactional analysis
applications of 196, 218–219
approaches (with)in xxvi,
    xxxiii–xxxiv, 4, 10, 32,
    135–136, 229, 254, 256
co-creative **265**
(TA) "101" (Introductory
    Course) xxiii, 186, 251–261
applications of 218–219, 235,
    253
(in a) cross-cultural setting
    161–165, 186, 188, 229
differences with other forms
    of transactional analysis
    133–138
and the educational field 131,
    170–174, 193–196
influence of xxiv–xxvi
non-verbal aspects of 93, 102
principles of xxiii, 3–5, 122, 161,

167–168, 186–188, 211–212
theoretical influences
    on 122–127, 133–136,
    141–142, 146
concerns about/critiques of
    xx–xxi, 228–231
conservatism of 229–230
currents within 158, 184
development of 255–256
integrative 4, 40, 131–135,
    145–146
method xxiv, xxvii, xxxvi–xxxvii,
    58, 60, 120–121, 129–132,
    144–145, 261
methodology 32, 54, 58, 64,
    120–122, 125, 127–129, 136,
    143–144, 149–150, 220, 228,
    253, 256, 260–261, 266
as organismic psychology 39–41
orientations within xxvi, 185
relational xxiii, 133–139, 145–147,
    154–155, **267**
value base of 252
Transactional Analysis Journal xxii,
    xxiv–xxvi, 1, 29–31, 119
Trautmann, R. L. 6, 119–120, 122, 131,
    169, 266
Tudor, K. (work other than that
    reproduced in this book) xxi,
    xxiii–xxv, xxix, xxxii, xxxv,
    xxxvii, 6, 17, 27, 27n.1, 35, 38,
    48, 59, 64, 67n.7, 76, 80–82,
    84–85, 99, 105, 108, 111,
    120–124, 126–128, 133–134,
    149–150, 136, 152, 154–155,
    172–173, 185–186, 188, 196,
    199–200n.1, 202, 220, 229,
    253, 256, 260, 265, 267

unconscious xxxv, 53–54, 75–76, 82,
    89–94, 96, 98, 101–107, 110,
    112, 114, 116–117, 130–131,

136–138, 144–147, 149, 155,
   168, 187, 193, 197, 209,
   216–217, 228, 264
co- 12, 197
co-created 175–178, 197
dynamic 90–91, 100
plan 163, 187
relational third 175–178
unitary 40, 74, 76, 202, **267**
universalism 81, 155
universality 73, 81, 219

Valentine, J. 196
Van Beekum, S. 52, 61, 218
Van Rijn, B. xxvi
von Foerster, H. 131, 145

Waitangi Tribunal 189, 229
Walker, R. 230
Wallen, R. 94
Wampold, B. E. 5
ways-of-being-with xxxv–xxxvi, 64,
   107, 126
Weinberger, J. 185
Weiss, E. 108–109, 118n.1
Wells, M. 72

"we"ness 3–4, 122, 161, 171, 186–187,
   220
Werner, H. 80
Wheeler, R. H. 80
White, J. D. 22
White, T. 22, 61, 86
Whitehead, A. N. 80
Widdowson, M. xxv, 64, 81, 169, 218
Wild, C. xxvi
Williams, R. xxi, 53
Winnicott, D. W. xxxvii, 142
Wittgenstein, L. 263
Wong, G. 218
Woodworth, R. S. 39
Woollams, S. 14, 35, 56
Worrall, M. xxiv, 48, 80–82, 105, 121,
   134, 196, 229
Wyckoff, H. 212

Yalom, I. D. 219–220
Yontef, G. 150

Zimmerman, J. 147
Žvelc, G. 72, 165–169, 192
Žvelc, M. 16